My Story

CONFESSIONS OF A WISCONSIN FARM BOY

Stories about the trials and tribulations of growing up and stumbling into a magical world.

By Donald Edmund

WITH REGARDS

Don Edmund

My Story

Confessions of a Wisconsin Farm Boy

Copyright © 2017

By Donald Edmund

My Story

This book is dedicated to my loving wife Dona; and to my wonderful daughter Linda. I could not have lived the life I have lived without their love and support.

And to my parents, now deceased, who taught me to love GOD and my neighbor, and taught me the value of a job well done.

My Story

Contents

My Story

My Story

Chapter 1: IN THE BEGINNING

It all started for me on October 14, in the year of 1932, in a tiny village in northern Wisconsin. My father, Harold R (Rudolph) Edmund had taken a job as Principle and High School teacher in Morse, an ex-logging village in Ashland County in the northern part of Wisconsin. It was in the middle of the Great Depression, and an influential friend of my fathers had suggested he take that particular job to get experience so he could qualify for the same type of job at his home village at Irma, in Lincoln County, Wisconsin.

My Dad married Irma Cummings in 1927, at the Bethany Lutheran Church in Irma, Wisconsin. He was a school teacher in one of Lincoln County's many one room schools, and his brother Carl Edmund was a teacher at the Cloverbelt School, in the township of Scanowon. Dad had accompanied his brother Carl to one of the school functions at the Cloverbelt School, and there he met this beautiful young girl who would become his wife. Within a year or two, Dad and Mom were married and living at Irma, and Dad was teaching at the Irma State Graded School. My older sister Verna and brother Jerry were born while they lived in a small house in Irma. Dad's friend, a member of the local School Board, suggested that Dad move the family to the small village of Morse, in Ashland County in northern Wisconsin, where there was a job opening for the Principle's position. The friend was aware that the same position would eventually be open at the Irma

My Story

State Graded School, and with more experience, if Dad could qualify, it would be a good career move for him.

I mentioned that my birth occurred during the Great Depression. I don't remember it being such a bad time. I do recall my Dad and Mother telling that he worked for a full year with out getting a pay check. By luck the local store owner was the Chairman of the local School Board, and knew full well that Dad would eventually be paid. He willingly carried them 'on the books' until the pay check finally arrived. My little sister Charlotte Anne was also born while we lived in Morse.

I remember my Dad telling me that men were working for a dollar a day, when they could find work. He said that one source of work was fighting fire in the surrounding forest lands. He said some of the men found that they could cause a fire by filling a certain kind of bottle with water and setting it on a dry snag. The sun shining through the glass and water was like a prism, and would concentrate the rays enough to kindle a flame. Another source of work was shoveling the train out of the snow after some of the severe blizzards. It seemed that the rails ran through a cut in the hills in the area, and at times they would drift full of snow. If the train got stuck, it had to be shoveled out. I guess life was pretty rough at that time in that place. He told that it was fairly common for the woodsmen living in the lumber camps to get into fights. He said there were times when some one would be killed in a knife fight in the winter,

My Story

and they would freeze the body and wait till spring to bury it. He and Mom told of being at a dance when two men got into an argument. One man pulled out a pistol, and pointing point blank at the other man's head, pulled the trigger. The man who was shot dropped to the floor, and the other man ran. Soon the man on the floor sat up, looked around and asked what had happened. His head was all bloody, and of course, every one thought he was badly hurt. It seems that the bullet split and went around his head under the skin, causing some bleeding but no serious damage. My mother was a gentle person, and when she and Dad told the story, I could see that it had a pronounced effect on her.

I believe that I have some memories of those early days of my life. I seem to remember how our house was located just one door from a curve in the road that ran through the village. The road came down a small hill, turned the corner to the right, and a short distance out of town crossed the Bad River on a small bridge. I seem to remember going to the bridge over the Bad River with my sister Verna and some other kids, probably the Fritz kids. Joanne was Verna's age, Shirley was Jerry's age, and there was a Janet, but I don't think she was along. What I remember about that particular time was that the 'big' kids would throw something into the water on the upstream side of the bridge, and then we would all run to the down stream side to watch it come out from under the bridge. For some reason, it seemed terribly exciting.

My Story

It may be because we had been told repeatedly NOT to go near the river.

I remember my Mother telling about a blind man who lived up the hill from our house. Once a day he would walk down the hill, around the curve in the road, and down a block to the store. He always walked without any help. One day as she and a neighbor lady were talking in the yard, they saw him coming down the hill. Another neighbor walking up the hill stopped and the two men talked a while. When they parted, the ladies noticed that the blind man was having some trouble finding his way on the road. They called out to him to see if they could help. He asked if they would help him get started in the right direction on the road. He explained that he could navigate because he kept track of the number of his steps until he had to make the turn. When talking to his neighbor, he had forgotten his count! The ladies got him started, and off he went counting as he walked.

When I was 3 or 4 years old, we moved back to Irma. where we rented a huge house directly across the road from my Dad's parents' farm. I don't remember much about that period except that one of the teachers at Dad's school lived in a small house near us. His name was Pete Smith, and I had a contact with him many years later when I was in the Air Force at McCord Air Force Base near Tacoma, Washington. He had a passel of kids, and it seemed his wife went off the deep end, (mental) and

My Story

they divorced. He eventually remarried and moved to Washington, near Tacoma. Somehow he found that I was stationed at McCord AFB and he got in touch with us. We visited with him and his new wife and his kids several times. Dad eventually moved our family to a farm one mile west of Grandpa and Grandma Edmund's farm. It was a small farm, and I believe the reason we had a farm was that my Dad thought that raising kids on a farm was better than raising kids in town. To this day, I believe he was right.

My Story

Chapter 2: MY BOYHOOD ON THE FARM AT IRMA

The farm was on the northeast slope of the Irma Hill, supposedly the second highest hill in Wisconsin. My very young days were spent in doing things little boys do. Some of the things got me into serious trouble, and some others should have, but the authorities (Mom and Dad) never found out. For some reason I seemed to break an awful lot of windows. I was a pretty good 'rock thrower' but the windows just seem to get in the way. One day when I was 'throwing things', I found that a stick that was heavier on one end than the other could be thrown a great distance. In fact, I could throw it completely over the barn! I was pretty proud of that, and when my Dad drove into the yard that afternoon I was anxious to show him what I could do. When I explained that I was going to throw the stick over the barn, Dad reminded me that there was a window in the peak of the gable. I knew I could throw higher than that because I had several times already. I wound up and threw that stick but it did not go high enough. The window was a four pane job, and my stick took out all four panes AND THE FRAME! My Dad and I made several trips to the wood shed over broken windows, and that was one of them.

Another thing that got me into trouble was experimenting with gasoline. I had been told that gasoline would explode if exposed to fire. I proved that

My Story

was false, but I failed to get rid of the evidence, and another trip to the wood shed was made. What I did was get a little gasoline out of the gas barrel and put it in a glass jar. Then I built a fire in the field behind the barn. I put the glass jar with gasoline into the fire and waited for the explosion. None came, and when the fire went out I lost interest and left to tackle some other project. When Dad stumbled on the evidence of the fire with a bottle of gasoline still in it, I professed not to know any thing about it. Of course, that never worked, so the trip to the woodshed was made.

Another experiment I made was to prove once and for all that cats could or could not swim. I methodically put an entire family of cats in the stock tank, one at a time, so I could perform a rescue if required. I can state categorically that cats can swim. In fact, if they were placed in the tank slowly they never got their heads or tails wet. If they were to dive in (with some help) they quickly surfaced and dog paddled (pun intended) to the nearest tank edge. Since no permanent damage was done, this experiment did not require a trip to the wood shed.

The farm and its location was a perfect place for me. The surrounding country was big enough so I never felt constrained. I could always find some place to go or some thing to do. There were two small creeks on the farm. One was very small, but had water year around. I found that there were minnows in it. I could bend a

My Story

common pin to form a hook, tie it onto some store string, and fish through the cracks in the plank bridge my Dad had made. An angle worm made perfect bait. I found that I could sell the minnows that survived, to my Dad for his Bass fishing trips. Later I found that you could wade into the creek with a home made net and catch them by the dozens. Then I could sell them to the neighbors also. I can remember one day fishing through the crack, of course always kneeling down so I could see my bait through the crack; I saw the largest monster I had ever seen. It was gigantic, and there were no minnows in the creek. I ran to the house and told my dad about the huge monster in the creek. When he finished what he was doing, he went with me to the creek. I showed him the monster. He explained it was a snapping turtle, and it was a big one. He grabbed it by the tail and yanked it out of the water. He carried it up to the house by the tail, and I remember each time the turtle would swing past his pant leg, it would snap at him. Dad put it in a stock tank, and announced that we would make turtle soup. I knew for sure that I would never eat any thing as ugly as that turtle was. I can remember teasing the turtle with a stick. I found out that when he snapped at the stick and got it in his mouth, I could lift him up. He would hang on with his beak. I also found out that he would hiss when he got mad. He would also eject blood from a hole in the bottom of his mouth. We got an unusually heavy rain one night. The tank filled to overflowing and the turtle got away. I can remember a

My Story

feeling of relief that I would not have to eat him, but I also missed teasing him. Eventually I found the larger creek, and that started a love affair with trout fishing that lasted many years.

I think the name of the larger creek was Crystal Creek, or maybe that is just the name I gave it. At first when I found that creek, I was only exploring. I named every twist and each turn that the creek made. I also named the banks on both sides, and some of the trees that grew along the banks. I followed the creek from where it came onto our property to where it ran along the road and finally disappeared on a neighbor's property where I was afraid to go. At some point I realized that there were BIG minnows in there. I rigged up a bent pin and store string, but now I had to have a pole to get the bait out to where I wanted it. Naturally I used a branch from some creek brush. I found that these minnows liked grass hoppers. I also found out that once they bit, I had to yank fast to fling them onto the bank or they would get off the bent pin hook. One day after I had caught several I took them home to show Mom. She said they were trout, and she would fix them for my dinner. I remember that she fixed them with the heads on, and I made her cut them off. She said if I could catch more, she would get me some real fish hooks. I did and she did. Dad let me use one of his casting rods, and with the real fish hooks I did pretty well. In fact, I some times shirked my chores to spend more time on the creek.

My Story

I also found out that our farm and the surrounding farms had lots of woodland around them. In fact the forests were dense and vast. At first the woods were a place to explore much like the creek had been. I spent a fair amount of time discovering and then naming places that I was sure no white man had ever seen. Eventually I became the owner of a BB gun. When I was not shooting at my brother Jerry, I was hunting for big game, mostly chipmunks. I remember getting one, but when I picked it up it came alive in my hand. I guess I had only stunned it. The BB gun was not strong enough for the squirrels that abounded in all the forests. When my Dad thought that I was mature enough to go hunting, he would take me with him. I did not get to carry a gun, but I did get to romp through the brush making as much noise as I could. It was some time before I realized I was the 'dog'. While I was hunting with him, Dad made me realize how a gun was to be handled. Eventually under his supervision, I was allowed to shoot at targets with both the shotgun and his rifle.

While I was still quite young, I traded a jack knife to Peanuts (Alfred Jr.) Denetz, for a 22 caliber rifle. It was a Winchester pump. I soon found out why Peanuts was willing to trade the gun for a jack knife. The rifling in the barrel was gone, and the gun would not shoot straight. I was a pretty fair shot, but not with my new gun. Dad tried it and also could not hit any where near a target. About that time we found that we had lots of mice in the granary, and Dad bought some 22 Cal. fine

My Story

shot for me to shoot them with. I tried to get them with the 22 rifle I had traded for. I could shoot at a mouse within a few feet, and he would run away. I concluded the reason was that what ever rifling was left in the barrel was spinning the shot, and scattering it too much. To solve that problem, I cut the barrel off so it was only about 12 inches long. I still could not kill any mice. I was in the yard with my "modified" 22 rifle one afternoon when Dad got home from work. I told him I could not hit any mice even though they were close. To demonstrate, I aimed at a barn cat that was about 30 feet away and pulled the trigger. The cat yowled, flipped a summersault, and headed for the barn. I guess it lived, but my modified 22 didn't. Dad took it and I never saw it again.

Eventually, after I had demonstrated more maturity, I was allowed to order a Mossberg 22 Cal. Rifle. It was a beauty! It had a beautiful golden wood stock that extended all the way to the tip of the barrel. It was a bolt action, and had a clip that contained seven cartridges. It had a trap door in the butt plate that could hold an extra clip. It had a variety of front sights that you could select, and also several rear sights that were easily selectable. One of them was a peep sight. I equipped it with a scope sight, and practiced shooting until I was pretty good. I showed my Dad that I could drive a nail into a fence post behind the barn from a 'leaning' stand at the tractor shed, a distance of about 100 feet. I am ashamed to admit how many rabbits and squirrels I shot. I am also

My Story

ashamed to admit that one day I lined up a bunch of sparrows along the barn roof edge. If I remember right, I got six of them with one shot. Grandma Edmund saw me, and bawled me out pretty good.

Shortly after I bought my Mossberg, Jerry bought an automatic 22 Cal. rifle. If I remember correctly, it had a magazine that held around 15 shots. I couldn't wait to get my hands on it and try 'rapid fire' at some thing moving. I finally got my chance when I got home from school and Jerry was not home yet. I grabbed his gun, strapped on my snow shoes, and headed for the 'back 40'. Just before getting to the wooded area, you crossed over a small hill. As I topped the hill, I surprised a red fox eating a partridge about 50 feet from the edge of the woods. As he took off, I started firing. I think I got off 5 or 6 shots before he got to the woods. When I got to where he started, I found blood, so I knew I had hit him. I followed the tracks to the woods, and he was there dead. I had hit him with 5 shots. There was a serious predator problem in the countryside at that time, and the County was paying a bounty on both foxes and wolves. The fox was worth $5.00, and I sold the hide to Sig Johnson. I don't think I ever paid Jerry for the use of his gun.

One time Donnie Lutzke, Dale Peterson, Kenneth Johnson, my brother Jerry and I were exploring our back 40 acres, and we stumbled across a skunk den. I think we had seen the female skunk leave the den. We

My Story

investigated, and found four small skunk kits in a nest. We liberated them and took them to our place, found a box for them, and put some milk in for them to eat, as we planned to make them into pets. One of the boys with me said he knew of an animal doctor who could remove their smell apparatus. When my Dad found them, he asked what we planned to do with them, and we said we were going to have them de-fumigated. He asked how we were going to pay for the operation so we told him we would sell one of the kits to pay for the operation. He said he was not too sure the Doc would go along with that. Anyway, it was going to be several days before any of us would be able to go to Merrill to get them to the Veterinarian, so we planned on starting the taming process right away. The next morning we found the kits had been "kitnapped". The box was tipped over and all the little skunks were gone. Dad said he thought the mother skunk came and got them, but the shed where we had them was a long way from where we found them in the field. After years of wondering about it, I have come to the conclusion that my Dad probably helped the escape.

Grandpa Edmund had built a couple of wooden row boats at some time before I knew what a row boat was. He gave one to his cousin John Samuelson, and gave the other one to a family named Blood, who had land around Gerbig Lake. When it rained in the summer time and we could not work on the farm, we would some-times go fishing. We would drive to Cloverbelt past

My Story

Grandpa Cummings place to where the Bloods lived. We would park in their yard, and walk the next half mile to Gerbig Lake. There we would launch the boat which the Blood family left on the beach. (Grandpa Edmund was not so dumb) There was no road to the lake, and very few people fished it, so it was always productive. Grandpa, Jerry, and I fished with cane poles and some sort of bait. Dad always used a casting rod and reel. We would get awful wet walking through the wet brush to get to the lake, but as soon as we got on the water and caught fish we would warm up. Sometimes Dad, Jerry and I would take the tent and go there and camp a few days. That was always great fun. There was a man who lived on the next lake, called Bass Lake, who had raised sheep at one time. I remember my Dad stopped to visit with him one day. While there Mr. Warren Eager asked if we wanted to see his two-headed lamb. Of course we did. One of the lambs born on his farm had been born with two heads. It did not live very long, and Mr. Eager had it mounted.

Since our farm was one mile from Grandpa and Grandma's farm, both Jerry and I often helped them with 'chores'. Grandpa had homesteaded his farm in 1910 when he arrived from Iowa. For some reason, he picked the hilliest and rockiest 80 acres in that part of Wisconsin. One of the 'chores' was to help pick rocks every spring before planting. Grandpa had built a stone boat, a small raft like thing on skids that could be pulled by a team of horses. I remember going to a field with

My Story

Grandpa one day. On seeing the entire field covered with rocks, I said "Grandpa, we can't pick up all these rocks". He said "we don't have to; all we have to do is pick up one rock at a time". All of his fields had large rock piles in them, and I eventually came to look at them as 'monuments to hard labor'.

I can clearly remember shooting my first deer. It was with Dad's 30-30 Rifle, on the Chase Hill back of our place, and was probably a little bit before the season opened. We would go bird hunting in the fall before deer season to "check out the territory". Usually, Dad carried his rifle, and I would have a shotgun and act as "bird dog" down in the swamp. On this particular day, Dad gave me the rifle, told me where to wait, and he acted as bird dog. It was not long before a young buck loped up the hill and crossed the open area in front of me. I shot just once, but got him. The major thing I remember about hunting with my Dad and his friends was the camaraderie. Although all of them were very careful with guns, and would brook no carelessness from any one else, they were always pulling jokes on each other, and kidding each other. I found that when they included me, they accepted me as an equal, even though I was still a kid. Although I have hunted in many states with friends and co-workers, I have never felt that kind of camaraderie at any other time or place.

Another very pleasant memory from my boyhood was swimming at Silver Lake. When I was very young, our

My Story

whole family would go to the lake on Sunday afternoons. Mom's sister, Aunt Lila and her family would also be there. We would picnic, and I guess the grown ups would nap while we kids would frolic in the water. The water was crystal clear, and there was a white sand beach that extended much further out than any of us could wade. I remember one particular time, probably on a Sunday, when several families were at the lake. A bunch of us little ones were in the water and our parents were sitting on the bank napping or talking when there was the sound of a car careening through the brush along the road toward the lake. Our parents scurried around and rounded us out of the water just in time to see an old model T Ford come dashing almost into the lake. Two very dirty old men jumped out and into the lake. Soon they began taking a bath and washing their clothes all without undressing. They had soap with them and they sure stirred up the water. They were the Dishaw Brothers. They lived in a small shack near my Mother's father (Grandpa Cummings), and did woods work or farm work for whoever would hire them. One of the men was severely crippled, and was bent over forward at his hips. I remember it was difficult for him to see when he walked or was standing, because he could not look forward, but he could drive that old model T because he was sitting down! Our folks told us he was crippled that way because he dove into very cold water when he was over heated from strenuous work.

My Story

When we kids got a little older, we would ride our bicycles to the lake. It was about 7 miles from home to the lake. I remember the trip to the lake was easy, but after swimming and playing in the water all afternoon, the ride home was tough. One of my more bitter memories about the lake was after we started driving. Both Jerry and I had to work pretty hard in the summer time helping to farm. Invariably, on the hottest day, we would be making hay and sweating up a storm, when Victor and Gene Cottrell would drive into the yard and say "We are going swimming, do you want to go along?" Was the Pope Polish? Certainly we wanted to go, but we had to finish our work first. In the long run, I think Jerry and I were better off. We learned a good solid work ethic.

I learned to swim in a kind of scary way. There is a little lake just south of Irma, called the Irma Lake. It had a mud bottom, and black water. It was not a nice lake at all, and so was usually ignored by every one until it froze over and was great for ice skating. Some older boys, Kenneth Johnson and Donnie Gothberg, invited me to go to the lake with them to try out a boat they had made. When I got there I found that the boat leaked pretty badly, but they had a can that we could bail with. I told them I could not swim, but one of them said "that's OK; we have a set of water wings for you. The water wings were two small canvass bags tied together with a short length of strap. When wet, you would blow air into the canvass bags and they would more or less

My Story

hold the air. To use them, you would put the strap across your chest and under your arm pits with the bags (wings) behind you on your shoulders. With that assurance, we shoved off. We were not out very far when we had to start bailing. It soon became obvious that we did not have enough cans (or people) to bail with. Water was coming in faster than one tin can could handle. As the boat sunk, Kenneth and Donnie started swimming. I grabbed for the water wings, and then realized we had not made them wet nor had we blown air into them. As empty canvas bags, they sank! As the boat disappeared from under me, I realized that I was dog paddling, and was making slow headway toward shore. I can still remember the icky mud when I finally got near the shore. I never went near the Irma Lake in the summer time again, but the next time we went to Silver Lake I learned that I could really keep afloat by dog paddling. I become proficient enough at swimming that I could probably save myself, but I never was as good a swimmer as those cats!

The Irma Lake in winter time was a completely different place. With the ice thick enough to support us, usually by Thanksgiving time, we spent a great deal of time ice skating there. As little kids, we would walk the 3 miles on Saturday and Sunday afternoons, and many times in the evenings. Some of the bigger kids would build a fire. When we got too cold, we would sit by the fire to warm up. As I got older, I was one of the ones to shovel the snow off from the skating area after each snowfall. With

My Story

a number of us, it was never too big a job. We would shovel a large area for us to play hockey, and an equally large area for just skating. We would also shovel fairly narrow 'pathways' into remote parts of the lake, and usually behind the islands. Yes, this little lake had a number of islands that floated. They were made up of brushy growths with the roots so entwined that they appeared to be real islands. They were spongy to walk on, and you would frequently step completely through the root systems into the water. The islands would float about the lake depending on the wind. It seems they always froze in place 15 or 20 feet from the shore on one side of the lake or the other. That is where we would shovel the paths. In case you have not already guessed, we made the pathways behind the islands so that we could try to steal a kiss from our favorite girl friend. I was better at hockey than I was at skating behind the islands, but I kept trying. I remember walking home after skating and getting my feet unbearably cold. As we walked, my feet would start to warm up and they would ache. I was afraid they would break off! If we had any money we would stop at the Gingham Girls, a saloon on the highway on the northeast side of the village of Irma. I have forgotten the lady's name that ran it, but she would allow us to come in and sit in a booth near the door. She would not allow us to go to the bar to ask for what we wanted. She would come over to the booth and ask. Since it was winter time, we would bring our sleds, and since the Irma hill was between our house and the

My Story

lake, we could slide almost a mile on the way to the lake, and almost 2 miles on the way home.

Winter time was a special time for me. In addition to the skating, there was skiing, snow shoeing, sledding on Irma Hill, and especially hunting. As I said earlier, our farm was on the northeast side of the Irma Hill. It was one half mile up hill to the south to the cross roads where County Road H crossed County Road J. The Church was located at this intersection. It was another one half mile further south, mostly down hill, to Grandpa Edmund's farm. From the intersection where the Church was, if you went west you would climb the steep part of the Irma Hill. It was about one half mile to the top, then another one half mile down a very steep part of the hill to our school, then about another half mile to U.S. Highway 51. As you can see, we could use our sleds no matter which way we were going, to or from school or to or from Grandpas place. Of course the steeper the hill, the faster you would coast. I suspect we would approach speeds of 25 or 30 miles per hour when coasting toward our place from the Church. We soon found out we could increase that considerably by starting at the top of Irma Hill and going toward the Church. If we were just out sledding, we would shoot through the intersection at full speed and continue on down the steep slope toward Otto Peterson's place (Dale's father). We never worried about meeting a car at the intersection because there was so little traffic. When we slid down the hill past the school toward Highway

My Story

51, we had to drag our feet (as brakes) in order to stop short of the highway. It was a paved road, and carried lots of traffic. If we were going home, we also had to drag our feet (as brakes) to make the turn from Highway J to Highway H to head toward our place. It seemed that we wore out our overshoes rapidly in the winter time.

Some of the kids had toboggans, and with them you could slide down the steeper hills in the fields or open spaces. They would carry from 4 to 8 kids, depending on how many were willing to pack on them. Usually, the kid in front, who normally was the owner, would get his face full of snow as we plowed through the loose snow. Some times the farmer who owned the land with the steepest slopes would take down his fences so we could slide through with out the danger of hitting fences. One night Jerry and I were sliding on the top of the snow drifts in one of our fields. The top snow had melted slightly and then refroze. We did not realize how fast or how far we would slide. Jerry was ahead of me, and at the end of the field he sailed right through a barbed wire fence. He was severely cut around his face and around his throat. I remember helping him get home, and then found out that neither Mom nor Dad was home. Mom was at a Church Women's meeting, and Dad was at a school board meeting. Big sister Verna was in charge and quickly took over. Since there was no telephone at the school, she called the store keeper in Irma and asked him to get Dad. Dad stopped at the Church on the way home and picked up Mom. By the time they got home,

My Story

Verna had stopped most of the bleeding. They took Jerry to the doctor in Tomahawk, and he had to put in a lot of stitches. He eventually outgrew the scars, but we had learned a lesson. Check for fences before sliding at night!

I think all of us kids had skis. It never was very popular with us because you had to walk up the hill to ski down. We did ski at school during noon break and at recesses. We would ski down through the woods across from the school on Earl Cottrell's land. He was the one who would open up his fences so we could toboggan through. We decided to build a ski trail down through a different part of his woods because it was steeper. We did not want to ask him to open his fence in another place, so we built a ski jump over the fence. One day before school started, we had a contest to see who could jump the farthest. I won hands down, but suffered a broken leg when I hit a tree. The problem was that the trail had a fairly sharp turn shortly after the jump in order to miss a thick grove of maple trees. My jump was so far that I was still airborne when I came to the turn. Try as I might, I could not turn in midair, and I hit one of the trees, resulting in a broken ankle. Dad was the Principle of the school, and the high school teacher. He could not leave to take me to the doctor, so he called Mom. We went to Doc Henderson at Tomahawk, and he put a rather large cast on my leg. They kept me in the hospital a few days, but when I got home, I found that the cast worked real well as a brake when we were sledding.

My Story

Eventually I broke the cast and had to go to have another put on. When I broke the second one the same way, the Doc announced to Mom that he would fix it so I couldn't break the next one. He had the nurse wrap my leg with the normal cast, and then he added a contraption that had steel rods going up the side of my leg outside the cast. Then they made a separate cast over the top of the first one encasing the steel rods. The contraption had steel rockers on the bottom so that I could walk on the rockers on that leg. The cast was very heavy, and was so big it would not fit in my trousers pant leg. Mom had to slit them down the seam and put in a zipper. I wore that cast until the next June, and I can tell you it itched something awful. I had a little trouble walking for a while after it came off but I soon got over that also.

There was a student living at our place for a time so that he could attend high school at Irma. His name was Art Hilgendorff. His Dad had made a large bob-sled called a 'ripper'. It would carry about a dozen people sitting down with their feet on the runners. It steered with a regular steering wheel. It was too heavy for us to pull back up the hill, so when we used it one of the Dads would tow it up the hill behind a car, then drive back down to the cross roads to flag any car traffic while we sailed through.

One day when I was about 9 or 10 years old, I was at the railroad depot at Irma. While in there I saw two pairs of

My Story

snow shoes. I believe they were about the prettiest things I had ever seen. I immediately decided I had to have a pair. Both of my parents said NO. Not long after, I found an ad for Army surplus snow shoes. The advertisement said they were genuine Army issue, and were brand new. They were priced at $2.50 per pair. Now it just so happened that I had that much money, so I ordered a pair. When they arrived I was chastised severely for wasting my money, but I didn't mind. I could strap them on and fairly fly over the deep snow. I soon noticed that when we went hunting my Dad would always wind up with my snow shoes on. Mom ordered two additional pairs for Dad for Christmas so that he could have his own and one pair for who ever went hunting with us. I would arrive home from school, rush through my chores, and then head for the woods with my snow shoes and my 22 rifle. I have used the snow shoes hiking or hunting in several states, and until recently, they hung on our wall as a decoration. I still have them somewhere in storage.

I can remember that even as a little boy I was engrossed with airplanes. When I heard one overhead, I would rush out into the yard and watch it until it was out of sight. I always wondered who was in the plane, and where they were going. I also wished I could see what they were seeing from up that high. As I got a little older, I like lots of other boys, built scale models of all kinds of airplanes. One time, my family was at Tomahawk, Wisconsin visiting Mom's sister, Aunt Wilma and her

My Story

family, I am certain it was on a Sunday. While we were there I had taken one of the cousin's bicycles to ride around town. Someway I wound up at a little airport right in town. I remember that a small plane was taking off and flying around town, then landing. The takeoffs and landings crossed a railroad track that ran right through the runway. When the pilot shut the engine down, I went to talk to him. He was giving 15 minute rides over town for $5.00. Man! Only 5 bucks, but I didn't have it. I pedaled back to Aunt Wilma's house, and pleaded for the $5.00. Dad decided he would pay for both Jerry and I. I think Grandpa Cummings paid for Jim and Bob Street. We all went back, and **I HAD MY FIRST AIRPLANE RIDE**. I was hooked! Of course everything looked like toys from up in the air. I suspect we were never over 1000 feet up, but I know I could see the whole world. It rained a little bit while we were up, and I could see rainbows in almost every direction. The airplane was a lowly Piper J 3 Cub, but at that time it was the most beautiful thing I had ever seen. **I knew that I would some day be a pilot!**

My Story

Chapter 3: I DISCOVER THE AUTOMOBILE

Ah- the automobile! As farm boys, both Jerry and I began driving at a tender age of 8 or 9 years old. At first we drove only the old Model T Ford truck we had. Then the tractor, and always on the farm from field to the barn or vice versa. It was a necessity because of the amount of farming we did in the summer time. Eventually, we began to drive the road between our place and Grandpas' place. I suspect I was around 13 before I was allowed to drive the car to go swimming in the summer time, or skating in the winter time. I remember taking the driver's test for a 'Farm Boy' driver's license. We had a 1936 Nash 4 door sedan at that time. Dad and I drove to Merrill to the Sherriff's Office at the County Jail. We went inside and Dad told the Sherriff that I needed a driver's license. The Sherriff said "I will have to give you a test, Boy, are you ready". Then without waiting for an answer, he asked me four questions. I don't remember what the questions were, but before I could answer them, he would answer them and say "Aint that right Boy?" And his belly would jiggle. He was very fat. When that test was finished we walked out to the car parked at the side of the street. The Sherriff told me to get in and start the car. I did, and sat there waiting for him to get in. He stood on the sidewalk talking to Dad. Finally he said "Aint you ever going to get started? Drive around the block", and he waved his arm to indicate I was to drive without him in the car. When I got back and parked the car, he said "Well,

My Story

come inside and we will see if we can find the right form." He had the correct form and I got my Farm Boy license which allowed me to drive during daylight hours.

Grandpa Edmund had a Model T Ford coupe that he and Grandma drove to church and also to the village (Irma) for their shopping. They would even drive it to Merrill, a distance of about 12 miles. You must remember that at that time, the 12 miles to Merrill was a long way from where we lived. Grandpa kept the Model T in a shed. I can remember that when Grandpa was going to take Grandma in the car he would jack up one rear wheel, and then crank the car until it started. The wheel would spin like mad until the car would warm up, then he would lift it off the jack and back it out of the shed. He would pick up Grandma at the yard gate and off they would go. Eventually Grandpa decided he needed a more modern car, so they bought a 1931 Model A Ford coupe. He had a hard time learning how to drive it because of needing to push in the clutch to shift. One day he and Grandma had driven to Merrill to shop. They had angle parked on Main Street in front of the bank. After they finished shopping they were ready to head for home. Grandpa started the car, selected a gear, pressed on the gas pedal (hard) and dropped the clutch. The problem was that he had put it in low gear (forward) instead of reverse! The car leaped forward across the side walk and came to rest against the concrete bank building. Luckily no one was in line with the car, so the

My Story

only damage was a slightly bent bumper, and Grandpa's confidence. He never again drove the car. He called Dad's office to get him to drive them home. The car stayed at Grandpa's place. When they needed to go somewhere they would call us. Either Jerry or I would walk the mile to their place, drive them, usually to Irma to Rene Schultz's store, drive them back home and park the car in their shed then walk back home.

There came a time when the Model A stayed at our place, and was more or less Jerry's and mine. I remember driving it to a basketball game one night in mid-winter. Gene Cottrell had gone with me and several others were packed into the car. I drove Gene home, and then started toward Dale Peterson's place. There was a sharp curve, actually a 90 degree turn down the road from Gene's place. Someone said "how fast can you take that turn?" so I stepped on the gas. I suspect we were going around 35 or 40 miles an hour when we went into the turn. The car slid up against the snow bank on the left side, then slid along the bank and eventually tipped over onto its side on top of the snow bank. Eventually we all got out and by pulling and pushing we got it back onto its wheels on the road. The engine started up ok and seemed to drive ok, so I took the rest of the kids home then I went home. The next day my Dad drove the model A to work to leave the 'good' car for Mom to use. When he got home that evening he asked me what I had done to the Model A. I innocently said "I didn't do nothen". He said well you must have

My Story

done something, because you broke the 'wishbone'. The wishbone was a steel brace that anchored the front axle so it could move up and down but not horizontally, and was connected to the underside of the car with a ball and socket that would allow the car to steer ok. In tipping the car back on its wheels, the steel ball snapped off allowing the car to wander back and forth instead of being able to drive it straight. Dad said it was more like 'herding' it, instead of driving it because the car was going where ever it wanted to, and it took him a while to get to town. His mechanic repaired the car during the day.

Another experience I had when driving the old Model A was that the radiator would freeze up in cold weather. One night Jerry and I with two other kids drove the Model A to Tomahawk to the ice skating rink. We had a great place to skate on the Irma Lake, but the Tomahawk girls were prettier. It was bitter cold and on the way home the radiator froze up. We knew that the way to thaw it was to pour hot water on one side of the radiator to get water flowing through one side of the radiator, which would then thaw the rest of the radiator. We had no hot water. You guessed it! We all lined up and one-at- a- time and peed on one side of the radiator. It worked. We quickly threw a blanket over the front of the car and drove slowly the rest of the way home. The reason we had only water in the radiator in the winter was that the radiator leaked and we could not afford to put alcohol it. I tried filling it with Kerosene and that did

My Story

not freeze, but my Dad made me drain it out because of the fire hazard.

In 1947 Mom and Dad got a brand new 1947 Pontiac four door sedan. It was black and was it ever a beauty! I got to drive it on special occasions, and did I ever think I was hot stuff. Our folks kept the Nash and that became Jerry's and mine. That arrangement really did not work very well. We usually wanted to go in separate directions and with different kids. The Model A had become a 'work' car by then, and wasn't good enough to drive on dates, so we both started angling to get our own cars.

We had both had bicycles for many years by then. Our first one was one that Mom and Dad bought for Verna, I think maybe for her birthday. She didn't want us to ride it, so I would get up early in the morning and practice before she got up. I think it was an Elgin, and although it was used, it was a great bicycle. I was too small to peddle it so I would take it up on the hill in the drive-way, run beside it, and jump on. I could coast down the little hill and tip over at the bottom. Back up the hill and do it over again. I finally got so I could peddle it by sitting on the bars. At some point Dad bought both Jerry and I our own bikes. They were used, and the one I got had what they called 'high pressure' tires. They were the skinny tires that they use now days for racing. I hated it! The tires always sunk into the soft gravel or dirt or mud. Besides, it was the only one of its kind in our bunch. I

My Story

saved my money and when I had enough I bought a brand new Hawthorn bicycle. It was in midwinter when I got it, so I did not get to ride it much until the spring. By then I had a Farm Boy license and was allowed to drive a car. First the Model A Ford, then the Nash. My bike stayed pretty new for quite a while.

One day I was at Mr. Grosse's auto repair shop at Bloomfield, about 7 miles east of Irma. I do not remember what I was there for, but I remember he had a large field full of all kinds of old cars. I guess they were his 'parts store'. I walked around just looking at all the cars and I found one I fell in love with. It was a 1933 Chevrolet, 4 door sedan. I asked Mr. Gross what was wrong with the car, and why it was in his junk yard. He said an old man in the area had bought it new, and had now gotten too old to drive, so his family sold the car to Mr. Gross. Goats had gotten on top of the car and their feet had poked holes through the roof material. The paint was badly faded, but I still thought it was beautiful. I asked if he would sell it, and how much it would cost. He asked how much I had. After I got done squirming (because I did not have any money) I remembered that I had a practically new bike. Mr. Gross's young son was playing nearby with an old junk of a bike. I told him about my practically new bike, he looked at it and said he would trade if my parents approved. I peddled that bike the 7 or so miles home as fast as I could, and boy, did I go into sales pitch! I told my folks what a beauty it was, and I told them every

My Story

thing I could think of that was wrong with both the Model A and the Nash. I also pointed out that Jerry had just bought a 1936 Chevrolet, and that I should be able to have my own car.

After promising that I would be responsible for all expenses and maintenance, I got permission to make the trade. Mr. Gross had informed me that the car had been in his junk yard for several years. He said he would supply a used battery, but that I should be prepared to put on different tires as the ones on it were rotten. When I went to pick it up, my brother Jerry drove me over there, and Russell Cottrell went along. Because I was sure I would need tires, I took all the spares I could find that would fit. The 1933 Chevrolet had 19 inch tires and Jerry's 1936 Chevrolet had 16 inch, but the wheels had the same bolt pattern. We also found two 21 inch wheels with tires on that also had the same bolt pattern. With four spare wheels and tires of three different sizes we were off to get my "new" car. As predicted, we had tire trouble on the way home. I arrived in the yard at home with three different size wheels on the car. It didn't matter. I had a car all my own.

I was still younger than 16 so all I had was a 'Farm Boy' license, but that car sure changed the way I lived! I was required to let my parents know where I was going, and with who, and what time I would be home, but none of my friends had to know that. They thought I was as free as a bird. If they suggested we go somewhere that I

My Story

knew was not allowed, all I had to say was "I don't want to go". Unfortunately, that didn't last very long, and I soon began ranging all over the county.

My girlfriend at that time lived in a community called Doering. It was a settlement of German families with large prosperous farms. They frequently had dances in their Community Center (which was a retired school house) and I would drive the 30 miles or so to attend the dances with my girlfriend. Some of the local boys felt that I was encroaching on their territory, and they tried to dissuade me from coming. One night when we were ready to leave after the dance, my car would not go. It started ok, and shifted ok, but would not go forward or back up. I finally got out to look under the car to see what was wrong. I found that they had lifted it up and put blocks under the rear axle so that the tires were just barely off the ground. What to do? Everyone had left by then, and I had no jack to lift it off the blocks. I looked around and finally found some splinters of wood. They were thick enough to give me traction if I could get them driven under the tires. A large rock served as a hammer and I got them forced under the tires. Viola! It worked and I got my girlfriend home just before her curfew.

At the next dance an accomplice of mine (from Doering) told me the plan was to crawl under my car and disconnect the driveshaft U joint. I asked him to watch, and let me know when they were under the car. He did, and when two of them were under the car working on

My Story

the driveshaft, I went out and whopped both of them with a tow chain I had left in the brush beside the car. I got both of them a couple of times before they got out from under the car. Several years later one of them said the chain on their legs hurt some, but not as bad as bumping their heads on the car frame when they sat up quickly!

I began to make improvements on my car. First I had to get some decent tires. I do not remember for sure, but I believe I got them from Bert Schreader in return for helping him in his garage. If I had a mechanical problem, I could usually get Bert to help me fix it, and then do a little work for him to pay the bill. He did not work me very hard, but he did make me wait to work on my car until his real customers were taken care of.

One day when I was working at Schreader's Garage, Chris Neilson, our neighbor, brought his car in to have the speedometer fixed. It was a 1937 Chevrolet. He left his car and was going to walk to the store at Irma; then pick it up on his way back. Bert asked me to take the old speedometer out of the dashboard. I went out and looked in the car and got sick to my stomach. I tried to work on the car, but actually started vomiting. I went back into the garage and Bert asked me if I had the speedometer out. I said I couldn't do it. Bert suggested that I owed him, and that was how I was supposed to repay him. I said I could do other chores, but could not do that one. Bert went out to the car, took one look inside, slammed

My Story

the door shut, and sent me out to take some other parts off one of his junkers in the back yard for some other repair. When Chris returned to get his car, I heard some very loud and very profane language being used and the last I heard was Bert saying "and don't ever bring that car in here again". The problem was that Chris chewed tobacco. Most people who chewed were reasonably careful where they spit. Chris was not. He apparently would not even turn his head to the side when he was driving. He just let'er go. The steering wheel and the dash in front of him were covered in tobacco juice spit. The whole front area of the car was full of it. It stunk to high heaven. As a matter of fact I thought his son Donnie Neilson had freckles until I realized it was spots of his father's tobacco juice spit all over his face. I guess he got it through the side window when it was down. I sometimes wonder if Chris's speedometer was really broken or if it was so full of tobacco spit that he couldn't see it.

As I started to say, I made several improvements to my car. The spare wheel and tire was mounted at the rear of the car above the bumper. It had no cover on it. I had noticed that in either Schreader's junk yard or in Gross's junk yard, an old car with a sort of a "continental" kit on the rear tire. Where ever it was, I bartered for it, and installed it on my car. This was the era of the 'sunshade' over the wind shield, and I needed one badly. They had not made them for cars as old as mine, so I made my own. It worked pretty well, but flapped a little in the

My Story

breeze when I drove, so I had to install a little brace from the center of the sunshade down to the cowl of the car. That solved the problem. I repainted the car. I think it originally was a dark blue, and that would not do. I bought some special paint and went at it. The paint was 'duck boat brown' and 'bittersweet'. The fenders and running boards were the brown color, and the body was a sort of yellowish tan. I liked it. Naturally, I had to label some of the parts. I lettered ENGINE ROOM on both sides of the hood. On the front doors I had ENTRANCE, and on the rear doors I had EXIT. In the middle of the rear panel above the spare "continental", I labeled THIS IS THE END, on the left rear panel I put PASSING SIDE, and on the right rear panel I put SUICIDE. At some point somebody else added a sign on the back end that said 'Don't laugh Lady; your daughter may be in here'.

I also began to install all kinds of lights and horns. If I remember correctly, I wound up with 37 lights, with some on the front and some at the rear. One night my Dad drove my car to a Church Board meeting. On the way, he messed with the light switches so he had all or most of them on. When he got to the Church, he couldn't get them turned off. Two things happened. First, all the neighbors apparently saw the car sitting in the Church yard with all the lights on, because they mentioned it several times over the next several years, and second, the battery was run down when Dad got ready to go home. Since jumper cables had not yet been

My Story

invented, he walked home. I had to go get my car from the Church yard the next day. I believe all I had to do was push it across the road and coast all the way home. I guess dad could have done that, but he would have had to drive it in the dark.

I also put several different kinds of horns on it. One was a 6 volt siren that sounded like the real thing. I had to be careful with that, because I think it was illegal. (By the way, I still have that siren!) Some of the horns were the "ooga' type with different pitches, and I had a couple sets of musical horns. The musical horns were not electronic like you can buy today. They were actual horns in sets of 3, 4, 5, or 6, and each horn had its own push button. I had the buttons mounted in a row on the steering wheel post so I could reach them easy. I could play several tunes with them. I could play 'Mary Had a Little Lamb', 'How Dry I Am', and some others.

During my high school years, I had cars of several different makes, but I always wound up driving my 1933 Chevrolet when I wanted to impress some one. One of the cars I had was a 1937 Dodge that I took away from Barney Cottrell. I had contracted with Barney to haul baled hay for him. To be able to do it, I had contracted with my Dad to use his Allis Chalmers tractor and wagon. I completed my job for Barney as I said I would. When I asked for my pay, he said he did not have it, and that I would have to wait. I went to see him several times to get my pay. Each time he would say he did not

My Story

have it. I pointed out that I had agreed to pay my Dad for the use of the tractor and wagon, and to do that I needed my pay. When he refused, I told him I would take his car in lieu of payment. He thought I was joking until I went and got it. One of my friends took me to his farm to get the car, but Barney said he would not give me the keys. I was ready for that. Bert Schreader had taught me exactly how to hot wire a car. I think it took me less that a couple of minutes to start the car and drive it away. It was a wreck and was not worth what he owed me. I put a toggle switch in instead of the key. Since it did not start easy, I left it parked on the hill at the end of our driveway so I could coast down hill to start it. All of my friends soon knew how to start it, so it became a neighborhood car. When the brake system leaked, I did not want to waste money fixing the leak, so I poured water into the master cylinder. That sort of worked, but of course it wrecked the brake system. My Mom told me that Barney must have been watching his chance to get his car back, because the day I left for Oregon, Barney came and got his car. Barney was a local character who had a reputation of being very undependable. I think my Dad let me agree to haul his hay to teach me a lesson! It worked.

For many years the Irma State Graded School had First Grade through 10th Grade. Dad was the Principle and the high school teacher. He seemed to know exactly what kind of, and how much, trouble I got into. Sometimes I just got a little shaking and a warning, but sometimes I

My Story

got a spanking. Often, if I got a 'likkin' at school, I would get one again when Dad got home from school. Once I said, "I already got a likkin, how come another? He said "because Jimmy Genrich is going to get one when he gets home". I guess we usually got into trouble together. I had Miss Lareiman for my first, second, and third grade teacher. She had been a friend of my parents for many years. I had Miss Dudley for my fourth and fifth grade teacher. She also was a friend of my parents.

I think I was in the fourth or fifth grade when Phyllis Natzke sat in the desk in front of me. She was the preacher's daughter. She wore her hair in long pigtails, and they were always dangling on my desk. When I yanked on them, she told the teacher on me. One day, just before recess, I tacked her braids to my desk. She almost jerked her head off when she jumped up. By that time I had cleared the room, so I didn't get in trouble until recess was over and the bell rang us back into class. Another time, I dipped her braids into the ink well on my desk. As soon as I did it, I knew I was in trouble, because as she flopped her braids around she got ink on her clothes. I quickly emptied my ink well into one behind me, so that I could claim mine was empty all the time. I don't remember how that turned out. I didn't like Phyllis too well. The teacher tried to fix the problem by making us exchange seats. Now Phyllis was behind me. I guess all was going well. I am ashamed to report this, but one day in class when everyone was studying and it was extremely quiet, I accidentally passed gas, I mean I

My Story

let a big FART. It was LOONG and LOUD. I quickly turned around and looked at Phyllis. She got real red in the face, and every one thought she had done it. She tried to protest, but just made it worse. As soon as she blushed, I was home free! Phyllis started to stutter after that, and I think she did for the rest of the year.

What I remember about grade school most is recess and lunch time. Both times were play times, and we played hard. As little kids we played Cowboys and Indians. If there were a skirmish just as the bell rang, it was common to yell "you are dead next recess" if you knew you had made a kill. In winter time, we spent the play time sliding down the hill. The main trick here was to know about when the bell was about to ring. Just before the bell, you wanted to run and jump onto your sled so that you would be whizzing downhill as it rang. Every one knew that a round trip down the hill and the long trudge back up could easily take ten minutes. If you went ahead and started AFTER the bell rang, you were in deep trouble. Even if a teacher did not see you do it, there were all those dopey girls who would tell on you. As bigger kids we played soft ball or football during the warm months, and either went sledding or played 'ground hockey' during the winter months.

My Story

CHAPTER 4: MERRILL HIGH SCHOOL

By the time I got through the eighth grade at the Irma school, they had changed things so that the Irma School had grades one through eight. You went all four years of high school at Merrill. Boy, what a change that was, from being a BMOC (Big Man on Campus) at Irma to being a pipsqueak at Merrill. We usually rode a bus to school, unless I had some after school function such as football practice. Then I would drive my car. Since Dad was now the Superintendent of Schools, and his office was in the Court House at Merrill, he would some times pick me up after foot ball practice. On a few occasions, I would hitchhike home after practice. In my later years at high school when I would get a little bored, I would take a little time off (skip school) and go around to all the used car lots to look at, and drive the cars, if I could convince the dealer I was really interested in buying.

One time I found a really beautiful car. It was a 1939 Graham Page. Its styling was radically different than any other car I had seen. It was two tone blue, and had white side wall tires. It had square head lights, and square tail lights. I wanted to drive it real bad. In fact, I wanted it! The dealer happened to be Lox Newell, who had been a resident of the village of Irma, and was a very good friend of my Dad. Lox would not let me take the car out alone, but he let me drive it with him beside me. I guess the car must have been too expensive for me. I cannot remember ever seeing another like it. One time when I took a little time off from school, I really stepped in it. I

My Story

went to Wausau, 20 miles south, to drive cars as I had worn out my welcome at the used car lots in Merrill. I was supposed to be back to school in time for football practice. But hitchhiking is sometimes slow, and I got back to Merrill too late. I decided to just hitchhike on home as the school bus had already left. When I got home I was amazed to find my Dad was there but the car was not! He had decided to ride the school bus home and leave the car for me. He had given the car keys to the high school principle to give to me after practice. What a bummer! In one swell foop Dad, the school principle, and the coach, all knew that I had played hooky. And besides, we were both at home and the car was 12 miles away in Merrill. Ah, life was so unfair!

My high school days were something less than brilliant. I believe I worked harder at not studying than if I had buckled down more. The one class I really liked was one that I accidentally took because it sounded easy. It was American History. I believe it was in my freshman year. By my last year, I had most of the credits (barely) that I needed in my morning classes, so I spent a fair amount of time in the pool hall. I really had no desire to continue my education at college, so I skimmed through as easily as I could. I expected to be a truck driver or some such vocation. I knew by that time I was not going to be a farmer. I tried boxing, but really did not like it. I was too short to play basketball. I took up wrestling and kind of liked it, but our school was not big in that sport. I played football three years, and was never a star, but I earned a

My Story

letter each of those years. I played a left guard position most of the time, and I weighed only 140 pounds. During the summer months I practiced running. I could outrun most of the players that played back field positions. I really wanted to play in the back field, but could not overcome two problems. Number one, I had no one to practice with at ball handling, and number two, the city kids had practiced with each other for years and did not want to hand off to, or throw to, anyone outside their own crowd. Even if the coaches knew what was happening, there was not much they could do and still field a team.

During my high school days, I had an event happen to me that I have given a lot of thought to in recent years. This thing of kids shooting up their schools has brought it back to me. They claim that these kids are usually loners who feel rejected and they strike out by shooting up their classmates or their school officials. Here is what happened to me. Our city had a semiprofessional football team called the Merrill Foxes. They did pretty well in their league, and I liked to watch them. One night I had driven in alone, and since I had gotten there late, I had parked my car way out in back of the parking lot. There were lights, but not where I was parked. I had gotten out of my car and was on the way into the stadium, when this kid I recognized as a student hailed me. He said "Come here, I have some thing to show you". I knew this kid was a loser. He was always alone, dressed different than most, and did not participate in

My Story

any school events that I knew of. I walked over to him, and in the dim light, I realized he was pointing a pistol at me. I can remember I got a kind of a hot feeling all over me. I thought he was going to shoot me. I said "What are you doing". He said "I am just fooling; I wanted you to know I have a gun". Of course, I have lost track of him, and I have no way of knowing how he turned out, but I wonder what he really had in mind. I wonder if he is the kind that have now taken that crap one step further and wind up shooting some one.

While in high school, I joined the National Guard. My agriculture class teacher, Mr. Ekert, was the commander of the local National Guard unit, which was just being organized. You could join at age 17 with parental permission, so I did. The Unit was a Tank Unit, and he needed tank drivers. He knew all the farm boys drove tractors, so he recruited several of us as tank or truck drivers. At first we all learned to drive trucks. Big deal. I had been driving trucks since I was 10 years old. Eventually our outfit got its Tanks. Now that was something different! Several of us were selected to go to Tank Driving School, and I liked that. Naturally, the National Guard was called on to put the tanks in every parade that came along. I became one of the ones who got to drive a tank in whatever parade was going on at the time. After the parade was over, usually near the west end of town, we would be turned loose to take the tanks back to the Armory near the east end of town. If I remember correctly, there were four tanks that we used

My Story

in the parades. In one parade, I was the lead tank, and when we finished, and turned around, I was the last tank in line heading for the Armory. Since I was not leading, I decided to cruise past a girls' house that I wanted to impress. So instead of making a turn that would have kept me on a concrete street, like all the others did, I continued straight to this girls' house on a black top street. As I neared her house, I down shifted so that I could make as much noise as possible, then turned around in front of her house. Now with a tank, like with any tracked vehicle, you usually have to go back and forth several times to complete a 180 degree turn around. I did that, and then I realized I was on a black top street in a 50 ton tank. It was a hot day and the tar was soft, and did I ever make a mess of that street! I guess I cut ruts a couple of inches deep. Not only was my unit Commander mad at me, the city was mad at me, and worst of all, the girls' father was mad at me because, even though the city repaired the street, every time a car went over it, night or day it made a terrible rumble noise.

My Commander eventually forgave me, and that year at our annual two week training session at Camp McCoy, I was selected to drive the tank that would make a "rapid fire" demonstration for the Governor. That was kind of neat. The target was a fake tank they had made out of old car bodies with a wooden pole sticking out the front to look like a cannon. My task was to drive my tank across the little river, come up out of the brush, swing

My Story

the tank both directions as if searching for a target. The
tank crew commander and the gunner were both
experienced men. They would swing the turret around
also looking for a target. Once the target (fake tank) was
spotted, they would open fire. First with a 50 Caliber
machine gun, with tracer bullets, then with the 105
Howitzer cannon. We did not know that just before the
demonstration started, they had soaked the fake tank
with gasoline and oil so that when we hit it, the
explosion would be spectacular. When we hit it with the
50 Caliber tracer bullets, the whole thing blew up. Our
gunner quickly fired about 4 rounds with the cannon
into the already burning tank. I guess it was impressive,
as we were complimented by the Governor for a fine
demonstration!

Some of the local dignitaries from Merrill had been
invited to Camp McCoy for Governors Day. Among
them were my Dad and Mr. Elroy Rundle, Dad's boss.
After the demonstration, I was given permission to take
both of them for a ride in my tank. Mr. Rundle got into
the right front position, where the machine gunner sits.
Dad got into the turret where the tank commander sits.
To get out to the driving ground we had to cross that
little river. I decided to give them both a thrill, so I hit
the water at nearly top speed (probably 20 MPH). I had
not noticed, but they had removed the 50 caliber
machine gun from its mount in front, leaving a 4 inch
hole where the gun would normally be. As I hit the river,

My Story

water poured through the hole left by the absent machine gun right into my Dad's boss's lap! Oh God, nice going!

My Story

CHAPTER 5: OUT OF HIGH SCHOOL
(THE WORLD IS MY PEARL)

I had worked several jobs during the summer vacations besides hauling hay for Barney Cottrell. One of the jobs I had was working on a roofing crew in Merrill. It was hard work but I liked it. One day the Boss, (the Owner) called me aside and said he would like me to go with him to learn to sell roofing jobs. It would pay more, so I agreed to try it. We would go to some house that looked like it had an old roof and call on the owner. The Boss would ask if we could give them an estimate on a new roof. Usually they would say yes, you can look at it. Once on the roof the Boss would do things that would make it leak. He would peel the roofing back from a chimney, or find a loose shingle and tear it. Then he would go to the home owner and tell him what he found that would be leaking soon if not fixed. Then he would give him an estimate that I knew was way too low. The idea was that if we got the job, he could tell the owner that we ran into things he didn't see at first, and he could jack up the price. Most of the time the homeowners were elderly people

I did not like what he was doing and I asked my Dad what I should do. My Dad said I should quit, and that I should tell him why I was quitting. When I told the Boss I was quitting, he said he would double the salary increase he had offered, but that I should not tell anyone else on the crew. I left at noon, and the roofing company

My Story

folded up later that summer. I think the word got around town that he was crooked. I graduated from Merrill High School in the spring of 1950.

All during my high school years I dreamed about going to the West Coast as soon as I could. First of all, I wanted to see more of the world than I could if I stayed in Wisconsin. Secondly, I did NOT want to get stuck on a farm for the rest of my life. I do not mean to disparage farmers. I knew several who I greatly respected, and who were very successful, but I knew it was not for me. Thirdly, I had lusted for a motorcycle ever since my friend Jimmy Karoba had gotten one. Jimmy was several years older than me but that did not register with me. What registered was that my Dad said "no motorcycle while you live at home". He was not being mean; he was looking out for my wellbeing. Both he and Mom were scared of them.

Graham Rankin, John Thompson, and I had made plans on how we were going to bust our bonds and head west as soon as possible. I was going to furnish the transportation, my '33 Chev. Both Graham and John agreed to furnish most of the money we would need. The morning we agreed to leave, I drove across the road to Thompson's farm and tooted for John. He didn't come out, but his Mother did. She said "John is not going". It was pretty obvious that John was not going to be part of the plan. I next drove over the hill to the Rankin farm. Guess what? The same thing happened,

My Story

except this time it was Mr. Rankin who came up from the barn. He said "Graham is going to be pretty busy working the farm this summer, maybe he can go next fall". I only had a small amount of money because they both had agreed that my car would be my share. What to do? **GO!**

I heeded Horace Greely's advice. He said "go west young man, go west". So I did. I was not just blindly heading into the nowhere. I headed to Salem, Oregon, where Mom's sister, Aunt Lila, and Uncle Bert lived. I had several great experiences driving out there by myself. One I remember was in Yellow Stone Park. I had seen a number of bears of all kinds. They seemed to lay around the picnic areas, and were often lying on the roads. I was tired of seeing them, and sort of anxious to get on with the trip. Wouldn't you know a bear was lying on the road and tying up traffic. I stopped several cars back from where he was and waited. After a while I decided to try to get around the "camera clickers" and move on. It occurred to me that the best way might be to get the bear to move. I had a bag of apples that I had been living on, so I reached into the bag, got an apple, and threw it at the bear. The apple landed in front of him, and he jumped up and ran after it. I had not realized that a man on the far side of the bear had gotten out of his car and approached the bear, I guess to get a better shot with his camera. The apple rolled toward the man and the bear chased the apple. The man sped back to his

My Story

car, and as I drove past both him and the bear, he shook his fist at me!

My Story

Chapter 6: I Arrive in Oregon

Although my car was pretty slow I arrived safe and sound in Salem, Oregon with less than two dollars left in my pocket. My Aunt and Uncle welcomed me, and said they had room for me until I could get a job and a place to stay. They had three sons. Richard was my age, Jack was three years younger, and Raymond was five or six years old. The first week there, I began looking for a job.

One day I was down near the railroad yards, and I went into an eating place. It was called the 'Blue Moon', and they were advertising that they had a special called 'the Blue Plate Special' that cost 85 cents. I was hungry and nearly broke, so I ate. I was sitting at the counter, and there was an older man on the adjacent stool. Some how we started talking and I told him I had just arrived in Salem. I told him I had a place to stay at my Aunt's house, but that I was broke and needed a job. He finished eating, paid his bill, and then asked the waitress for a page of her order book. On the back he wrote 'come south 3 blocks to the Blue Lake Packers'. There was that 'Blue' thing again. I asked the waitress what the Blue Lake Packers was, and she said it was a fruit and vegetable canning factory. I sauntered down there after I finished eating, asked for the Boss, and said that I wanted to apply for a job. They directed me to the office, and guess what. The Boss was the guy who was on the stool next to mine, and had suggested I come down there for a job! He put me to work that night. My

My Story

job was helping the man who ran the cookers. We were located on a circular stage kind of place, about 4 feet above the regular floor. There were about ten large silo type boilers all around the stage. Each one could hold four large metal baskets of canned stuff. There was a crane that swiveled all around the 'stage'. It was used to put the metal baskets into the boilers, and to take them out when they had cooked the right amount of time. My job was running that crane. The cook knew how long each basket was supposed to be in the boiling water. Each basket could have different stuff in it; therefore, each needed to cook different lengths of time. Believe me, he sure kept me busy. I would be pulling baskets out of one boiler at one side of the stage, when he would be hollering to pull baskets out of a boiler on the other side. We worked from 5:00 P.M. until we ran out of stuff to can. Usually it would be around 3:00 A.M. I do not remember what my wages were, but with my overtime, plus working Saturdays and Sundays, I was making more money than I had ever seen before. I immediately began looking for a motorcycle!

I found a shop in Salem that had a bunch of used motorcycles on display outside, and new ones displayed inside. As soon as I got inside and looked at prices I went back outside. I found one that looked pretty tattered. When I asked the price, I found that I could afford it. It was a 1941 Harley Davidson 74, which meant it was a big bike. I tried to act like I knew all about Harleys so the guy would sell it to me. As soon as

My Story

I got on it and fiddled around trying to find out how to start it he knew I had never ridden before. He let me suffer for a little while, and then said "Let me on it". I got off. He straddled it and kicked something and it started to roar! What a beautiful sound! He said "climb on behind me". I did, and he drove us out into the country onto a deserted road. He stopped and got off. Then he showed me how to start it and how to shift it. When I got it started, he said "go down the road a little ways, then turn around and come back". When I got back, he said "you will be ok, let's get back to town". He rode in back and I drove us back to his shop. Now I had the transportation that I had gone out west looking for! For anyone who is familiar with the weather on the Oregon coast, you know that I was wet nearly all the time.

Like my first car, I had to make some improvements. It already had a double saddle, saddle bags, and a windshield, but I bought new fenders that were a later style, and then bought a bunch of chrome stuff to put on it. I also bought some handlebar streamers. Man, was I something riding my 'bike'. I did not have any days off, so mostly I was riding to and from work. The Boss let me keep the 'bike' inside the factory storage room where no one could mess with it.

In September of 1950, I had a chance to go deer hunting with several others, in the eastern part of Oregon. In was in the area called the 'high desert' east of a town called

My Story

Prineville. I had never seen a mule deer, and that is what we would be hunting. I was also excited about hunting in the desert. The other hunters left for Prineville a day or two before I could leave, so I planned to ride the motorcycle over. I was told to go to Prineville, and then head out to the east on the Crooked River Road. I would eventually come to a large house on the right about 30 miles from Prineville. I was to stop there, and the ranch lady would tell me where to find my hunting partners. I bought two boxes of 30-30 cartridges, and had a large lunch packed. I put both in the same saddlebag, and headed out. I rode up over the Cascade Mountains on the North Santiam Pass into eastern Oregon.

What a beautiful ride. The scenery changes radically as you top the Pass. You have big timber all the way up from the west, and when you cross over, you are suddenly in desert type country. No large timber, just scrub brush and rocks. When I got to Prineville, I thought about stopping for some lunch, but decided to save my few dollars, and ride on and find a place to eat the lunch I had in the saddle bag. I found the Crooked River Road, and followed it east. I have never seen a rougher road. It had wash-board bumps a foot deep! It was very slow going, and seemed to be shaking everything a part. After several miles, I found a place with some shade right near the river. I stopped to have my lunch. Much to my dismay, the rough road had ruined it. The 30-30 cartridges had worn through the shell boxes, and then through the sandwich bag and the

My Story

paper they were wrapped in. I had one big gob of bullets and cheese sandwich! None of it was edible. I continued on to try find the ranch house.

I found it about mid afternoon. It was impossible to miss. First of all, there were no other buildings around for many miles. It had been a Stage Coach Stop at one time. It was a mess hall and bunk house all in one. It was three stories high, with many bed rooms on the top floor. The second floor had the living quarters for the ranch family, and the first floor was the dining room, kitchen, store rooms and stuff. It had a Veranda all the way around the ground floor. The Veranda was 12 or 14 feet wide, and was roofed. It had benches scattered on all four sides. There were several old men sitting on some of the benches. I was told later that they had been the original cow hands on the ranch. When they got too old to ride, they were invited to retire and stay on at the 'big house'. As I had been told, the lady of the house came out to tell me where my hunting buddies were. She said just follow the road on east from here. You can't miss it.

My Harley 74 soon became a dirt bike as the road disappeared in a creek bed, but I could follow their old tracks. I rode up higher in the canyon and eventually found their camp. There was no one in camp, but I found the rifle they had for me in the truck, so I loaded it and started out to hunt. I started up a mountain near camp where I knew I could find my way back to camp. I kept

My Story

climbing higher and the weather started to deteriorate. Soon I had mist drifting around me. I figured I had better start back down. At one point I saw the biggest deer I had ever seen. I tried to get a bead on it, but the mist closed around me, and when it cleared a little the 'deer' was gone. I worked my way back toward camp and arrived there as it was getting dark. The guys in camp knew I had arrived because my motorcycle was there, but did not know which way I had gone. They were about ready to mount a search. They told me the mountain I had climbed was called Black Butte. When I described the big deer I had seen, they decided it had been an elk, and if I had shot it, I would be in big doo-doo.

The next day we all went out together to hunt, and they explained to me how we were going to do it. I was told to climb down to the bottom of a canyon, and just walk along slowly. The others would also be walking the same direction. I was also told not to "shoot down". What they meant was that the canyons were so deep, if you shot a deer in the bottom, it would be easier to just eat it down there than to try to get it out. Shortly after we started out I realized their strategy. They were all walking along the canyon rimrock above me. They had easy walking, and they could see down into the canyon. If I spooked a deer, they are the ones who would get to shoot. The bottom of the canyon was littered with boulders and fallen trees so it was difficult walking and I had to stop often to rest.

My Story

On one such 'rest' I was watching one of the men hunting with us. He was about 100 yards ahead of me, and walking on the top of the rimrock, being as quiet as he could. As I watched him, I realized there was a deer below him maybe 100 feet, and looking up toward him. The deer stayed there, and my hunting partner walked well above and past him. I began to think I was going to get a shot. I looked more carefully, and found that he really had large antlers, but not as large as the animal I had seen the day before. If I remember correctly, I took a leaning aim using a dead snag to steady me. I held the aim a long time, as I had to make sure the guy on the canyon top was not in line with the deer. By this time I was starting to get shaky, because I knew if I missed and the deer ran, he would go to the bottom of the canyon and would be a sitting duck for the guy on top. I fired once, and the deer dropped where he was. The guy on top yelled "stop shooting at squirrels". I told him I had a deer down, and I needed some help to get it out. That was a major job.

It was about 100 feet up to the top of the canyon wall, so we could not get him out that way. We wound up taking him back down to the bottom of the canyon, struggling through the brush, boulders, and fallen trees, to a place where the canyon walls were not so high. It was a large mule beer buck, by far the largest deer I had ever shot. If I remember right, he had six points on each side, and the spread was almost four feet. Unfortunately, my good luck was more than the ego of my hunting partner could

My Story

stand. He had been the instigator of the hunting trip, was the oldest and most experienced of all of us, and fully intended to be the one to get the first and biggest deer. He found all kinds of fault with about everything I did, including shooting the deer. He felt it was my duty to signal to him where the deer was, and let him shoot it. Because his attitude changed so suddenly, and because he became so sullen, and because one of the other hunters suggested it, I felt it best to head for home that evening. After we had cleaned the deer and had it hanging, I announced that since I had no place to stash the deer, and no place to show the head, I was giving it to them, and that I had to get back to my job. I rode that Harley Davidson 74 cubic inch trail bike out of the mountains in the dark, and was never so happy to get back onto that wash-board road along the crooked river.

This time when I got to Prineville, I stopped at a Café to eat. When I finished eating it was dark, but I headed toward the west in a light rain. By this time I had bought what was called a lap-cloth. It was canvas, and connected to the lower part of the front crash bars on either side of the front wheel, and then fastened to your belt. It caught most of the water that was driven up from the front wheel, and helped to keep you dry. As I started up the east side of the Cascade Mountains, again on the North Santiam Pass, it was still raining. As I got higher, it turned to snow. I kept thinking I would soon be over the top and start down and would get back into the rain. The snow was building up on the road, and I was riding

My Story

very slowly with my feet nearly dragging on the road to keep from tipping over. A semi trailer truck caught up with me and passed. He stopped quite a ways ahead of me, and got out of the cab. When I got up to him, he said "If we can lift that thing onto my flat bed, I will carry you over the pass". Naturally, we could not lift the motorcycle. He said he would drive slowly, and I should ride in his track. We started out that way, but even though he drove slowly, I could not keep up with him. He was soon out of sight. I kept going and eventually started down the west side.

Shortly before I got to the little town of Sweetwater, the snow changed to rain. When I got to Sweetwater I knew I had to get warm, and I needed fuel. It was about 6:00 A.M. and I feared I would have to wait for a station to open. As I rode along, I saw a man through the window of a small gas station. I pulled up to the gas pump and tried to get off the motorcycle. I could not get off! I was so stiff I could not get off the bike. The man came out and literally lifted me off. He said, I am not opened yet, but I have a fire going in the stove. He got a chair, put it behind the stove, and helped me into it. I don't know how long I sat there, but it was the best chair and stove and gas station I had ever seen. While I was warming up, I told him about my hunting experience, and how come I was riding back to Salem during the night. When I got warmed up and limbered up, he filled my gas tank and wouldn't take any pay for it. I thought I would catch

My Story

pneumonia or at least catch a cold. I don't remember getting either one.

My Story

Chapter 7: I GET A REAL JOB

I had heard that the Southern Pacific rail road was hiring, so I rode the motorcycle to Portland to apply for a job. They told me I had to be 18, but they were only looking for a few people and my chances were not too good because I had no experience. On October 14th, the day I turned 18, I rode the motorcycle back to Portland to apply again. It rained all the way, about 30 miles, and when I got there I was soaked through. The railroad was the Southern Pacific, and they had a great big beautiful building. I parked the motorcycle as close to the main entrance as I could, and went inside. I was soaking wet and leaving tracks all down the hall. I saw a door that said PERSONNEL in big gold letters, so I walked in. There was a girl at a desk, and when I said I was looking for a job, she said I would have to go to some other office. I was asking how to find it, when an older lady came out of an inner office. She listened awhile, then asked me where I came from, how come I was so wet, and what did I want. I answered her questions in reverse order. I told her I needed a job, that I was wet from riding to Portland in the rain on my motorcycle, and that I was from Wisconsin. She said "Come with me". We went into the office she had come out of, and she introduced me to a man behind a gigantic desk. She told him I had ridden from Wisconsin in the rain to get a job! I corrected her, and said that I had just ridden the 30 miles from Salem. It turned out that she was originally from Wisconsin, and so was the man behind the desk.

My Story

He was the man who did the hiring for that Division of the Southern Pacific. I got a job! He told me to report to Mr. George Rhodes, foreman of a work crew at Woodburn, Oregon. I was to report to him the next morning before 8:00 AM. I had no way of knowing where it was. I figured I would ask when I got back to Salem.

I have to talk about my motorcycle ride to Portland that morning. It was raining so of course I was soaking wet. In Oregon, even if it is not raining, you still get wet because it has been raining, and the front wheel throws all that water off the road up into your lap. The route I took into Portland that morning went over the Burnside Bridge. It was an old bridge, and the roadway was made of thin metal strips that ran parallel with the roadway. I had been over that bridge one time before in a car, and I remember seeing a guy pushing a motorcycle across. I wondered why. I found out why the morning I started across to get the job. The problem was that the metal strips were badly worn, and as you rode across they would twist sideways. First they would twist one way, then the other. When the front wheel would move one way the rear wheel may move the same way, but it also may move the other way. As soon as you corrected your balance, every thing would slip the other way. With the bridge wet that morning, it was as bad as riding on ice. I was about half way over the bridge that morning before I could get to the side and stop. I wound up pushing the motorcycle over the rest of the bridge.

My Story

On the ride back to Salem, I saw a sign that said WOODBURN, with an arrow pointing to the right. I followed the arrow, and within a few miles arrived at a small town with a railroad running right through the middle. I rode to the depot because I thought they would know where George Rhodes' crew was located. The agent there pointed to the rail yard out in back. I said "Is that where they work from?", and he said "That is where they live". I guess I looked kind of dumb, so he said they live in those 'outfit cars'. I went over there and there were four or five old box cars that looked like they had been made into bunk houses, and maybe six or so that were just freight cars, all hooked together. I parked the motorcycle, and was wandering around wondering what was going on when an older lady came out of one of the bunk cars and asked if she could help me. I explained that I was supposed to report to Mr. Rhodes in the morning to go to work, and I was looking for him. She said that I was at the right place, but that he was out on the tracks with the crew and would not be back until evening. She suggested that I come back the next morning well before 8:00AM, because that is when they started loading. I didn't understand what she meant by loading, but figured I would find out the next day. I rode on back to Salem, went to the Blue Lake Packers, and found the boss. I told him I had a real job and had to quit. He was not angry. He said it was just as good that I found a job because the packing season was about over.

My Story

I left Salem on my motorcycle early the next morning. I got to the rail yard at Woodburn well before 8:00 AM, and found a crew already working. I found an older man and asked if he was Mr. Rhodes. He was, and he was expecting me. I don't know how, but he had been told that I would be there. He assigned me to work with an older man named Shorty McRenalds, and do whatever Shorty told me to do. We loaded tools and supplies on what they called a 'motor car', and on a trailer attached to it. It looked like a flat bed trailer, but had a small gasoline engine under it, and small train wheels on each corner. The motor car had benches to ride on. There were 3 or 4 of them being loaded by other people also.

By 8:00 AM, we were all on the motor cars and heading out toward the main tracks. Shorty jumped off from our car and opened a switch so we could get onto the main track, and we headed out of town. Our job was to install wires on the poles along the track which would eventually operate the new signaling system we were installing. Some of the crew were doing the wiring in big metal boxes along the tracks, some were setting poles, some were climbing poles and setting cross arms and pulling wires up. I was what was called a "grunt". I was on the ground and ran and fetched anything the guy on the pole asked for. He would drop a handline, I would attach whatever he had asked for, and then he would pull it up. There were about 30 men on the crew, and I learned that several of us were brand new, a few having started before me, and a few came a few days

My Story

after I started. The S.P. Railroad was just going from a completely visual signal system, to one that was partly electrical using both signal arms and signal lights. This program was to provide traffic signals to the train crews and also crossing bells or crossing arms for motorists where they did not already exist. To do this, they had to set power poles where there were none, and run new electrical wires. Where there were telegraph poles, we would run our wires on them. In exchange for this privilege, we would repair broken telegraph poles, cross arms, and wires.

The crew lived in what were called 'outfit' cars, and the other freight cars held supplies and tools. The whole outfit could be hooked up to an engine and pulled where ever there was work to do. I eventually learned that our crew had started this project a few weeks before in Portland. We would work the entire length of Oregon, winding up in the Rogue River area at the southern end of Oregon. I became acquainted with another new employee within a few days of starting, and learned that he was living near where I was staying in Salem. His name was George Matson, and he had a car. He offered to pick me up in the mornings if I would help with gas money. Since I was tired of being wet all the time, I took him up on his offer. The first morning I rode with him, I was dismayed to find that we got to work a little after 8 AM. Since every one else was working by that time, I suggested we start a little earlier. The next morning the same thing happened. The third day, Mr. Rhodes came

My Story

to me and said "Move into one of the outfit cars this weekend. You can have any bunk that is empty". That was on a Friday, and I moved into an outfit car during the weekend. The next Monday, when George arrived about 10 minutes after 8 AM, the boss fired him. I over heard George Rhodes tell him that his tardiness was an indication of his disregard for all the other workers. If he felt he was important enough to hold up that many people he should look for a position where his importance would fit better. That is a lesson I have never forgotten!

In the outfit car that I chose, lived Shorty McRenalds, who I was assigned to work with, and two other men. One of them was about 50 years old and was mad at the whole world. I solved that problem by just ignoring him; the other was named Kurt Terry. Kurt had been raised in South Dakota, and had joined the Army in 1940. He was stationed in the Philippines when the war started, was on Corregidor when it fell to the Japs. He survived the Bataan Death March, and had been a prisoner of the Japanese in several locations, the last being in Manchuria. He was one of the "pole climbers", which I thought was the best job on the project. We hit it off pretty well, and spent some of our free time (weekends) together. Since we could ride certain trains for free, we would some times hitch a train ride somewhere, spend a few hours in some little Oregon town, then start trying to find a way to get back by work time on Monday.

My Story

Kurt was a little guy, but he was tough as nails and when he would have a few drinks he would be ready to take on anybody. I had to talk us out of trouble several times because of his big mouth. One time we wound up in a little town on the coast in the southern part of Oregon. After we ate, we found a bar and went in to have a drink. They had one of those little Shuffle Board games, and we played a couple of games while we drank a beer or two. I noticed that most of the crowd seemed to be loggers. First by the way they were dressed, and also by their size! After we had played a couple of games and consumed a couple of beers, Kurt loudly proclaimed that between us, we could beat anybody else in the place. Almost immediately two women stood up to play against us. We had bet a dollar per game, rather Kurt had bet a dollar a game, but he didn't have any money, and I didn't have much. Those two women beat us about five games in a row, and when we tried to quit, they insisted we keep on. I tried to convince them we only had enough money to eat and find a way to get home. About five great big loggers stood up and convinced us we did not have to eat, and that we should keep on playing until we were broke. When we left that joint we had about a dollar and a half between us.

Kurt had been starved when he was a prisoner, and he frequently had night mares. We could have a big dinner, go back to the outfit car and get into a card game or something before going to bed. Kurt's bunk was pretty well in the far end from mine, but I could sometimes

My Story

hear him screaming and/or begging for food. Kurt had had a bad experience, and was not too loyal to the U.S. What he told me was that when he went into the Army his father had several sections of fertile land in South Dakota that he grew wheat on. While Kurt was a prisoner, his father died, and since he had been reported as missing and presumed dead, the family farm was sold to neighbors. When he got home and asserted his claim to his place, the neighbors went to court to block him. He had money coming from the Government for all the time he was a prisoner, but they did not give him the money in time to fight in court for his land. While I was working for the railroad, he got a job in Saudi Arabia, working for the Am Arabian Oil Company as a lineman. He wanted me to try for a job with them also.

Shorty kept encouraging me to become a lineman. He pointed out that my pay would be about double that of a ground man (grunt). I had already decided that is what I wanted to do, but the boss wanted his line men to be experienced. Shorty decided we could take care of that. With Kurt gone, I was spending weekends in Salem at Aunt Lila and Uncle Bert's place. Shorty convinced me to stay at the rail yard and practice climbing. He found a set of 'hooks' for me to wear. They are a steel contraption that has a shank that you strap on your legs. There is a steel bar that fits in your instep, and up the shank a few inches is a pointed piece of steel pointed down. That is what you stick into the pole you are climbing. Shorty also rigged me up with a tool belt and

My Story

the belt you loop around the pole and that you lean back into when you are working on the pole. There was a pole in the rail yard that apparently had been used for practice climbs for ages, because it was sure splintered. When we went out to climb, it seemed we drew a crowd. Several of the crew stayed in the bunk cars on weekends, and I thought they were all coming out to see me fall. They actually came out to help show me how to climb. The crew leader was there with his hooks on, and helped get me started. After I got the hang of it, it was fun to run up the pole almost like a squirrel.

Eventually I stuck a hook into a soft spot on the pole and it slipped out. As I started to fall, I grabbed the pole with both arms. That stopped my fall but you cannot get the hooks into a pole unless your butt is quite a ways out from the pole. I was about 50 feet up, and I was stuck! My arms were bleeding because of the splinters I had gathered in the short distance I had slid when I hugged the pole. The crew leader climbed up behind me and convinced me to let go of the pole and lean back into him. When I did that I could get my own hooks into the pole and then let myself down. By then I was shaking and was ready to try something else. After lunch Shorty convinced me to try climbing again, but to not go so high. We also found another pole that was not as badly splintered. It was a newer pole and was solid. Again I soon found that I liked climbing. When we got back to the outfit cars, the crew leader had found a set of newer hooks, a new tool belt with a full set of lineman's tools,

My Story

and a new climbing loop. I tried them all on and they helped adjust them to fit me. The crew leader suggested that I practice more with the new stuff, and on Monday I was to include my new tools with my grunt tools on the motor car without the boss seeing them. I did that and within a day or two, at the south end of Woodburn, they needed another lineman for a job. The crew leader told the boss he knew how to do it, and sent me to the motor car to get my lineman's stuff. While the boss was busy somewhere along the track I went up the pole with another man to install new cross arms and help string the wire. We were tying in the new wires when Mr. Rhodes came back and saw me. He said "What do you think you are doing?", and The crew leader said "He is getting experience". That settled it. I worked poles whenever it was needed after that. My pay increased, but it did not double.

One of the jobs I got after I started climbing was to replace broken insulators on the cross arms. The crew had several small two man motor cars that ran on the tracks, but one man could lift them off when a train came. I would take three or four gunny sacks full of new insulators, then patrol along the tracks looking for broken insulators. When I found one, I was to pull the motor car off the track, take a new insulator, climb the pole, cut the tie wires on the broken insulator, put on the new insulator, retie the wires, then climb down, put the motor car back onto the track and start all over. When I was first assigned to this job, I was thrilled because I

My Story

had some responsibility. When I worked poles in the little towns, I usually had an audience, and I enjoyed showing off. When I was working the miles between towns, the job sure got boring. As a kid, I had been known to try to shoot the insulators with a 22 rifle. I decided that had been a foolish thing to do.

On one of my runs down track one day, I met another worker with a motor car like mine. He was with a stationary crew out of Salem, and his job was to check for proper bond cables at the places where rails joined. I had him show me what they were supposed to look like, and how to correct them if they were broken. His name was Cliff Furlott, and he was from Antigo, Wisconsin. We found that we had played football against each other while in high school a year or two earlier. Some time later after our outfit cars had been moved to Eugene, Oregon, our crew was asked to supply a man to work with a 'Gandy Gang' to bond the new rails they were installing. I told the boss I knew how to do that, and I got the job. That got me out of replacing insulators for a while, and got me involved in a new task. The Gandy Gang was replacing several miles of track. They would bring the new rails out on a flat car that was backed up the new track as they laid it. An earlier crew had upgraded the rail road bed with new gravel, and had set the ties. The gang I worked with would take the new rails off the flat bed, carry them to the right place, position them, and then drive the railroad spikes into the ties to hold them. What a hard job! On this crew, only

My Story

the boss was white. All the others were Blacks or Mexicans, and all of them were big. The boss was very young, only a little older than I was. One day there was a little bit of trouble with quite a bit of yelling and pushing and shoving. I noticed the two biggest Black men I had ever seen go to the boss and just stand there. He got every thing quieted down eventually, and every one went back to work. I learned awhile later that the young boss's father had been the boss of this crew for a long time, and the son was the assistant. When the old man had to quit because of health problems, and the son got his job, the old man asked the two big Black men to help him if he got into trouble. He treated them right and they were sure backing him on the occasion I saw.

My job was to install a bond cable on the ends of the rails as they laid them. This was to electrically tie the rails together to make the signals work properly. I guess this job lasted a month or so. Another job we had was to maintain the telegraph wires on the poles along the track. They carried a little bit of voltage, and you would get a shock when you touched them and when you let go. I got so that if I was working on the telegraph wires, I would make contact, then lean on the wires until I finished whatever I was doing, then let go. That way I only got it twice instead of every time I touched the wires.

By the time winter started, we were in the mountains way south of Eugene. They had a lot of snow down

My Story

there, and wires were constantly being broken, usually by the weight of snow and ice on them, but some times by snow slides. Most of our time that winter was splicing broken wires. The rail road had installed what they called 'snow fences' in places where the tracks ran close to steep mountain sides where there was danger of snow slides. If there were a snow slide, it would pull the fence wire, which was actually a net, and that would trigger a signal for the engineer that there was a slide over the tracks. The company would then send out equipment to clear the tracks, and then we would go in and rewire the snow fence trigger mechanisms. We would also have to splice all the broken telegraph wires.

I remember one time in a whale of a snow storm, we were trying to pull several telegraph wires close enough together to get a splice on them. There were probably six or seven men pulling on each end of the wire to get it up out of the snow. When we got close enough together, one man reached out to the men on the other wire to help pull the ends closer. When they touched, we all got a terrific shock, and we were all knocked down. Some how, our wires had gotten mixed up with a set of electrical wires that we were not supposed to mess with. I remember that the boss was one of the men that got knocked down, and he said "to hell with it, leave it alone".

My Story

One time we were working on a slide near the summit of a mountain pass. There was a Section Station located there, with one section worker. We were there to help him clear up the slide and get the snow fence back into place and rewired. While we were there, there was a terrible snow storm, and we could not get out. The Section Hand had his family there with him, so there was no room for us in his house. He had a fairly large tool shed, and it had a stove. We fired it up to stay warm, and worked in shifts because there was not enough room for all of us at a time. All we had to eat was potatoes and baloney. We fried them on top of the stove because we had no pans. We were there two days before they got an engine in to get us out.

The engines they used in the mountains were called "Malleys". They were about twice the size of the normal engines, and had either twelve or sixteen drive wheels. They would stop the trains at the foot of the climb at either the north side or the south side at a rail yard. They would take off the regular engines and put a Malley in front and one about 15 cars back. If the train was particularly long, they would some times put a third Malley about 30 cars back. These Malleys were diesel powered, and they caused severe problems for the Hobos who rode the trains. What was happening was the Hobos would hop into the empty box cars. When they went through the many tunnels, the diesel exhaust would seep into the box cars. When there were multiple Malleys, there would be that much more exhaust, and

My Story

they would frequently find dead Hobos in the box cars when they got to the rail yards at Eugene.

I remember one day we were working on poles along a long straight stretch of track. The SP was testing a new special engine that was extremely fast. The boss kept checking his watch. He had told us when he gave a signal, he wanted every one down off the poles and way back from the track. He was afraid the fast train would create a suction and we would be pulled off the poles. He needn't have worried. The train came through and it was fast but it did not create a vacuum.

All the while I was working on the railroad, when they moved our outfit cars to a new location, I would ride my motorcycle to the new place. I swear, I was never dry, and I was getting fed up with it. I began thinking about some different transportation.

My Story

Chapter 8: MY FORD ROADSTER

One weekend while in Eugene, Oregon, I began to do some serious car shopping. I looked at many cars, and drove a few. It sort of reminded me of when I was in high school and would skip school to go drive used cars for entertainment, only now I had some dollars in my pocket and a motorcycle to trade in. The bike was sort of a problem. I found a few cars that I liked, but in each case the dealer would not take the bike in trade, and I did not have enough cash. I remember being at a car lot on the edge of town, in a slight rain, and I found two beautiful CONVERTIBLES! I had not even thought about a convertible, but all of a sudden I wanted one bad! One of them was a gigantic 1941 Buick. It was black with a white top. It had acres of chrome, white wall tires, a continental kit, and the dealer would take my bike in trade. The problem was that I did not have enough cash even with the motorcycle to swing the deal. I began looking at the other convertible. It was a 1939 Ford convertible coupe. It was Robin Egg Blue, with a white top. It also had white wall tires, a radio, spot lights on both side cowls, and it had a Rumble seat! Wow! I can still remember how the paint shined because it was wet from the rain. I drove it around the block and knew I had to have it. I bought it that night, but had to wait till Monday to get it titled and licensed. What a change in transportation. When it was sunny the top came down, when it was raining the top went up. What could be better?

My Story

I began to make trips around Oregon that I had not seen on my train trips. On weekends, I would drive to Salem to Aunt Lila's place to eat and spend Friday night. Then on Saturday Richard (my cousin who was about my age) and I would take off for some place. One trip we made was to Coos Bay, Oregon, to see a gigantic big whale that had beached itself. It was still alive, but could not get back into deep water. They tried lots of actions to get rid of it because they were afraid of the smell it would make if it rotted there. I heard later they dynamited it and then buried the pieces. Another weekend trip was out to the eastern part of the state. It was called the John Day country, and was more desert than any thing I had seen up to then. One weekend we went up on Mount Hood. I believe it is Oregon's highest mountain, and it had lots of snow. We tried skiing, but it was not as much fun as skiing on the Irma Hill when I was a kid.

In the spring of 1951 I began to think that I really did not want to be a lineman the rest of my life. I looked at the guys that were much my senior, who were the experienced linemen. They were living just like I was. They spent the week in the outfit cars, and then on weekends they went home to their families. There really was not too much future in the job I had. I talked to Mr. Rhodes about it, and he offered me a pretty good raise if I stayed, but he agreed that the job did not have a real bright future. I think it was about June that I quit, and headed for Merrill, Wisconsin in my little blue convertible.

My Story

Chapter 9: I HEAD BACK EAST

I drove south out of Oregon down into California. I really did not stop to see much of the country, but I thoroughly enjoyed it as I drove through. The weather was nice, and I drove with the top down almost all the way to Wisconsin. My route took me out of California to the east into Nevada. Boy, did I ever see desert there. I was driving down out of some mountains early one morning, and I noticed there were icy spots on the highway. At one of them I stopped to investigate. I found a large pipe about 3 feet in diameter, made of wood, running along side the highway. At some places there were holes in the pipe, and the pressure would shoot a stream out onto the roadway where it was freezing. When I got into a little town below I asked what the pipe was for. They told me the Mormons had built it in the 1800s to bring water from the mountains to the desert below for their crops. I drove through Reno and Elko in Nevada. They were both small towns. I drove through a portion of Utah, and then into Colorado. I remember descending from the mountains into Denver. It was at night, and the lights were beautiful. The next town I remember was Omaha, Nebraska. I stopped there to try to find a school friend. I found him just as he was leaving for work and he dared not be late or he would lose his job. I sure did not envy him! I pressed on and soon arrived back in Merrill about a year after I had left for the west.

My Story

When I arrived in Merrill, I was not sure where my Mom and Dad lived. I knew they had moved off the farm at Irma while I was gone. I knew it was a big house on 3rd street, and I soon found it. As I had driven pretty hard, I slept for a couple of days, and then started looking for work.

I soon got a job on a roofing crew. After all, I had experience because I had worked at roofing while in high school. One of the guys on the crew had been an assistant football coach, as well as my biology teacher in high school. I thought why aren't these guys better off than me? They have been at it longer than I. The work was hard and we worked long days, but I reveled in showing off how good a shape I was in. I was the only one on the crew who could carry a full bundle of shingles on each shoulder up the ladder and deposit them on the roof. After all, I had been a lineman climbing poles for almost a year.

My next job was driving a taxi cab. The Cab company had brand new 1951 Chevrolet cars. The owner drove during the daytime, and I had the night shift. I worked from 6:00 P.M until 8:00 A.M. My pay was $5.00 per shift and all my tips. The problem was Merrill does not tip! In fact, many of my customers were little old ladies going home from shopping. They paid in nickels and dimes, and very often would short change me. Since the cabs were radio dispatched, the office knew exactly how much I should turn in at the end of my shift. When I was

My Story

short, they expected me to make up the difference from my tips. My time from 6 PM until about 8 PM was usually taking people home from the office, or from shopping. The fare was 25 cents for a ride any where inside the bridges. If I had to cross any of the bridges, there was an extra 10 cents added per bridge. All of the passengers knew this, yet many of them would count out the fares in pennies, nickels, and dimes, and would short me a few pennies. I soon knew who they were, but the office also knew who they were and often would warn me via radio.

I had a couple of unique experiences in the short time I drove cab. One was an attractive lady who was probably in her 30s. On Wednesdays and Saturdays, at 7 P.M., she would request a cab pick her up at her home about 4 miles south of Merrill. That was on my shift. I would pick her up and take her to a Saloon in the sixth Ward. She was always well dressed. At about 9 P.M., I would get a call to pick her up and take her to a saloon at Mid Town. By this time she would be starting to show a little wear. Around 11 P.M. I would get a call to pick her up and take her to a saloon downtown. By then, she would be pretty sloppy. At about midnight I would get a call to take her to a saloon out on the East Side. By now I would have to help her into and out of the cab, when we got to the next saloon. At 2:00 A. M., (Closing Time) the bar tender would call for me to pick her up and take her home. By this time she was pretty limp and usually incoherent. I would drive her back to her house. The

My Story

first time, I wondered how I was going to get her into the house. I needn't have worried. Her husband (I think) met us in the driveway and carried her into the house. He always tipped well. I didn't know who she was, or what her background was, but she certainly had a routine. I was told later that she had been a 'working girl' in her younger days. After she married, her husband paid her bar bills and took care of her in return for her staying with him.

The other incident that I can clearly remember was a fare that I picked up at a saloon on the west side. It was around midnight, probably a week night. There were four men, and I had transported them to a couple of bars earlier. They told me they were salesmen from out of town and were in Merrill for a meeting. Anyway, shortly after I picked them up and headed toward the east side, I smelled cloth burning. I looked in back, and they had started the seat upholstery on fire with a cigarette. I stopped, and we put it out. I called into the office and asked what to do about it. They told me to charge them $25.00 for the damage. The men heard it on my radio and said "by God, they were not going to pay a cent for the seat upholstery". While they were singing at the top of their voices, I called the office and told them the men would not pay. The cab owner came on the radio and told me to waste a little time, and then drive past the Merrill Police Station. There would be a cop on the side walk. I did that and when I came near the Police Station, sure enough, there was a cop waiting for us. The

My Story

men got out thinking we were at the next saloon. The Cop grabbed one of them and said, you guys are done drinking in my town, you are going to jail. There was a short argument, and the men agreed to pay for the upholstery, only by now the price had gone up to $50.00. They also agreed to pay for their fare to the Police Station, which they did, and then the cop drove them to their motel. Driving a cab 12 hours a night is not conducive to safety. While I was driving cab, Jerry had an appendicitis operation. One night Emily, his girlfriend, called me to see if I could drive her out to the Hospital to see him. I guess her car was broke or something. Any way, I drove her out there and later picked her up to go home. For years, she told me that going both ways, I was stopping for green lights, and driving through red ones. Maybe! I soon got tired of driving around Merrill. It was a pretty routine job. Before going off duty in the morning, I drove the same people from their homes to where they worked. One man who worked in the courthouse was wheelchair bound. I would help him into the cab at his house, then out of the cab at the courthouse. I remember that I would drive right up to the steps on the west side of the courthouse, but I cannot remember there being a ramp there. The morning hours up to 8 AM were just like running a bus route. The few day times that I drove, most of the time I was hauling old ladies shopping then back home. At night it was mostly hauling party goers around from tavern to tavern. About the time I was

My Story

severely bored, the Paper Mill at Tomahawk came to my rescue.

My Story

Chapter 10: I HEAD TO OHIO

My brother Jerry had worked at the Tomahawk Paper Mill for a while, and one day he told me the Mill was looking for people to go to Ohio to work in a paper mill they had purchased down there. He was planning to go on a temporary basis, as were several other mill workers. I asked about outsiders, and he said they were looking for additional men. I promptly went to the paper mill at Tomahawk to put in an application. They immediately accepted, and within a week or two I was on my way to a new adventure. If I remember correctly, the people from Wisconsin were all going down there on a temporary basis, so they did not let us drive our cars. They sent us by train. I guess the ride was uneventful as I do not remember any thing exceptional happening.

When we got there, the Jaite Company (the mill that had been purchased) had made arrangements for a number of us to board in private homes. They had a barracks building near the mill with dining facilities, but that was filled with other workers, so we were assigned to private homes. The place where I was assigned was at Mrs. Conger's home. Mrs. Conger was an older lady who reminded me much of Grandma Edmund. She had a large house that was located about halfway between the villages of Peninsula and Boston. My brother Jerry and two older men were also assigned there. I don't remember how we got to work, as none of us had a car. I guess the mill must have had some one pick us up.

My Story

I bought a motorcycle within a few days, so my transportation problem was solved. Within a short time, the temporary workers began drifting back to where ever they had come from. Jerry and I were still there, and some other men from the Tomahawk Mill were still there. It looked like we would be for a while. We convinced the company to send us back to Wisconsin and let us bring our cars back down. They agreed. I guess there were four of us who all caravanned back to Ohio after picking up our cars in Wisconsin. Jerry had a new Plymouth, and I drove my Ford convertible.

At work, I was assigned to yard work, which was the lowest form of employment the mill had. As I remember it was mostly cleaning up debris that had accumulated over the years. After most of the temporary workers were sent back home, those who were chosen to stay were told to move into the barracks. The two older men who originally had stayed at Mrs. Congers had long since gone home. Jerry left to go back to his job at the Tomahawk Mill, and I stayed on. Mrs. Conger asked me to continue staying at her place, and that suited me fine. She was a good cook, and her house was much more comfortable than the barracks. I had both the motorcycle and my car down there. Mrs. Conger had a garage that I could keep the car in, and I usually rode the bike to work. Mrs. Conger (and all the others who had workers in their homes) was paid by the Company for our room and board. I thought that Mrs. Conger had asked me to stay so that she could continue to be paid by the

My Story

company for my room and board. I found out much later, after I had joined the Air Force and was home on leave that she was not being paid by the company, and neither had I paid her! When I apologized, she said having me there was like having her sons back home. It turned out that Mrs. Conger was fairly wealthy, her two sons were very successful businessmen, and her daughter and husband, who lived across the street, were owners of a large successful trucking company

One day when I was at work doing menial tasks in the mill yard, someone asked me if I was interested in earning some overtime pay on the next weekend. Was I ever interested! I agreed to meet a Mr. Leslie Smith the following Saturday morning. I should explain that in addition to making paper, this mill also made paper bags. They were the types that were sewn together at both ends for stuff like fertilizer, cat food, etc. The bags were made in a wing of the paper factory. Between the paper factory and the paper bag factory was a large storage room. When the rolls of paper were made they would be delivered to the storage room and placed in stacks according to the type of paper. The rolls of paper were approximately 5 or 6 feet in diameter, and the stacks could be 20 or 30 feet high. When the paper bag factory needed a certain kind of paper, it would be delivered from the storage room to the bag factory via an overhead crane. The rolls of paper were handled by a gigantic crane that was mounted in the storage room ceiling. By working levers in the crane cab, one could

My Story

move in any direction, while other levers were used to lower or raise a boom that had a device which would squeeze the paper roll. The squeeze device also was controlled by levers in the cab. This whole thing ran on rails that were electrified.

My job that weekend was to climb around on these stacks of paper and call out the identification information on the paper rolls to Mr. Smith on the floor. The reason we had to be taking this inventory was that the man who was supposed to be operating the crane, and keeping track of which paper was on which stack, had not been doing his job. He was also the Postmaster at a little nearby village. It later developed that he would come to work at the mill, clock in, stack what ever paper had been made during the night shift, and find and put down whatever paper the bag factory would need in the next shift. Then without clocking out, he would go and do his Postmaster job. Later on in the afternoon he would come back in and clock out. In other words, he was cheating. I did not know all of this on that weekend I was working with Mr. Smith, but I told him that I thought running that crane would be about the best job I could imagine. Think of it, you would have some responsibility, and you would sure be in the center of activity. You would interface with the paper factory to store their output, and you would interface with the bag factory to get them the material they needed. When there was no paper to store away or to put down, you could mess around. Above all you would not be outside on the

My Story

grounds crew! To facilitate getting the information from some of the paper rolls that weekend, there was a man in the crane to move paper rolls if they needed to be moved. The man was not used to the crane, and was having a hard time restacking paper rolls.

Would you believe that within a week I had that job? The operator who had been cheating was fired. I was asked if I would take the crane operators job on the night shift until I had learned how to operate the crane (which was easy) and learn the identifications of the many different types of paper that was manufactured. Certain kinds of paper were stacked in a place where they could be moved out to a loading ramp for shipment. Other types were to be stacked so that they could be moved down to the bag factory floor. I worked night shift for a few weeks then was assigned to day shift. When the bag factory worked night shifts, I would work overtime to supply them with the paper they needed. This job gave me lots of free time, but I made sure I was always around where they could find me if paper needed to be moved.

Like I said earlier, I had bought a motorcycle shortly after arriving in Ohio. I never was a 'wild biker' but I did ride with a bunch of rough bikers. One Saturday we were in Akron, Ohio on Howard Street which at that time was sort of a slum, and was mostly Black. We pulled into a coffee shop, raising about as much dust as we could raise sliding to a stop. We strutted into the

My Story

café, and sat at the counter. A very large Black lady asked for my order. I said "coffee". She said "How do you like it", I said "Just like my women, hot and sweet" She said "Do you like it black too honey?" I guess she cut me down to size quick! The tough bunch I rode with never let me forget that exchange.

My Story

Chapter 11: I meet my Dream Girl

One Saturday I went to an annual celebration event in the village of Peninsula. There I met a young local girl. I was pretty much smitten, and asked some of the people I knew, who she was and where she lived. Her name was Dona Wise, and she lived in the Village of Boston. I told Mrs. Conger about my meeting her, and Mrs. Conger said "Oh yes, I know her family well". I guess I found out Dona was working at a restaurant in the little town of Hudson, so I started hanging out there, and eventually got brave enough to ask for a date. We went to movies, and I guess to dances. On Halloween, we went to a costume street dance in Akron. Dona had picked out costumes for both of us. We parked the car and started to where the dance was in progress. Some dizzy female shouted "Look, here comes Julius La Rosa," and that started a mad rush of lots of people toward Dona and me. We quickly ducked back into my car, and we got out of there. For all of you young folks who may wonder who Julius La Rosa was, he was a singer on the Arthur Godfrey Evening Show. I guess he was a 'flash in the pan' because his career was short lived.

I was surprised one day at work to find out that I had known Dona's Mother quite awhile before I met Dona. Dona's Mom worked in the bag factory, and was one of the ladies I talked with when I was not in the crane. I found out some time later that there was a conspiracy to get us together! Mrs. Conger had known Dona's Grandfather for many years, and apparently they

My Story

respected each other greatly. When Dona's Mom found out that I was visiting Dona at the restaurant where she worked, she asked the older gentleman to check me out with Mrs. Conger. I guess Mrs. Conger gave them a good report on me. Some of the characters who went to Ohio to work the mill were hard drinking ruffians, and after all, I was riding a Harley!

One of the lessons I had learned when I was a boy in Wisconsin, was that it never worked out good when you loaned out your car. I really liked my little Ford convertible, and although I was asked several times to loan it to people I worked with, I never did. One evening, probably a Saturday evening, Dona and I were double dating with another couple. The guy was from Chicago, and had not been on the crew very long. We met at a saloon locally called 'Dirty Dick's', and then were going to pick up our dates. He convinced me to let him take my car and drive the couple of miles to where his date lived to pick her up, then we would pick up Dona. He never made it. On the way he smashed into a cement culvert, and that was the tragic end of my beautiful little blue convertible.

My Story

ODE TO A '39 FORD

I was fresh out of school

and bum'in around.

When I found myself

in this west coast town.

It was rainy and wet as I rode along,

But I was happy and I was hum'in a song.

I had left my home a year before,

And was doing the things I had come here for.

I had felt a need to see the world,

So I set out with my old 'Chevy' girl.

She was old and slow, a sedan you see,

and she proved to be too slow for me.

She got me to the Oregon coast,

without a breakdown I could boast.

My Story

But I wanted a faster, more stylish ride,

so I found a Harley that I could abide.

I rode her around the Oregon west,

and when it was sunny I felt the best.

It rained a lot, and I was always wet

so for a dryer ride my heart did set.

It was misty and rainy as I rode by

when something shiny caught my eye.

I quick turned back for a closer look,

and what I saw just fit the book.

She was Robin Egg Blue and a beautiful thing,

And tho not new, she was fit for a King.

She was slim and trim and ready to go,

And I could see at a glance that I wanted her so,

My Story

I parked my Harley in the Used Car lot,

and headed for the office at a rapid trot.

I grabbed the man who ran the place,

I got right up in his 'used car' face,

I told him of the deal I'd make,

if he could see clear to give me a break.

He didn't, he wanted my gold hoard,

but I left that lot with a '39 Ford.

As I said before, she was Robin Egg Blue,

she had a white top that folded down too.

She had a leather inside and a Rumble Seat,

And when I cruised 'top down' she was really neat.

We toured the breadth of Oregon some more,

through desert and mountains and down to the shore.

My Story

It was over a year since I'd started to roam,

So I turned south and headed for home.

We traveled beside that shiny sea

on 101, my '39 Ford and me.

We passed Mount Shasta on the trip,

and drove down Reno's famous Strip.

Then we headed back east in bright sunshine

my Ford and I followed the center line.

We rode through Death Valley and out on the plain,

then up through the Rockies, and plains again.

We drove through towns both large and small,

My Ford and I enjoyed them all.

We crossed many rivers, including big Miss.,

then turned north toward home in Wis.

My Story

It was good to be home, but I soon got bored

so I fueled up my trusty old Ford.

We headed down south, on the road once more,

past old Chicago and Michigan's shore.

We drove on east toward the rising sun,

sort of job hunting, and I found one.

It was in Ohio at a paper mill,

And I found lodging on the side of a hill.

In a short time I found a cute girl,

I thought what the heck, I'll give her a whirl.

She looked at me and she looked pretty bored

but she sure did like my '39 Ford.

When we went driving, we'd put the top down,

I sure felt good driving up town,

My Story

with a pretty girl in the car with me

and the top down so all could see.

Alas and alack, I broke my rule.

I loaned out my car like a damn'd fool.

He used the car to get him a date,

And he sped away because he was late.

Before he had driven very far

he had totally wrecked my car.

I realized when it was too late

that my '39 Ford had met its fate.

Now I had a problem. I was seriously courting Dona and all I had was a motorcycle. To make matters worse, her father was still not sure I was good enough for his daughter, and he certainly did NOT like my motorcycle. He forbade her to ride it with me. She did only once, and that was when she needed a ride home from her job, and we had specific permission from her Mom. Her Dad never knew! Part of my troubles were since she could

My Story

not ride the bike with me, we would stay at her place and watch TV, or swing on the porch swing. About 10:00 PM, I would head for home, and there is no way you can start an old 'kick start Harley' quietly. Her Dad worked a night shift at a tire company in Akron, and he usually got his sleep in the evening before going to work at midnight. He was not too happy at being rudely awakened way too early by a roaring Harley. By the way, I loved the noise. I used to ride with my head sideways so I could hear the exhaust noise!

Since my courting Dona was severely crimped by not having a car, I decided I would buy a new one. I went to the local Chevrolet dealer in Peninsula, and put in an order for one. At that time you had to order your car and it could take up to several weeks to get it. My 19th birthday was coming up, and I wanted to have my car by then. The dealer assured me I would have it by then. The car I ordered was a 1951 Chevrolet four door sedan, iridescent green. I did not order fancy add-ons because I could not afford them. Another of my coworkers ordered a similar car at the same time, from the same dealer. A few weeks later, on arriving at work, my coworker had his new car. He said my car was there also. We were on a night shift at the time.

The next morning I dashed to the dealership to pick up my new car, and the dealer said "Yours did not come in". I said "Yes it did, that is it right there". He said he had just sold it to another guy. When I protested, he said

My Story

the other guy had a trade in that he could sell, while all I had was a motorcycle that he did not want. He told me my car might be on the next load in several weeks, I told him I thought he was crooked, and that I would not buy a car from him under any condition. I told him I was going to go into Akron and I would buy a car that day if it had to be an old Model A Ford. He laughed, and I left. I went home and told Mrs. Conger what had happened. She suggested I get some sleep before going into Akron to look for a car.

When I woke up she told me she had talked to her son who had a Ford dealership in Akron. He had suggested I go to a Chevrolet dealership in Akron, I think it was "Dutch's' Chevrolet, and they were by far the largest dealer in the area. When I got there I found that they had literally blocks of new cars. I was walking around the lot looking for one like I had ordered, and I found one exactly like it. A salesman showed up and I told him my woes, and that I wanted to buy that car that day. He said, "Wait a minute, most of these cars have been ordered, and have just not been delivered yet". We went into an office and lo and behold, the car I wanted was one they had ordered on speculation, meaning it was available. There was a problem however. I had ordered my car pretty bare because it was cheaper. I told the dealer I would take the car if they took off the fancy bumperetts, the extra chrome, and the fancy seat covers. I said I would keep the radio. They told me if I wanted the car, I would take it all. They said they were selling the car at

My Story

cost, and they had to make a little money on the accessories. I quickly caved in when we discovered I had just enough money to swing the deal.

I drove my new car directly to the dealer in Peninsula and parked in front of his gas pumps. I went in to find the owner, and asked him to fill my gas tank. He was some flabbergasted when he saw my new car exactly like I tried to buy from him. He thought he had me in a bind and I would have to wait to get my car from him. Within a few years (by the time I got out of the Air Force) his dealership had failed. Now I had an automobile, and my courtship of Dona flourished.

I had decided that she was the one I wanted for my wife. At work one day, I showed Dona's Mom the engagement ring I had picked out, and asked if she thought she and Dona's Dad would let Dona go to Wisconsin with me at Christmastime to meet my family. I planned to give Dona the ring at Christmastime. Dona's Mom thought it would be OK, and I knew she would 'run interference' for us with Dona's Dad. We finally gained his approval.

Would you believe the day we were to leave, a few days before Christmas, we started to get snow and rain. Both Dona and I were working day shift, and we planned to leave as soon after work as we could. We had agreed to stop at Chanute Air Force Base, in Illinois, and pick up my brother in law, Capt. Ray Schwartz. My Sister Verna and their kids had gone to Wisconsin a few days earlier.

My Story

When we got out onto the highway, a very busy two
lane (Interstates had not been invented yet) the rain
began to freeze on the road surface. Traffic was very
slow. Dona slept a while as the plan was for her to sleep
a little then relieve me when I got too tired. We were
somewhere in Indiana when I could not keep my eyes
open any longer. Dona started driving and before I could
even get my eyes closed, we went off the road. The road
was glare ice, and many cars were in the same fix. We
had gone off on the right-hand side of the roadway, and
down into a fairly deep ditch. There was no damage to
the car, as our speed had been very slow. Shortly after
we had climbed back up to the road, a car, I think from
New York stopped to help us. They could not pull us
out, but offered to take us into the next town to get help.
It was a few miles, probably 5 or six, to a little town.
They let us out at a service station. The man there had a
small wrecker, and said he would go out to pull us out.
He did. I think he charged us 15 or twenty bucks, and
there were seven or eight other cars in the ditch that you
could see from our car, so he was going to make out
pretty good.

Once back on the road, we pressed on and got to
Chanute AFB shortly after daybreak. We found Ray,
and as soon as he checked out of the Base, we headed
for Wisconsin. Ray was driving because he had gotten
some sleep the night before, and neither I nor Dona had.
We left the Base in a snowstorm, and it continued to get
worse. We were in a long line of automobiles, and were

proceeding very slowly. By nightfall, we were about adjacent to Chicago, and a few miles to the west. We had managed to refuel some time late in the day, and this turned out to be an important thing. The traffic was proceeding at the speed of the snow plow we were following. As cars ran out of gas, the column would dig a path around them. And we would continue. At some point during the night, the entire column of cars was stopped. The snow plow was hopelessly stuck.

We were near some kind of country store with gas pumps. We could not get the car up to the pumps because of snow, but we still had lots of gas. We did not have much to eat, and it looked like we were going to be there a long time. Ray got out of the car, waded to the store, and came back with lots of snack type stuff to eat. It seems to me that we wound up with several others in our car because we had gas to run the engine and keep the heat on. Some did not. We also had stuff to eat, and some did not. About daylight they got several snow plows together, and we began to move along again. We had now been in the car all one day and all one night and had traveled less than 100 miles. Besides that, Dona and I had been in the car all night the night before. We were informed that if we turned west and got on whatever the next major highway to the west was, we would have easier going. We did, and it got better. It took us a full three days to get from Chanute Field to Wisconsin, where it usually took Ray and Verna one day. When we got home we found out that the officials had sent rescue

My Story

trains out from Chicago to rescue the travelers who were stranded on the highway we had been on. We did enjoy a nice Christmas at Merrill. I got to show off my intended, and she accepted my engagement ring! Then trouble struck!!

My Story

Chapter 12: A Change in Plans

While we were in Merrill, I believe the day after Christmas, I received my Draft Notice! I was in a state of shock. I had just turned 19, and they were drafting 26 year olds. I knew that my time was coming, but expected it was a couple of years away. My Dad checked with the local draft board to see why I got my notice at age 19 when they were still drafting 26 year olds. The answer was that I was changing my address too often, and was apparently just bumming! When I signed up for the Draft at age 18, while in Oregon, they made my Draft Board be at my home in Merrill. They also instructed me to keep them aware of my current address each time I moved. I did this religiously, and because the railroad moved us frequently, then I returned to Wisconsin, then went to Ohio, I guess they figured I was fair game. I dashed to the Air Force recruiter and attempted to enlist as that had been my plan.

The Recruiting Officer told me he was sorry, but that his quota was filled, and I would have to wait a month. I did not have a month. I had been instructed to report to Milwaukee, Wisconsin for my physical the day before New Years day, and then leave immediately for Boot Camp. I went home and told my brother-in-law Ray (Captain Schwartz) that I could not enlist because the quota was full. He went to the Air Force Recruiting Office with me. After a fair amount of discussion, I was

My Story

sworn into the Air Force, providing I passed the physical which was the same one I was scheduled for the Draft.

Because the physical was scheduled for the last day of 1951, December 31, and I was to leave for Basic Training immediately, Dona and I had to change our plans severely. We had planned to stay in Wisconsin through the New Year's holiday, and then drive back to Ohio. The plan we quickly put together was this: Dona and I would leave immediately for Ohio. I would then drive back to Milwaukee for the scheduled physical. Since there would not be time to drive back up to Merrill, I was to leave my car in a commercial parking lot when I left for Basic at Lackland AFB in Texas. When I got to Texas, I was to contact Dad to let him know where the car was, and he would pick it up as he had a meeting in Milwaukee within a week or two. That was the plan.

Here is how it actually went down. We drove back to Ohio, and I had to leave immediately to get back to Milwaukee in time for my physical. Of course I passed. They let the Army Draftees go home to wait for their call up, which was to happen in a few weeks. The Air Force enlistees were sworn into the United States Air Force on December 31, 1951. We were lined up for inspection, and immediately given a Three Day Pass! Wow, this was a whole new event. What do you do with a 3 day pass? You don't drive your car to Merrill, in northern Wisconsin; you naturally go to see your

My Story

Girlfriend who lives in the opposite direction! I drove back to Ohio, spent New Years Day (and the next day) with Dona, and then drove back to Milwaukee, found a good parking lot, phoned my Dad to tell him where the car was, and hopped the train for my new career in the Air Force.

I remember a particularly funny thing I witnessed when we had our physicals. There were probably 100 young men from all over Wisconsin. They were draftees for the Army, and enlistees for the Air Force. We all went through the same line and got the same treatment. There was a fellow two or three places ahead of me who was quickly identified as a real "hay shaker". Almost every time he was asked to do something, he would say "Who, me?" in a high pitched voice. It was pretty obvious the Doctors were getting fed up with him. At the last stop in the line, the medic said to each man, "Give me a urine sample" and he would point at a row of small bottles on a table about 10 feet away, and indicate a privacy screen in a corner. The hay shaker said "Who me" and then "What?" The Medic repeated the same instructions again. The hay shaker said "What?" The Medic yelled "Damn it, piss in the bottle". Hay shaker said, with an astonished look on his face, "From here"? I guess every one was watching the exchange by this time, and everybody laughed. I have often wondered how Hay Shaker made it in the Army.

My Story

Chapter 13: MY MILITARY CAREER

We arrived at Lackland Air Force Base, near San Antonio, Texas, on January 4th, 1952. We were immediately assigned to a tent in 'tent city'. They had many empty barracks on the base, but I guess putting us in tents was part of the training. The tents held 12 men each, and each man had a cot and a small foot locker. They woke us up at 4:30 A.M., and we marched for about an hour. Then we had a one half hour free time (trip to the toilet), then we were marched to the Mess hall for breakfast. I always had enough, but some of the really big guys were always hungry. We did not get any G.I. clothes or equipment for several days. We wore what we arrived in, and we marched in what we had on our feet. Neither clothes nor shoes lasted long. I had on a bright yellow shirt, and that damned shirt got me into more trouble. It seemed if the Drill Instructor wanted to show how to do some thing, or make an example of some one, he would yell, "Hey, you in the yellow shirt, front and center". Then he would use me as a demonstration dummy.

Eventually we got our military clothes. Naturally, nothing fit, so when you got back to the tent area, you went looking for some one who had your size clothes, but needed the size you had been issued. They did take enough time to fit our boots. Of course they also issued a duffle bag, and you soon learned how to roll your clothes so that every thing would fit inside. We spent an awful amount of time learning how to march. They

My Story

called it 'close order drill', and we did it all day long. For some reason that I never knew, after about two weeks, they piled us all into buses, and transported us to Sheppard Air Force Base at Wichita Falls, Texas.

This base is in the northern part of Texas, and it got bitter cold at night. We were still in 12 man tents, and each tent had a stove in the center. There was a pile of wood outside each tent which the occupants were to keep replenished. We were supposed to take turns standing a 2 hour fire guard during the night. It was so cold that it was common to over heat the stove and the metal chimney that went through a hole in the canvas would catch it on fire. When a tent caught fire, you would see men rolling out from all sides. I don't remember any one getting burned, but we sure burned up a lot of tents. We soon learned that in addition to standing Fire Watch, we also had to stand Fire WOOD Watch. Since we had to carry the fire wood from a pile a half mile away, it was easier to steal it from someone nearer. Even though we had a stove in the tent, it was impossible to stay warm, so we would sleep with both pairs of fatigues on. When the Drill Master found out we were doing that, he would keep us at drill in the morning until it got hot and every one was ringing wet with sweat. Usually at noon, after mess, we would have enough time to peel off one pair of fatigues.

We started out with a Flight of about 110 men, and halfway through Basic we were down to less than 50,

My Story

the rest being in the hospital with pneumonia. They combined two Flights of trainees to get enough to continue the stuff we were supposed to do. Most of the Trainees spent their 'off' time griping about how bad off they were. I sort of enjoyed Basic Training. I was in pretty good shape when I went in, and other than holler at me a bunch, they did not abuse me.

When we had first arrived at Lackland, they decided we needed to have hair cuts. They marched us to the base barber shop. It had about a dozen barber chairs in a row, and tiers of seats facing the barbers. They marched us in, and instructed us to take seats. The barbers were all ready and were looking over the new recruits. One barber beckoned to a kid who was from California, and had him sit in his chair. The barber elaborately put an apron on the kid, and a scarf around his neck, then he said "how do you want it?" The kid had an elaborate 'duck tail' with big pompadours on each side of his head. He was busy showing the barber exactly how he wanted it, when the barber said "do you want those sideburns?" the kid said yes, and the barber said "Well catch 'em, here they come", and then he shaved the kids head as close as he could. The kid was almost in tears. The lesson was, keep your hair short! My haircut was a butch, and was about as short as they required so the barber was done with me in about a minute. When I started to step out of the chair, he said stay here a minute. He said you were required to be in the chair at

My Story

least 3 minutes so that each barber had an equal chance at the same number of hair cuts. A hair cut cost 75 cents.

When we were not doing close order drill, or picking up pebbles, we were learning Air Force history or taking aptitude tests. I was a little worried about those tests, because I did not want to be a cook nor did I want to be an Air Police. I wanted to be on an Air Crew. I do not know what my tests showed, but I was judged to be a candidate for electronics training, specifically, airborne electronics, which was taught at Scott Air Force Base at Bellville, Illinois. I thought great, I will be flying, and at Scott Field, I will be close enough to get to Ohio once in a while. To make a long story short, I was trained to work on airborne equipment, but not to fly with them. Upon graduating from school at Scott AFB, I was assigned to a Fighter Squadron to work on airborne communications in Jet Fighter aircraft.

I mentioned 'picking up pebbles'. That was one of the ways they kept us busy. If we were not doing close order drills (marching), we picked up pebbles. They issued a 3 pound coffee can to every one, and you used it to transport the pebbles. At some point in time way before I got to Basic Training, the Air Force had hauled in several truck loads of pebbles. They had dumped them in a pile at the end of our tent area. Our task was to pick up a can full of pebbles, carry them to the place in the area that was presently being 'graveled', carefully spread them about an inch thick on a pathway, and go

My Story

for another can full. Some times there were thousands of guys with cans full of gravel. While we were there, we used up the piles of pebbles. Guess what. The next task was to go back out to the pathways and PICK UP the pebbles and carry them back to the piles. By the time I left, the pile was getting pretty big. Out of Basic Training, I was promoted from Airman Basic to Airman 3rd Class which corresponded with the Army Private First Class (PFC), then on to school at Scott Air Force Base near Bellville, Ill.

Once I got settled into my routine at Scott Field, I made arrangements to get to Wisconsin to get my car. I think it may have been on a three day holiday or a three day pass, but I hitchhiked to Merrill. I had a bear of a time getting up there. Although it was late winter, or early spring, it was fairly warm at Scott Field, so I was not wearing heavy clothes. When I got up into Wisconsin it was just plain cold! I got a ride north of Madison with a bunch of young folks who said they were going to go to Wausau. I thought great, that will get me pretty close to Merrill. But better yet, it was about midnight, and this ride would take me through the night when it is nearly impossible to hitch a ride. The problem was that we got just north of Stevens Point, and they decided to go off some place to the east instead of continuing north. They invited me to stay on with them and party through the night, but I wanted to get to Merrill. They let me out at an intersection of two highways way out in the country at about 3 A.M. and it was blowing snow! I had a light

My Story

jacket, suntans, and oxford shoes. I walked north along Highway 51, hoping a car would come along, but none did. The highway had water on both sides, and the wind was blowing snow across like a blizzard. I was about frozen, and began to wonder if I was going to be able to make it when I saw a light on the right side of the road well up ahead of me. When I got up there, there was a small building that I think was a small country store. I went over to it, and banged on the door. An older man came to the door and opened it just a crack. I told him I was hitchhiking home to Merrill, and had run out of rides several miles south of there. I was in my uniform (which helped when hitchhiking) so I guess he trusted me. He let me in, and it turned out that he was there early to make doughnuts which they sold in their store. It was warm in there, and I decided I could not hitchhike any more. He let me use his telephone, and I called home and told Mom and Dad where I was, and that I was stuck. Dad said they would start out right away to pick me up. The man fed me doughnuts, and gave me a place to sleep until Mom and Dad got there.

I drove my car back to Scott Field, and there I was a big wheel, because I had a new car and I was only a student. Students were not allowed to have personal cars on base. We were required to keep them in a large parking lot at the edge of the base. This was bad news, as cars were routinely stolen and/or vandalized. I solved that problem by making the acquaintance of the Air Policeman who dispensed 'permanent party' windshield stickers. He was

My Story

from Ohio, and I convinced him that I had gone to high school there, and that we had played football against each other. He gave me the permanent party sticker, which allowed me to park the car right beside the barracks I lived in.

That solved that problem, but I had another. When I bought the car a few months earlier, I had financed it with a loan from the bank at Merrill. I don't remember what the payments were, but I remember I could not afford them. There were two solutions to the dilemma. One was to sell the car, and the other was to have Dona make the payments. I chose the latter. Since she was making the payments, it seemed only fair that she should have the car in Ohio. We sort of traded off. I would drive the car to Ohio, and then hitchhike back to Scott Field. Next time I had sufficient leave time, I would hitchhike to Ohio and then drive the car back to the base. I did that several times. Dona and her Mother came to the base to visit me a couple of times, and once or twice, I rode to Ohio with them, then drove the car back.

Early in the summer of 1952 while I was at Scott Field, Dona and I began making plans to be married just before I finished my training. We did not know what or where my duty assignment would be, but we figured we could manage about any thing. We picked a date in September, and I put in for a week of leave time. Dona made most of the plans. I told my parents that we would be married

My Story

in September, and that I hoped they could attend. When we first talked about getting married, we talked to Dona's Mom. She said "OK, but you will have to ask her Father". Dona's Dad worked a night shift, starting at midnight, so he went to bed in early evening. I waited until he was settled one evening, then asked if I could talk to him. I told him I wanted to marry Dona. It got awful quiet for a long time. Finally he said "How will you take care of her?" I told him that we would both work, and that we loved each other. It got awful quiet again, and finally he said "If you take her away, you cannot bring her back". I told him again that we were in love, and we would make it work. I guess he agreed, because we continued making plans.

While I was stationed at Scott Field, I hitchhiked to and from Merrill, to and from Chanute Field at Rantoul, Ill., and, of course, to and from Boston, Ohio, where Dona was.

When hitchhiking, I always wore my uniform. So did the other military travelers. Several times I would have members of several branches of the Armed Services in the car when I drove to or from Ohio. One time I had another Airman in the car, and I stopped to pick up another one. When the guy got in the car, I could see he had on only parts of his uniform, and they did not match at all. The first Airman I had picked up was going to a small detachment just south of Indianapolis, so I agreed to drop him at the Base Gate. As I drove up, I decided to

My Story

turn in the second hitchhiker, as I had decided he was an imposter. When I got to the gate, I asked the Air Police to take a look at my passenger. They did not look long. One glance and they jerked him out of the car and had him in a patrol truck and off to the Guard House.

One time I was hitchhiking back to Scott Field and late at night I was picked up by a car full of young ladies. It had been a long and hectic weekend for me, and I soon dozed off. Soon I realized that we were traveling at an extremely high rate of speed. Now usually I liked going fast because it got me there quicker, but it seemed that the driver was more involved in talking than driving. To call attention to her speed, I said "Won't this car go any faster?" It did, and she did! Eventually the other passengers convinced her to slow down a little. It turned out they were all from the St. Louis area, and had been to a small Air Force installation south of Indianapolis, where they had spent the weekend with their husbands and boyfriends. It was the same place where the Air Police relieved me of the imposter. They were very considerate when they learned that I had been to see my girlfriend, and they detoured out of their way to take me right to the main gate at Scott Field. Actually, that happened to me several times, where someone would detour off the main highway to deliver me to the Base.

One time I was hitchhiking back to Scott Field from Chanute Air Force Base, where Ray and Verna were stationed. It was at night, and had been raining, and I

My Story

was wet. An old couple with an old car picked me up. One of the rear windows was broken and the wind was blowing in and I was cold. I sort of dozed off, and all of a sudden I felt the car sort of lurch. I looked out and realized we had driven off the road. I was beginning to be alarmed when the driver came to a stop off the roadway, beside a corn field. The lady got out and disappeared into the corn field. The man said "Every weekend in the very same place". It turned out their only son was in the Air Force at Chanute Field, and every weekend they went to spend time with him. They also, delivered me right to the main gate at Scott.

Another story about hitchhiking. I think I was on the way to Merrill, or maybe Chanute Field. Anyway, it was late at night when I caught a ride with two men. We started out and I realized they had been drinking. The driving was pretty erratic, and I had a policy of getting out of a drunk's car as soon as I could. I started watching for a highway intersection so I could say "this is my stop", but we were really out in the country, and there was no other traffic. They were only driving about 25 miles per hour, so I started to relax. Eventually I could see some red taillights on the road far ahead of us. The two drunks in front noticed it about the same time I did, and one of them said "If it wasn't for this heavy traffic, we could make better time". I decided the ride was a safe one, and rode most of the night with them. I found that on some trips, I could make about the same time hitchhiking as I could driving.

My Story

Remember I said earlier that as a student I was supposed to park my car at the student parking lot off Base, but since I had connived to get a Permanent Party sticker, I had my car parked next to our barracks. During the summer, it got unbearably hot in our classrooms, and they would sometimes curtail class early. At such times it was common to go somewhere and have a beer and shoot a little pool. On one particular such occasion several others and I decided to take my car, which was parked near by, and go to town to drink our beer. On the way off base, I took the route I normally did, except this day they had a sign on the road that said 'road closed'. I drove through the intersection anyway as I could see no reason not to. Unfortunately an Air Police unit was following me, and he decided I should have stopped. He pulled me over to tell me so, and it probably would have been over at that, but I had some wise guys with me who proceeded to tell the cop how to do his business. The result was that I was issued a citation that included having my cherished Permanent Party sticker shaved off the windshield, and my car banned from the Base for a week. In addition, I was to report to my Squadron Commander who would mete out my punishment. My punishment was a "Week of Hard Labor".

Now this turned out to be a blessing. Our Squadron had been assigned to a detail that was building new sidewalks out of used brick during all of our non-class times. It was hard, grueling labor, digging out sod, carrying the bricks from a truck and placing them

My Story

adjacent to each other to make a sidewalk about 4 feet wide. When the Squadron Commander sentenced me to hard labor, he turned me over to Lt. Goldberg. Lt. Goldberg had the responsibility of getting the sidewalk completed. When I reported to Lt. Goldberg, he asked me if I could drive a truck. Could I drive a truck? Wow! Do bears do it in the woods? Naturally I could drive a truck. I was a farm boy! My week of 'hard labor' turned out to last the rest of my assignment at Scott Field. My hard labor consisted of driving the truck to a place in Bellville, Ill., and parking it next to a building that had been demolished. Someone would load bricks on the truck while Lt. Goldberg and I went for a cup of coffee. When the truck was loaded, I would drive it back to base, park it in the Squadron area, and then watch as my barracks mates unloaded it. Then if there was time, we would make another trip. I continued to drive the truck well after my 'sentence' was completed. There was a downside to getting the citation.

After the base windshield sticker had been shaved off and after my week of suspension was over, I went back to get another sticker. Of course, by this time, my make believe buddy from Ohio was long gone. The best I could do was to get a 'student' sticker. I parked near my old place near the barracks any way, and naturally, within a few days I had another ticket. I just left it on the windshield under the wiper blade. When I used the car, I would put the ticket up on the visor, and when I would park, I would put the ticket back under the wiper blade

My Story

as if I had not yet found it. Somehow I acquired three more tickets within the next several weeks. I treated them the same as the first.

I had arranged to leave the base on my leave to get married on a Friday after class. While in the 'ready' room on Thursday after class, I reminded the First Sergeant, who was the biggest Black man I had ever seen, that I was scheduled for leave to get married. Since I was to be married on Saturday, I would have to drive all night to get there. He said "Why don't you go on your Honeymoon first, then marry her when you get back? I said "Her Dad wouldn't allow that". He said "how do you feel? Aren't you too sick to go to class tomorrow? I said I was not feeling at all well, and he said "Get outa here". I quickly loaded my stuff in the car and started for Ohio and my wedding. As I pulled out of my parking place, I noticed an Air Police pickup behind me. As I turned on to the main street, another Air Police truck pulled up beside me, and indicated for me to pull over. I did. The cop came over and said, "Give me that ticket on your visor". I did. "He said give me the rest of them". I did. He said "Follow me". I did. We went to the Guard House, and the Air Police truck that was behind me followed us all the way. When we got inside, the Captain explained in a rather loud and nasty tone that when you got a ticket, you were supposed to do what it said on the ticket. I told him that I had not had time to read it. He reminded me that I had several, again in a loud and nasty voice. He then said they were going to

My Story

shave the sticker off my windshield, and I would have to take my car off base immediately, and they would follow me to make sure I did leave the base. How lucky could I get? I was going to have a police escort off the base where I was going any way. He also said I would have to report to my Commanding Officer "As soon as you can". I did not tell him I was leaving for my wedding and a week of honeymoon. I was not worried about not having a sticker. Our plans were for Dona to keep the car in Ohio as I was about finished with school and would soon be going to a new assignment somewhere.

I do not remember the trip to Ohio, but I know when I got there things were in a tizzy. Dona had just learned that in Ohio wedding participants had to have a blood test. That test was to be at least 3 days before the wedding, and the check to make sure of the time delay was that the sample had to be sent through the mail. I guess that would indicate that the test had been timely. I had not been available to have my test done. What to do? Dona's big sister had the solution. She knew someone who worked in a Post Office, and had made arrangements for us to bring my blood sample to her. She would get it stamped and post marked, and we could get the license that day on Friday. The next day, Saturday was the big day!

We were married in Dona's home Church on September 20, 1952. Dona was just a few days past her 19th

My Story

birthday, and my 20th was a few weeks ahead. My parents and my sister, Verna, and her husband, Capt. Schwartz, came for the wedding. All of Dona's family were there, as well as many of her family's' friends. After the ceremony, there was a reception in the church basement. Lots of people had brought gifts, and it was the custom there to open the gifts at the reception. I remember that as Dona opened them, I was supposed to thank the people who had brought them. Since I did not know many of them, I found that I would be thanking in one direction only to find out that the people I was thanking were in the other direction. We did get through it ok, and it was a memorable event for me.

It had been a long several days for both of us, and we were anxious to get started on our Honeymoon. We planned to take a slow leisurely trip to Wisconsin, then up into Upper Michigan, across the lake at Sault St. Marie, then down through Lower Michigan and back to Ohio. We left on our honeymoon shortly after the reception was over. I had hoped to drive to the closest town and stop at a motel. When we got into whatever the first town was Dona said "We can't stop here, they have polio". So we continued on to the next town, and the same thing happened. I swear I believe my new wife was afraid of me! We finally were just too tired to continue, so we spent whatever was left of our first night together in some little town either in Ohio or Indiana. We did thoroughly enjoy our honeymoon trip. When we crossed from Upper Michigan to Lower Michigan, we

My Story

were on the ferry boat because the bridge had not been built yet. We made that same trip when we got out of the Air Force in 1956 and then crossed on the new bridge. When I got back to Scott Field after my leave was over, I dropped back a week into a new class.

Remember when I left, I left with a cloud over my head. Because of the number of parking tickets I had accumulated, I was supposed to report to my Squadron Commander for punishment (again). While I was gone, they had combined my student squadron with our sister squadron. Our Commander, Major Johnson stayed as the Commander, but the First Sergeant came from the other squadron. He, like our old First Sergeant, was also a Black man. He was an old hand, and had a reputation of being tough on his people.

The Sargent was trying to get through the paper work of joining the two squadrons when I reported to the Orderly Room. Everything was in a mess. The clerk told me that Major Johnson was not available and I would have to report to the First Sergeant. I went to him and told him who I was, that I had a citation, and I was supposed to report for my punishment. He glared at me and said "What kind of citation?" I said a parking ticket. He said "Do you expect me to stop getting this squadron squared away just to deal with your damned parking ticket? I said "No Sir, I can deal with it myself". And he said "Then do it, and get out of here". Man, did I ever get out of there. I had a buddy who worked in the

My Story

Orderly Room, and I asked him to back me up and tell how it all happened if my parking ticket (s) ever came up. He said he would.

My Story

CHAPTER 14: McCord AIR FORCE BASE

When my old class graduated a few weeks later, almost all of them were sent to Minot, North Dakota, or to an Air Base in Texas. When I graduated, the students were scattered all over, and I was sent to McCord Air Force Base at Tacoma, Washington. I had done fairly well in class, and I had received my Corporal stripes before I left to get married. I sure was hoping my 'tickets' would not catch up with me because they would pull my hard earned stripes.

I had a few days off before going to McCord Air Force Base, so I went to Ohio. This was kind of tough. When I was at Scott, I knew I could get to Ohio or Dona could come to me, but now we were going to be pretty far apart. What we decided was that Dona would stay in Ohio and continue with her job, and I would go alone. We would both save our money, and we would try to get together the next spring. I got to McCord at the end of October, 1952. I was assigned to the 318th Fighter Interceptor Squadron, which had F-94 Jet Fighter Aircraft.

McCord Air Base is located near Tacoma, Washington. It was primarily an Air Defense base, which meant Fighter Interceptor airplanes were the main component. There were two Fighter Squadrons, ours, and the 317th. Of course there was a fair amount of competition between the two Squadrons. We both had F94 Fighter aircraft. They were pretty early Jet Fighters, and only

My Story

had eight 50 Cal. machine guns. By now, most 'new' fighter aircraft also had rockets. Since the Cold War was in full swing, our Squadron's task, along with our sister Squadron, the 317th, was to fly 'guard' in the area from Alaska, east into Canada, and south to Washington, both inland and out to sea. The pilots were supposed to intercept any and all unknown aircraft flying in 'our' area. You may remember that a number of American aircraft had been shot down by the Russians over Alaska and the Bearing Sea, so we knew they were not an idle threat.

My job was in the Communications section. We were responsible for maintaining any type of communications and navigation equipment on the airplanes. Most of our work was preflighting our equipment before a flight, and removing and replacing any piece of equipment that did not work. We did very little trouble shooting on the individual pieces, as there were base shops that did that work.

The Squadron was pretty well self sufficient. We had three barracks that the enlisted personnel lived in. They were old World War II buildings, two stories high with private rooms at one end for Non Coms. Every-body else lived in open bays. There were about 40 cots down each side with a fairly wide aisle down the middle. The Squadron had its own Supply building and its own Mess hall. When I checked in, they sent me to the supply room to get my bedding and foot locker. They told me to

My Story

pick any open bunk in any of the three barracks. I picked out the barrack nearest to the Mess hall, and chose a bunk on the upper floor near one end. I made up the bunk, hung my clothes, and got fairly settled before the daytime work was finished and the troops came in. One guy who was in the Communications Section came over and said "I don't think you want to be there". When I asked why, he just said "I think you will want to move". I soon found out why. There was a guy there who was trying to get a 'hardship discharge' and he was rotting his feet. He would keep water in his boots all day, and keep his feet wet at night. The result was a horrible smell around him and everything he owned. Needless to say, I moved my stuff.

I took to Barracks life pretty easily. Of course, I missed Dona, but there were lots of things to learn about my job, about the airplanes, and about the people around me. The Mess hall was small enough so that the cooks knew every one in the Squadron, and we really had good food. If you worked on the Flight Line late, you could go in and the cooks would fix whatever you wanted if they had it. We, along with people from other maintenance sections, were required to be on the Flight Line whenever we had airplanes landing or taking off. If they were taking off, you had to be there to resolve problems during pre-flight and start -up. After landing, you were there to make sure the equipment you were responsible for worked ok during the flight. Our Squadron's task was flying 'alert' out over the Pacific,

My Story

and up to Alaska. The fear at that time was that the USSR was going to attack, and would be coming either down the West Coast, or down over the polar route. The polar route was someone else's responsibility.

Our airplanes or those of our sister Squadron were in the air 24 hours a day, usually in twos. Our Squadrons alternated being on 'alert status' 30 days at a time. When on alert, in addition to the airplanes that were in the air, we kept two of them on the Flight Line with electrical power on the airplane, and all systems turned on. Since it rained most of the time (it seemed) we kept them in a large tent that had both the front and the rear open. Each airplane had to have an armed guard during hours of darkness. Because only Squadron personnel were allowed on the Flight Line, we had to stand guard. That was kind of a bum job. First of all, they would not give us any ammunition for the 45 Caliber hand gun, but worse than that, the power unit was a large gas powered generator that made an awful lot of noise. You were supposed to stand out of the light, so anyone attempting sabotage could not see you. If you did, and if it was raining, you got wet. Needless to say, we slacked off pretty bad when we realized we were probably not going to be sabotaged. The worst thing that could happen was to get caught sleeping by whoever came out to check on you. Since whoever was going to check on you would also have to be out in the rain, there was not too much to worry about.

My Story

Jumping ahead a couple of years, I remember one time we were on alert status, and working on airplanes late at night. We had several new Airmen just out of school assigned to our section, and I put two of them out in the tent to guard the standby airplanes. I told them they would be court marshaled if they let any one get near the aircraft. Sometime during the night, Jim Terrill and I decided we should check on our new Airmen guards. We walked out to the side of the tents, then when quite close, stepped out in front of the airplanes, but still in the rain. One of the kids came rushing at us with the gun in his hand pointed at us and said "Halt". We did. Then he said "Advance two paces, lay your identification on the ground, and back up two paces". It appeared this kid was serious. We knew the gun was not loaded, but was it? We did not want to lay any identification down on the wet ramp, so we finally convinced him to let us turn around and back into the tent so he could see us. Jim and I were both Sergeants by that time, and the kid tried to apologize. We told him he did the right thing, but I never tried to sneak up on anyone after that.

One day I was called into the Orderly Room to take a long distance phone call. It was from Mom. She gave me the sad news that my cousin Richard Lengely had been killed in a shooting accident at an Air Force Base in Rapid City, South Dakota. Mom wondered if I could go to Salem, Oregon to be with Aunt Lila and Uncle Bert. I got a three day pass, and made arrangements to go by Greyhound Bus. When I arrived in Salem, I called

My Story

them and some relatives of Uncle Bert's picked me up.
When I got to their house, they had not made any
arrangements, but said they would like to have a
Military Funeral. I knew that there was a small Air
Force detachment at the Portland Airport, so I suggested
we drive up there to see what could be done. Of course
we were stopped at the entrance gate by the Military
Policeman. I went into the guard shack, explained the
situation, and said we were looking for some help. The
Sergeant said "wait right here". Within a few minutes an
Air Force car with an Officer driving arrived. He
introduced himself as the Base Chaplain. From then on,
he took care of everything. He was very supportive of
Aunt Lila and Uncle Bert, asked them a few questions to
determine what they wanted, and told them he would do
the rest. We went back to Salem, and the next day the
Chaplain arrived, again in the Air Force car, and
explained to them how everything would be handled.
Since Richard had been shot in the face, the coffin had
to remain closed. The Chaplain supplied 6 Airman for
Pallbearers, but then asked me if I would like to serve in
place of one of them, so I did. All in all, it was a sad
day, but was handled with great compassion.

The shooting accident happened because of carelessness.
I had grown up with Richard when they lived in
Wisconsin when we were kids. When Jerry and I were
taught how to handle guns, it appeared that Richard had
not had the same kind of attention. When I worked in
Oregon for the railroad, some weekends Richard and I

My Story

would tool around the country in my convertible. At times we would take 22 Caliber rifles with us and target shoot in the desert. Richard was just plain careless. One of the Airmen who was involved in the funeral told me that Richard and some other Airmen at his Air Base in Rapid City, were at a private shooting range, target shooting. Richard was using a pistol, and I could have guessed immediately what happened. Richard liked to practice 'quick draw', then he would spin the gun with his finger through the trigger guard like the slicks in the movies. I had seen him do that many times. That is how he got shot. He spun the gun with a round in the chamber and it fired. The bullet caught him in the eye. He never regained consciousness although he lived long enough for Aunt Lila to get to the hospital at the Rapid City Air Force Base.

On one of my trips to base shops to take in a piece of equipment for repair, or to pick up something that was fixed, I got to talking with a civilian employee who worked on the equipment. He told me he had to sell a special car that he had been working to restore. It seems he had brought it up from California in pieces and was working on it at his girlfriend's house. They got into a spat, and she threw him out. She was also going to throw out the car. It was a 1933 Auburn Sportster. I didn't know any thing about it, but mentioned it to a senior level Non-Com in our section. I think he was a Tech. Sergeant carryover from WW II. He got all excited about it, and wanted to go see it. We went back

My Story

to base shops and found the guy who had the car. We made arrangements to go see it that afternoon. When we got there, the car was still in pieces, but you could see it would be a beauty if we could get it all together. All of the body and fenders had been repaired and were primed. The engine was mostly together, but there were lots of parts in boxes. The Sergeant asked what he wanted for it, and the guy said $500.00. We talked it over and found that neither of us had enough money, but we did if we pooled our funds. The Sergeant lived off base, and had a small garage where we could work. We bought it. To get it to the garage where we would work on it, we had to put the wheels on the axles, and connect them to the frame. Then we piled all the loose stuff on the frame, and pulled it home sort of like a trailer.

When we got to the Sergeant's house, his wife raised holy hell with him. Apparently, he had spent the rent money and also their food money for the month. I told him I had a little more money, and that as fast as I could, I would buy the car from him if I could keep it in his garage to work on it. That sort of settled his wife down, and she said I could work on the car there, but he could not spend any money on it. I really could not blame her. He had agreed to buy it with me with out talking to her, and they had two little kids that needed food and clothes. The bottom line is that we worked on the car together. I had no transportation, so I would ride home with him, work on the car until dark, then he would take me back to the base. When the car was complete enough to drive,

My Story

he requested that I take it out to the base and work on it there. I did.

It had a 12 cylinder engine, and we found all the parts except the rod bearing babbits. A guy at the base showed me how to make them out of melted lead. It was originally built to be a road racer. It had seats for two people, although it was longer than our four door Chevrolet sedan. It was the 'boat tail' model, so it was almost all hood. It was a convertible, but the canvas top was completely missing. I used some heavy nylon material from an aerial tow target for the top material. I think I had someone on the base make the top for me. The windshield was made to fold down, and was only about 4 inches high. It had 19 inch wheels, which were 'knock off' type racing wheels. It carried two spare wheels and tires, and they were located on each side on the front fenders in front of the doors. The spares were incased in chromed cases, with a rear view mirror mounted on the top of each spare wheel mount. There was a strange little brass knob on the floor board that said "for fast driving pull up". I and several others puzzled over that for some time, but eventually I found an old man who had raced this type of car. He said it was to be connected to a cutout on the muffler, and when you wanted more power, you would pull it up and bypass the muffler. I never dared use it. It also had a knobs and cable system hooked to the shock absorbers that you could use to give you a soft or hard ride. Each side worked independently, so you could manipulate

My Story

them to raise one side of the car to put it into a lean (tilt) prior to entering a turn when you were driving fast. The standard headlights were gigantic. They must have been 15 or 16 inches in diameter. There were two smaller lights mounted on the side cowl above the front fenders. Neither of them were bright enough to pass the test required to get it licensed, so I had to install a pair of sealed beam headlights. When I got it sufficiently put together to try the state required inspection, I drove it to Tacoma.

The inspection building was a long narrow building about a block long. You drove through in single file, and there were numerous test stations as you went along. There was one to test the muffler system, one for the brakes, one to test front end alignment, etc. The test was very thorough. I passed them all including the headlight test, the horn test, and at the last test station the man said "turn on your windshield wiper". There was none. I pointed out that the car was not made with one, but he was adamant that it HAD to have a windshield wiper. He put a great big red 'rejected' sticker on the car. What to do? I went to a junk yard and bought a vacuum operated wiper assembly off an old Chevrolet (I think). I drilled a port in the intake manifold and threaded it. When I mounted the wiper motor and blade on the cowl, the blade was three times longer than the height of my wind shield! I cut the blade holder and the wiper blade way down so that it fit the wind shield. It worked like a charm. I went back to get the wiper checked. They made

My Story

me go through the entire inspection system again. Again, I passed all the tests, and when I got to the last place, he said turn on your windshield wiper. I proudly pulled the little knob and the little blade zipped back and forth. He said "Does that wiper wipe 144 square inches? That is the legal requirement". I said "I don't have 144 square inches in the entire windshield! After glaring at me for a while, he gave me a green sticker!

 By the time I got that far along with the car, the Sergeant who started out with me had come up for discharge, and he and his family left the area. I cannot remember his name, but I think he had a raw deal. He was in the Army during WW II, then got out, got a job, and started a family. When the Korean War started they recalled him. This time he elected to go into the Air Force, so that is where I met him. He really did not want to be in, so he was pretty unhappy. I guess his wife was unhappy also. My life was pretty routine. I spent nearly all my time on the Flight Line, or messing around with my car. Evenings, I spent a little time in the Squadron Rec. Room, where there was a pool table. I could make a little money playing pool, but it was always nickels and dimes.

There was a fellow in our Squadron who was from back East and had never driven a car. He wanted to learn, so some of the guys taught him how to drive the tow tractors that were used to move the airplanes around the ramp or in or out of the hangar. One day he approached

My Story

me and asked me to go look at a car with him. He was planning to buy it, and wanted my advice. I went with him to a parking lot off base, and there was a pretty little 1937 Plymouth 4 door sedan. An Airman was being shipped out and wanted to sell the car. We took it out for a drive and found that everything worked ok, so I recommend he buy it. He did.

I had a couple of funny experiences with him and his car. One evening he asked me if I would go skating with him. He had found there was an ice rink in some little town nearby, and he wanted to go but was afraid to drive out there by himself. I said I would go. On the way out we had to cross a street that had a stop sign. He stopped and looked both ways. It was clear, but he didn't move. Soon the car behind us got impatient and tooted his horn. Phil (that was his name) kept looking first one way then the other, and the guy behind kept tooting his horn. Finally Phil said "That's funny, every time I look to my left, my horn toots". I finally convinced him to go ahead and cross the street and we would work on his horn later. I don't think I ever convinced him that the horn tooter was in the car behind us.

Another time Phil invited me and two or three other guys to ride with him up into Mount Rainier National Park. We all agreed that it would be a good outing for us. Phil drove slow, so everyone on the road passed us until we got up on the mountain and on the crooked road, then they piled up behind us. Soon we got into

My Story

snow, and the roadway was icy. Phil continued on at his same speed; slow, but much too fast for the icy roadway. The road was a typical mountain road with cliffs on both sides, steep up on one side, and steep down on the other. We told Phil to slow down because of the ice, and he said "It's ok; if one wheel slips the other three will hold it". We all hollered at once "Stop this thing". We made Phil get out and let one other guy drive the rest of the way up to the Lodge. When we got there, Phil got out his camera and took a few pictures of his car in front of the Lodge, then said "Get in, we are heading back to the Base". We had not even gone into the Lodge yet! All Phil wanted to do was take the picture of his car at the Lodge because one of the guys at work had told him his car could not make it up there. We finally convinced Phil that we should at least see the Lodge. It was the Timber Line Lodge, and was certainly unique. Very large, and all built of huge logs. Phil was sort of weird in some ways. I knew he was from Rhode Island, and one day I asked him if it got cold there. He said not where he lived, he was from the southern part of Rhode Island! I think the entire state is about 50 miles across.

Dona and I had planned that she would join me in the spring. I was missing her, and really anticipating going home to get her. I put in for leave time for the next May or June. My plans were shattered pretty badly in March of 1953. Our Squadron was put on orders to ship out to Thule, Greenland. At that duty station no dependants

My Story

were allowed. The assignment would be at least a year, with possible extensions. What a bummer!

The entire Squadron and all of its equipment were to go. I, along with almost all of the Squadron enlisted men was assigned to "packing and crating". It was in a large warehouse where all the Squadron equipment was being readied for shipment. That included all the jeeps, trucks, power units, etc. We would prep them by draining all the fluids and packaging a certain amount of spare parts for each. We also were packing all kinds of equipment and spare parts for the airplanes. Everyone was working 12 hour shifts, so not much of anything else was going on. One day a runner from the Squadron Orderly Room came looking for Cpl. Edmund. I said that's me, what do they want. He said "They want your Butt there on the double". My mind raced to try to figure out what I was in trouble for. Then it dawned on me. Those damned Parking Tickets had caught up with me. They were going to jerk my stripes, and I just made 'time in grade' for Buck Sergeant! I was told to report to Major Garino. I knew the Major pretty well and figured he would go as easy on me as he could. When I got to the Orderly Room, the Major was busy so they told me to sit and wait. What misery. It is terrible what a guilty conscience can do to you.

Eventually the door opened, and he beckoned me in. When he shut the door, I knew it was pretty bad. He asked me a few questions about how I liked my job, and

My Story

how I liked it here. Finally he asked me how bad I wanted to go to Thule, Greenland. I said "I don't want to go worth a damn, but I will if that is my assignment". Then he asked if I would like to stay at McChord and help start a new Squadron. Wow, I could not believe what I was hearing. He repeated that he would be staying at McChord to start a new Squadron with the new F86Ds, and was looking for an NCO (non-commissioned officer) to run the Communications section. When I first got to the Orderly Room and he was busy, he was selecting his Adjutant, a Lieutenant that I also knew. He said he would select an NCO for the Radar section, one for the Mechanical section, and we would form a new Squadron called the 465th Fighter Interceptor Squadron. Then I realized I was not an NCO. I did not have enough stripes. Would you believe I had them that day before I left the Orderly Room. Wow, what a day. First, I got out of packing and crating, which I hated. Then I got out of going to Thule for God knew how long. Then I was selected (one of only 5 men) to help start a new Squadron. Then I was promoted to Buck Sergeant. And besides all that, when I told the Major that I had planned to go home and get my new wife in the spring, he said he saw no reason why I should change my plans! I was in a sort of state of euphoria for a while. The old Squadron shipped out very soon after that. Our new Squadron was so small that we cut back to one barracks building, and (bummer) we had to give up our Squadron Mess. We now had to go to the

My Story

base Consolidated mess hall, where everything tasted like whatever you had the day before. Also where you did not dare hang up your hat or field jacket because someone would steal it.

The F86s that we were promised were badly delayed and we did not have much to do. The Air Force eventually found some old propeller driven P51s (Mustangs) that they flew in for us to use. They had a pretty simple radio system, and no navigation stuff, so I did not have any trouble. There was one pilot in the area who had flown them in WW II. He was a Colonel from base Head Quarters, and one day he came down to the flight line to check out in one. I was there to help him get in. He couldn't. He did not fit. Even when we put his 'chute on his back instead of on his butt. He said it had been years since he flew one, and he had grown some. He could not get the hatch closed when he was in the cockpit. We had 7 or 8 of the P51s and I think only one or two ever flew. The problem that delayed the F86s was that the pilots' oxygen filter system was faulty. They had a flight of four F86s going cross country, and somewhere in the Midwest, they all crashed, one after another. Only one pilot got out by parachute. They found that he had been poisoned. Eventually they found the chemicals used to manufacture the face masks, when mixed with oxygen made a poisonous gas. While the new F86s were grounded trying to find and fix the pilot oxygen problem, I had a chance to go to Ohio to get Dona.

My Story

CHAPTER 15: I RETURN TO OHIO TO GET MY BRIDE

I did not have a very long leave. I think it was only two weeks, but may have been three weeks. I found out that it was possible to catch a flight on a Military Air Transport (MATS) plane. They did not often go to exactly where you wanted to go, but could sometimes get you within reasonable hitchhike distance. I found that there was a C130 flying to New York on the day before my leave started. I arranged with a buddy to sign me out properly the next day, so I grabbed my duffle bag and headed for the Flight Line. We left early in the morning. The air crew arranged for a box lunch to be available for all the passengers on board. This was a cargo plane, and it certainly was NOT comfortable. The seats were canvas sling seats that hung from the sides of the cargo bay. The metal frame work inhibited the blood from flowing to your legs so they went to sleep. You had to keep getting up and stomping them. I believe there were about 30 people on the plane, not counting the crew. There were members of all branches of the military, both male and female, and both enlisted and officer status. The flight was to take around 15 hours, but it took a fair amount longer than that. We ran into head winds which delayed us some, but when we got to where ever we were supposed to land, the weather was too bad. They diverted us to Suffolk County Airport out on Long Island. There was a small Air Force contingent at that airport. We got in there at about 4:00 AM.

146

My Story

We deplaned and all crowded into a tiny Operations Office. The Officer of The Day was a brand new 2nd Lieutenant, and he promptly told us we would have to wait until 8:00AM when the base would be opened for business. He said we could then start making arrangements for surface transportation to wherever we wanted to go. There was a full bird Colonel on the plane, and I had overheard him tell another officer that he was on his way somewhere overseas, and could not afford to miss his commercial flight out of New York. The Colonel and the 2nd Lieutenant disappeared into an inner office, and a few minutes later they came out and announced that they were bringing two Air Force buses in. One would run to the main airport (now JFK), and the other one would run to Grand Central Station. I chose the one going to Grand Central Station thinking I could find a way out of town and could start hitchhiking.

I learned two things that morning. First, Grand Central Station is a BIG station, and New York City is a BIG city. It was not easy finding out how to get to where I could hitchhike. I teamed up with two sailors who were also going to Ohio. If I remember correctly, we hired a cab to take us to the outskirts of town. He took us to a place where he said we could start hitchhiking after we crossed that little bridge. I don't remember which bridge it was. As a matter of fact it was not a bridge, but a tunnel. I remember that the sidewalk petered out as you got to the tunnel entrance, and there was no way to walk across. We stood there a while, and finally a man

147

My Story

stopped and held up traffic while we loaded our duffle bags and ourselves into his car. When we got in, he said "I can only take you through the tunnel", but when we told him we needed to get to where we could hitchhike, he took us a distance out of town. That is when I found out how big New York was. When we got out far enough so that we could hitchhike, we split up. It was much easier for one to catch a ride than it was for two or three. I guess the rest of the trip to Dona's place was routine, as I don't remember any other problems. With all that had happened wrong, I still made it home the day my leave started. Not bad for bumming across the U.S. from coast to coast, then back one third of the way to Ohio. Dona had things all ready, so we planned to leave within a day or two. Her family had a get- together planned for the night before we would leave.

All of Dona's sisters and brothers and their families were there for dinner, and afterwards we just sat around and visited. As we started to break up, and some of them leave, Dona's brother Bob said someone was messing with our car. We had it all packed, ready to leave early in the morning. We all ran outside, and sure enough, several guys ran in different directions. One of them ran full speed into the handle of Dona's Dad's power lawn mower. He laid there on the ground and groaned for a while. Another tripped over the dog chain when the dog ran out of the doghouse and stretched the chain in front of him. I had put some fancy wheel covers on the car before I left for McCord Field. I guess the thieves waited

My Story

until we were leaving thinking we would not miss them until we were on our way. They had pried them off, and that is what Bob heard. They were off, but still laying by the wheels. The car was locked, and they did not bother any thing else.

We left Ohio early the next morning, and stopped in Wisconsin to see my family on the way out west. This was sort of like a second honeymoon. We just lolly-gagged on the way back to Mc Chord Field. When we got to Tacoma, we had to find a place to live. The first place we found was an old motel that had been converted into several small apartments. It was fairly near the Air Base, being only a 5 or 6 mile drive to work. There were several other Squadron members near our place, and I was invited to car pool with some of the senior sergeants who had by then joined our Squadron. It seemed like a pretty good deal. I would drive only once a week so that would save gas money, plus it would leave the car available for Dona during the day. The good deal soon turned into a problem. The other guys all wanted to stop on the way home and drink beer. The first time was ok; we stopped and drank a beer and talked a little while, then proceeded on home. It seemed that each time we stopped, more beer was drunk, and it was later when I got home. This soon became a real problem for me. Number one, I did not want to spend the amount of money it was costing me, and more important, I wanted to be home. The other car poolers were all my seniors, and two of them were on the

My Story

Squadron Promotion Board, so it was a little difficult to break the car pool arrangement.

One evening it really got late, so I called Dona and had her come pick me up. The next day, when they started ragging on me, I told them I would much rather spend the evenings with my new wife than with a bunch of hairy Air Force Sergeants, and that I would not be in the car pool any more. Of course they made fun of my decision, and a couple of them were angry. Eventually they all got over it, and two of them said I was right to end the beer drinking evenings. It was not long after that I began carpooling with Jim Terrill, who was my age and rank. We socialized with Jim and Doreen Terrill and several others who were in the same fix as Dona and I. Away from home and family, and not much money to spend on entertainment. Our socializing amounted to visiting each others apartments and playing poker. We played 'penny ante' and could have an evening's entertainment at a cost of a dollar or two. I think there were five or six couples. Dona and I also went on picnics in the rain, and took a few short trips to the seashore or to Mt. Rainer. I was still working on my Auburn, and one day we decided to drive it up onto Mt. Rainer. We drove it all the way up to the Timberline Lodge, and were on the way out when I hit a deer. The deer went flying off to one side, and I thought I had damaged the car. When I got stopped and got out to look, I could not tell where the car had been hit. The front fenders were so heavy they did not even bend.

My Story

We had some friends who were from Maine. They had two very young kids, and he was only an Airman 3rd class, (PFC) so they had very little money. They could not afford a car. It turned out that she was expecting another baby, and one day Dona volunteered me to take her to the base hospital for a periodic check up. Of course she had to take her two toddlers with us as they also could not afford babysitters. She had them all dressed up, and they were well behaved. When we got to the doctor's office, it was filled with expectant women, some of whom also had little kids. One lady was Black, and she had a little boy with her. He was as black as she was, and was all dressed up. He had a little hat on and was as cute as a button. The little girl whose Mother I had taken to the doctor had never seen a little black boy. He had walked out to the middle of the room, and the little girl walked out to meet him. She walked all around him, really looking him over. She took his hand and tried to rub the black off. Then she lifted his little hat and tried to pull the crinkles out of his hair. Every one just sat and held their breath. Neither Mother dared to call either one of them back. It all wound up with them playing together.

One day when I got home from the base, Dona took the car and went to the grocery store a few blocks away. She was back home in a few minutes, and she was crying. When I got out to the car, she said that a man had backed his car into our car when he was trying to park, and when she told him that he had hit her car, he said he

My Story

could not have done so much damage. The rear fender had a significant dent and was badly torn. We jumped into the car and dashed back to the store. Dona pointed out the car that had hit her. It was a beat up old Dodge, and had an angle iron for a rear bumper. That is what caused the damage to our car. We waited until he came out and I confronted him. Again, he said he could not have done that much damage, but he admitted he had bumped into her when he was jockeying around to get parked. I told him I had just had some work done on the car that week, and the repair man would swear that there was no damage on that rear fender, and that I was willing to call the police. The man said "Where will you take it to get it fixed?" I named the repair shop that I had just been to, and he said "Take it to him and tell him that I will pay for the repair". He gave me his name, Miles (something) I have forgotten it. We drove down to the repair shop, told the owner about the accident, and that the man said he would pay for the repair. I told him the man's name, and the repair shop owner started to laugh. He said "I know him, he was dressed in dirty engineers coveralls, was driving an old Dodge with an angle iron bumper, and had on a ragged old felt hat, right"? He had described him to a 'T'. The shop owner told me that at one time the man had owned the largest timber operation in the state, and he had married the Madam of all the cat couses in Tacoma. He said between them, they had more money than anyone else in town, and that if he said he

My Story

would pay the bill, he would pay it. The owner agreed to fix the car.

Dona wanted to work, and got a job at the telephone company. She was a Comptometer Operator, and they liked her capability. She had been a Time Keeper at the Paper Mill in Ohio, so she had some experience at that line of work. We really enjoyed being there. By living off base, it was like any other job. There was some requirement to work evenings on occasion, and also on weekends if the Squadron was on special alert. Eventually Dona became pregnant, and we were going to need more space, so once again we looked for an apartment. This time it was in an old part of Tacoma in a huge old house.

There were two apartments in the upstairs, and we had the largest one. It had two bedrooms, a living room, closets, bathroom, and a kitchen. We were in 7th heaven waiting for our baby. We bought an 8 millimeter movie camera a few days before Dona's 'due date' so that we could make a complete record. When Dona said "its time to go" we dashed for the base hospital. I waited with her for a long time and nothing was happening, so the nurse said "You might as well go to work, and we will call you when it happens". I spent the day at work, but I suspect I didn't accomplish much. After work I went back to the Hospital and still nothing. Again, they said "Go home, we will call". I think I did go home, but I am not sure. I know it was near midnight when the

My Story

magic event occurred, and we had a beautiful little daughter. It was Friday the 13th of August, 1954. It being Friday the 13th, and near midnight, the Doctor asked Dona if she wanted to wait a few more minutes until after midnight. Dona told him she had waited long enough, and was anxious to see her baby. I can still remember feeling weak in the knees when I first saw Linda. She was perfect in every way. She changed our lives considerably immediately, and I cannot imagine what our lives would have been without her. The first pictures I took with our new movie camera were of Dona just a few days before she went to the hospital. All the rest of many reels of film are of Linda, or have Linda in them.

Shortly after she was born, I was told I was being sent back to Scott Field in Illinois for advanced electronics training. We decided that we would all go, and Dona and Linda would go to Ohio to be with her folks while I was in school. To see how we would travel with Linda, we decided to make an all day trip to Mt. Rainier National Park. Dona packed the things we would need for a long trip, and we wedged her bassinet in the back between the front of the back seat and the back of the front seat. No body had heard of strapping babies in at that time, but we felt that with the bassinet wedged she would be safe. Jim and Doreen Terrill went with us. We planned to make a full day of it, so we stopped to look at the scenery as we drove up the mountain. We pulled into a parking area at Nerada Falls, and walked down the

My Story

trail a hundred yards or so to see the falls. Since it was fairly cold at that altitude, we left Linda in the car asleep. We locked the doors of course. All four of us walked to the falls and spent a few minutes there. When we started back, we realized a woman was peering into the car window. Being a little anxious, we walked faster, and when we got near the car, the lady began to bawl us out severely for leaving an infant in there all alone. She said what made it worse was that it was an Ohio baby. She had seen the license plates on our car. As they pulled away, we saw that they also were from Ohio!

What she did not know, was that we were in real trouble. I had left my keys in the ignition, and it turned out that Dona did not have her keys with her. There was our new baby locked in the car! We tried several things to open the door but nothing was working. I was finally able to trip the lock lever on the driver's side wing window, and I could pry it open about an inch. That was not enough to reach in to get the keys, and when I wedged my arm in further, we could not use the crank to open the window. Doreen Terrill was very slender, in fact, she had skinny arms. She was able to get her arm in far enough to reach the window crank, but it was also too tight to unwind. I asked her to try one more time, and when she got her fingers on the crank, I pushed on the window as hard as I could. That relieved enough pressure so that she moved the crank a little. That was enough for her to finally crank the side window open, and then I could reach the keys. That taught us to check

My Story

to see where the keys were before we locked up. In fact, I soon learned to carry an extra key in my billfold. The final part of this story is that my trip to school at Scott Field was canceled. We would have liked to make the trip home, but we were not too sad about not going.

Linda certainly changed our lives. She was immediately the center of our lives, and that continued until she was grown up and on her own. I was very proud to be her Dad. Dona dressed her in cute outfits, from Cowgirl shirt, pants, and boots, to little lady outfits. We continued our social gatherings with our friends. The only difference was now we had to carry baby stuff with us. Several of the other couples also had small children, so they just got put to bed, sometimes with several in the same crib.

We wanted to see as much of Washington State as we could while we were there although we did not have much money. One weekend we drove out on the Olympic Peninsula, to the Pacific Coast. The scenery was unbelievable. The annual rainfall out there is over 100 inches in some places, and the trees grow like a jungle. We had driven out along the south edge of the Puget Sound, so there was big water on one side and the majestic Olympic Mountains on the other side. When we got to the Pacific Coast, we turned south on the coast highway. I believe it was Highway 101, and it was a narrow two lane black top road. It was extremely busy with logging trucks. They were huge vehicles and

My Story

frequently they carried only one log because the trees were so big. We had planned to drive around a big loop and wind up back home in one day. It was taking much more time than we had figured, and also a lot more fuel than we had planned. We were south bound on this Highway 101 and there were no towns. We were low on gas, and I knew we could not make it to whatever the next town on the map was. It was late in the evening, starting to get dark, and our gas gage was on empty. I was about panicked. Linda was tiny, and we would not have any heat if we ran out of gas. About that time, we saw a little sign pointing to the right that said LA PUSH. I figured if there were a town there, there would be gas. We started down that dirt road, and every mile was torture. I just knew we would run out of gas, and no one would even find us on such a remote road. We drove what seemed like an eternity (next day it showed to be about 20 miles) and finally came to the end of the road. There was no town! There was a Coast Guard Station, and just outside the perimeter gate was a tiny gas station! It was late and it was closed. I figured we would park by the pumps and get gas in the morning. Pretty soon a man came from somewhere and said the gas station was closed for the night. We told him we would need fuel so we could run the car for heat. He said "Why don't you rent one of my cabins?" Would you believe he had two or three tiny cabins right on the beach that he rented. We rented one, and as soon as we got our stuff in from the car, we walked the 100 feet or so to the Pacific

My Story

Ocean. It was getting dark, and looked sort of stormy. We stayed in the cabin that night, and the next morning we could not even get to the beach. The storm during the night had piled drift wood up almost to where the cabins were. They were huge complete trees. We wondered where they came from. Before we left that day, the man was out cutting a path down to the ocean. We also learned that this little place was the gateway to an Indian Reservation. Several years later in the 1970s we again drove to La Push. The change was unbelievable. It had become a major sport fishing destination, with service stations, restaurants, and motels, not to mention developed fishing boat facilities.

My Story

Chapter 16: I FINALLY GET TO FLY

One day while at work on the Flight Line, before Dona joined me at Mc Chord, I struck up a conversation with a new Squadron member. His name was Robert Bacheler, and he was from Valentine, Nebraska. He told me his family had vast ranch lands in Nebraska and stretching up into South Dakota. He said they operated the ranch using airplanes. He said he, along with his brothers, had learned to fly at the age where most farm boys were learning to drive. He had just come back from leave, and he had flown his own airplane back to the Tacoma area. He had it based at a small grass strip a few miles east of the Air Base. He told me it was a Piper Cub, and he would be glad to take me for a ride! We went out to his airport that afternoon, and after about 5 minutes in the air, I knew I had to do something about flying.

I picked his brains about every thing I could think of about flying. What kinds of airplanes there were, how much they cost to buy, how difficult they were to maintain, how much they cost to operate, and most important, how you went about learning to fly. From him I learned that there were several types of small, two place airplanes that would be good to get instruction in. I think that was all I talked about in the barracks. I got two or three others all excited about flying, and we decided to form a flying club, pool our money and buy one. I met a Squadron member who had been a fighter plane pilot in WW II, who had been reduced in rank to

My Story

Buck Sergeant. He had been in a crash, and his face was horribly scarred from being burned. He was a pilot, and had retained his license. He volunteered to help look for a suitable airplane. He and I went to Boeing Field at Renton, Washington. The runway was used by Boeing Aircraft to launch the airplanes coming off the assembly line at their Renton plant. In addition, there were a number of Fixed Base Operators that offered all kinds of General Aviation services, such as airplane maintenance, aircraft sales, flight training, etc. We went the rounds, up one side of the Flight Line, and down the other side, talking to every operation. Several had airplanes that were for sale, but all were priced above our limit, which was $700.00. We were nearly down to the last operation, and went inside to talk to the operator. He told us he had airplanes, but it turned out that all were priced too high. We had explained that we were trying to start a flying club, that we were all Air Force enlisted men, and had very little cash. There was a fellow in the room who it seemed paid no attention to us, but he followed us outside. When we were clear of the office, he said "I have an airplane I might sell".

We went with him to look at it, tied down near the end of the ramp. It looked like a very nice airplane. We asked him how much it would cost, and he said he would sell it cheap. I told him I had $450.00 which was correct, because that is how much I intended to kick in to make the $700.00. He sort of acted funny, hard to describe, but finally with tears in his eyes, said he would

My Story

sell it for that! We asked him to wait a little while, and we dashed back in to the office and asked the manager what he knew about the airplane and the man. He told us the airplane was in excellent condition, that it had just recently been completely refurbished by an aviation school, and had a brand new relicense. About the airplane owner, he said he was not stupid, but that he had such a lack of coordination between mind and muscle, that it seemed he was not right in the head. He had been taking flight instruction for several years, and had many hours of dual time, but no instructor would sign him off for solo flight. I guess he just decided he would give it up, and decided to sell on the spot. I paid him the money, and the sergeant I was with flew it home to the Spanaway airport, while I had to drive the car back home.

The airplane was an L2 Taylorcraft. It was built in 1941, and had served as a Navy primary trainer. It was a two place with a tandem seating arrangement. Unlike the J3 Cub, this airplane was flown from the front seat when flown solo. It had a 65 horse power Lycoming engine, and would fly at about 70 miles per hour. I do not know how the previous owner got a hold of the airplane, but just prior to my purchase of it, it had been refurbished by an aviation school in Renton, Washington, as a class project. It did need some additional work, so the other people who had signed on with me to buy an airplane agreed to pay for the additional work. The propeller had to be replaced because it had several nicks from taxiing

My Story

on gravel. The fabric needed to be rejuvenated, so we did that and then painted it red with white trim. We also had to replace the main wheel tires.

Finding Instructors to start giving me lessons was not a problem. As a matter of fact, there were more offers to give me instruction than I could use. The Squadron jet pilots that found out I had an airplane, lined up to fly with me. I usually flew with Major Garino, partly because he outranked the other 'would be' instructors, but also because I liked him. In addition, he was the one who invited me to stay at McChord and help start a new Squadron instead of going to Thule, Greenland. I can clearly remember my first solo flight. I had just had about an hour of 'touch and go' landings instruction, when the Major said I should stop and let him out at the end of the runway because he had to pee. When he got out, he said "Take it around and pick me up when you make your landing". I was surprised, but he said "Do it just like you have been doing". I only had about 6 hours of training. I taxied back to the end of the runway and started my take off roll. The airplane fairly leaped off the ground. With only me, it was that much lighter, and the take off was much quicker. I flew it around the pattern and started my approach. When I got to where I should be landing, I was still 50 or so feet in the air. I knew I could not get down and still have enough runway to stop, so I put on power and went around. Then it dawned on me that like the take off, it was going to be different with only me on board. Next time I came in a

My Story

little slower, and made the approach lower. I touched down with out any problem. I rolled on out to the end of the runway and picked up my Instructor. He said if I had gone around again, he was going to call out the Squadron and shoot me down! Kidding of course. When he got in the airplane he said "Ok, now let's go out and just fly and have some fun. He did the first loop I had ever been in, then we did some crazy eights and a few power on and power off stalls. He wanted me to be able to practice that stuff when I was flying solo to build time for my license.

Once I had soloed, I flew whenever I could get the time. I did my practice flying northwest of Tacoma, over the Puget Sound country. What a beautiful place. Water everywhere you looked, and lots of timber. When I had about 30 hours, my instructor suggested that I fly my cross country requirements. At that time, you needed two fairly long cross country flights, with landings at several different airports. The first one I flew was south to Portland, Oregon, to a small strip at Trout Dale just west of Portland. I landed there just ahead of a dense fog bank that was rolling in from the west. Several local pilots were caught out in it, and had to fly many miles inland to find clear landing fields. While waiting for the fog to clear, I talked to two helicopter pilots who had just flown small helicopters down from Alaska. They had followed the Alaskan Highway all the way down, and at one point had chased a grizzly bear. They said when he got tired; he lay on his back with his claws up

My Story

and was ready to defend himself. When the fog lifted, I headed up the Columbia River to the northeast to my next destination. I landed at a small grass strip, name forgotten, got my logbook signed, and took off for home. I was out most of the day, and saw some wonderful scenery that I could not have seen any other way.

On my second solo cross country, I was required to fly to the north. I flew a fair distance north of Seattle, to a small airport in Skagett County. When I got to where I thought the airport was, I could not find it. I circled the area several times, but could not pick out the runways. I was low on fuel, and had just about decided to land at an Air Force base (Pain, I think). I flew around one more time, and as I did, I saw them push an airplane out of a building. The shape of the airplane caught my eye. The problem was twofold. First, the hangar was built like a barn with a hip roof, not a round roof like hangars are supposed to have. Secondly, the Skagett River had flooded, and had run over parts of the runways. The parts that were not flooded had snow on them, and I could not make them out from the air. I landed at one end of a runway that was not flooded and taxied up to the office. A man came out and said the river was still rising and I had better be leaving. He signaled the fuel truck, and quickly signed my log book while they were fueling the plane. I think I was on the ground less than 5 minutes! As I took off, I could see the water creeping over the end of the runway I was on. The Skagett River

My Story

flood did a fair amount of damage in that area that year. I found that I really enjoyed flying solo. I could go pretty well where I wanted to.

The Hood Canal country on the Olympic peninsula is extremely pretty. There are waterways everywhere you look. The Puget Sound waters flow through and around the land there. There are small fishing villages located on the shores of many of the waterways, and overall is the gigantic Puget Sound. On any day you could see large naval vessels coming into or leaving the Tacoma area, and there were always freighters heading both directions.

I had moved the airplane from the grass strip at Spanaway, to the West Tacoma Airport, located just to the west of the city. The main reason was that the airport had hard surface runways, and had much more room for takeoffs and landings. At Spanaway, one had to takeoff and land over electrical lines, and the runway was only about 2000 feet long. West Tacoma was safer. The predominate wind was from the west, so one usually took off to the west. Immediately west of the airport was the waters of the Puget Sound, but the water level was about 300 feet below the runway. When you cleared the end of the runway heading west, you immediately gained an additional 300 feet of altitude. That was usually comforting; however, I remember on one occasion after taking off over the water, I could not gain any altitude. In fact, I was actually losing altitude. I

My Story

wanted to turn back toward the airport, but I did not have sufficient speed to start the turn for fear of a stall. Even if I had been able to turn, by now I was below the level of the airport. What had happened was that I had made my take off using runway 270, when the wind was a cross wind. As I cleared the end of the runway, I encountered a wind shift that actually became a tail wind. That had the effect of increasing my 'ground speed' but decreased my 'air speed', and it was airspeed I needed. I saw a small aircraft carrier type ship on Puget Sound ahead of me, so I began to make plans to ditch in the water as close to the ship as I could, if I continued to lose altitude. The reason the ship looked like a baby aircraft carrier was that it was called a 'jeep' carrier. It was designed to haul vast numbers of military vehicles, and was used for training a contingent of Navy Reserve, based at Tacoma. As I approached the ship, I began to gain altitude. When I had enough altitude, I changed course slightly and got rid of the tail wind. I believe that as I got nearer the water, I encountered cooler air and it increased my lift. With my new heading I was able to continue my climb out without further trouble. I discussed this event with a flight instructor when I landed, and he took me through the 'temperature vs air density' calculations. I learned from that experience that when the temperature was high you had to be aware of the length of runway required and the effect on the 'rate of climb'.

My Story

When I had only about 25 hours of solo time, my main instructor, Major Garino, suggested I hire a civilian instructor for an hour or two to get me ready for my flight test for my private pilots License. I didn't think I was ready, but made an appointment with an Instructor at my airport. On the day of our flight I was relaxed because I knew the instructor. I knew all I was going to do was fly and have him tell me what I could do better. Before we took off, the instructor looked over my log book to make sure I had my solo flights completed, and to see who had been signing off my dual instruction time. Major Garino had been signing for my dual time, although I had had a number of the jet pilots from the Squadron fly with me. It was uncanny. They would be flying jet fighter aircraft all day, and in the evening they were practically lined up to fly with me in my sod hopper!

Before we took off for our check flight, I did a complete 'walk around' preflight. The instructor asked about several of the things I did. I told him the military pilots did their preflight walk-arounds that way, and had taught me to do it the same way. When we took off, the instructor told me to head in a westerly direction. As I climbed out, I headed out over the area I had used for my practice stalls, "S" turns, and all the other things I was supposed to practice. When we got out pretty well over the Hood Canal country, the instructor asked me to do a few stalls and S turns and then to do a 'slow flight' where I was supposed to throttle way back to see how

My Story

slow I could fly with out entering a stall. I did all of those things, and then he said "I am going to give you a problem that I want you to work out on your E6B (a hand held circular slide rule) and give me the answers". He said here is the problem "You have been airborne for an hour, now when I tell you to, I want you to turn to a heading that will take you directly to Portland. I want to know in advance what that heading is, how much 'crab' you will have to carry to make that heading, what time you will arrive at Portland, and how much fuel you will have left when you arrive. When I began to work out the problem on my E6B computer, he said "I will take the airplane". I gave him the controls, and I busied myself working out the headings, crab, fuel usage and estimated time of arrival (ETA) at Portland. While I was struggling with the questions, I could see that he started a descent. He went lower and lower until we were below the treetops, skimming over the water in some of the waterways. When I had the problems worked out, I told him I had the answers. He kept control of the airplane, and asked me to recite my answers. I did, and he said "They sound good. Now take the airplane and give me a climbing turn so that you arrive at 1000 feet altitude at the same time you are on the correct heading for home". I know he did not know that I had done all of my practice flights over the area we were in. Knowing the correct heading for home was no sweat, so all I had to do was adjust my rate of climb to arrive at 1000 feet when I got on the heading. I did that all OK. By that

My Story

time we had been in the air for around an hour, and I thought we would practice some more maneuvers. Instead, he said "take me home".

When we landed he told me to come into the office when I had finished tying the airplane down. I then thought we would do some 'hangar flying' discussing what I did right and what I had done wrong. The purpose of the flight was to have a commercial general aviation instructor get me ready for my flight test for my private pilots license. When I got inside his office he was at a typewriter, and he said "What is your address"? I told him and he pecked away a little more at the typewriter. He asked a few more questions, did a little more poking at the machine, then took out a small piece of paper and handed it to me. He said "This is your temporary private pilot's license; they will send you a permanent one in the mail in a few days". Wow! I thought I was going up for some instruction, and instead I had passed my final flight test! I only had a little over 25 hours at the time.

When I told the folks at the air base of my good luck, they insisted I fly the airplane back to Spanaway airfield the next weekend for a celebration. When I got there, many of the pilots from our Fighter Squadron were there, as well as several of the enlisted men, some of whom were also taking instruction in my airplane. Major Garino was there to congratulate me also, and to insist that they cut a piece off my shirt tail. I have no

My Story

idea where that custom started, or why, but they did cut a little piece off my shirt tail. Then they all decided that I should take Dona for a ride. She was a little reluctant, but finally agreed to go around the pattern once. It started to rain just as we took off. I stayed in the pattern, and when I made my approach, I was not satisfied that I could see well enough for a touchdown, so we went around the pattern again. This time we landed with out any trouble, and Dona was my first passenger!

I continued to fly at every opportunity, usually by myself. Each time I would take off, I would wonder if I could get back down safely, so I would make a 'touch and go'. If that was smooth, I would head out to see whatever there was to see from my lofty perch. If my touch and go was rough, I would repeat them until I was satisfied I would have no trouble on my return. By the time my discharge date came up, I had around 80 hours of flight time. I sold my share of the airplane to Sgt. Talsma, who was the Squadron First Sergeant. I learned later that several airmen from the Squadron learned to fly in that little airplane.

I was fairly good at my job, and my superior officers must have noticed, because I made promotions immediately when I had 'time in grade'. By the end of my second year, I was a Buck Sergeant (Airman 1st Class). Before I had 'time in grade' for Staff Sergeant, I was selected to go to NCO Academy. The class was held at McChord Air Force base, so I was close to home,

My Story

however, like all the other students, I had to live on base. There were about 50 students, all candidates for promotion to Staff Sergeant. They came from all over the Western Air Defense Command, and I was the only 'slick arm' candidate. For each four year period you had served, you were encouraged to wear a slash on your uniform sleeve. 'Slick arm' meant I had less than four years in the military, and I was constantly reminded of it by the other students. The class ran for four weeks, and was intense. We were up by 4:00AM to start a regimen of close order drill, exercise, and classroom studies. In addition, we were exposed to the most intense inspection I have ever encountered. Every item in your assigned area had to be functional, and had to meet rigid requirements. Clothes were to be folded a certain way, shoes were to shine like a mirror, all personal items were to be lined up a certain way. There were two men to a room, and each occupant was responsible for his half. You would be 'gigged' for any number of reasons, during any number of inspections.

My roommate was a 20 year veteran, and besides being a Fireman, he was a slob! His side of the room was closest to the door. By the time the inspectors had inspected his side and gigged him severely, they hardly paid any attention to my side. He would nominally have 15 to 20 gigs a day and I had less than that in the entire four weeks. Both the exercises and the close order drills were easy for me, because I had just come through Basic Training two years back. Some of the candidates had not

My Story

had either exercise or close order drill for years. The class studies were also easy for me. I found that if I applied myself, I could do very well.

At graduation time, I had a very nice surprise. First of all, they had invited Dona and the other wives from McChord to attend the ceremony. As we marched in, I realized that my Commanding Officer was there also. When we received our diplomas, they announced that I had acquired the fewest gigs at 13, had achieved the highest rating of the current class, and the 2nd highest rating of the entire year. my Squadron Commander congratulated me, and asked if I would stop at the Squadron Orderly Room before I went home with Dona. When we got there, he gestured me into his office, and handed me a set of Staff Sergeant stripes. He said "Have those on your arm when you report in tomorrow". He had just promoted me, and I still was two months short of having time in grade for Staff Sgt.!

I thoroughly enjoyed my hitch in the Air Force. Basic Training was not as bad as most people felt it was. Some new recruits had a hard time because they refused to comply with the stupid orders given by the Drill Instructors. Once you realized they were Drill Instructors because they probably could not make it anywhere else, you just complied. If they said "Give me xx pushups", you did just that. When you realized it was only going to last a few weeks, you could just take it in stride. The men I knew who had a hard time in Basic

My Story

Training never did very well when they got out. It was actually fun to outwit the Drill Instructors. Here are a couple of examples.

When we first got to Lackland Air Force Base, we were told we would never have enough time to go into San Antonio. First of all, they said they would keep us too busy, and secondly, they said you could not go off Base without a pass, nor could you get back on Base with out a pass. So here is what I did. During our off time, they assigned us to dig dandelions with a small kitchen knife. I and a guy from Indiana decided to see if there was a way to get into town. We dug weeds down to the main gate area where we could see traffic coming onto the base, and going off base. It was not very long before we realized that a bunch of taxi cabs were both coming and going, and the gate guards never stopped them to check for passes. We dug dandelions for a few days until we knew the routine of how long we had before the Drill Instructor (DI) would decide to call the Flight to Order. We found out that early in the afternoon on weekends, our DI, along with some others, would go to the Non-Commissioned Officers (NCO) Club. They would stay until mess time at 5:00PM. The following Saturday, my buddy and I had our dress uniforms on when the dandelion detail started. The DI said, "Too bad, you guys, you are going to mess up your uniforms". We slowly worked our way down to the main gate. When we had a chance, we stashed our weeding tools in a trash area, and strolled out onto the main drag. When an

My Story

empty cab came along, we hailed it. As we went through the gate, we managed to be engaged in a heated conversation, and did not even look at the guard. He waved us through. The cabby said "OK wise guys, where to now?" We asked him to take us to town to a beer place that would not have other Airmen around. When he let us off at a run-down dive at the edge of San Antonio, we asked him to pick us up in half an hour. We each had a beer, then sat outside and waited for our ride back to camp. We could have had several beers, but neither of us had enough money. Eventually our cabby came back and we rode back to camp the same way. Again, we were engaged in animated conversation as we went through, but we needn't have bothered. The cabby waved at the guard, and the guard waved back as though they were on first name basis. When the cabby dropped us off a little ways from our tent area, he suggested we not try that too often! We didn't see much of San Antonio, and we did not need the beer we drank, it was just to test whether or not we could.

On occasion, we would be assigned to KP. The tasks were not as bad as some have made them out to be, and I never really minded the duty. I did notice one time, that when the Inspectors were around, the cooks got sort of riled up. I also noticed that the Inspectors always carried a clipboard, and either walked around doing nothing or sat at a table and drank coffee. I tried that and it worked. I borrowed a clip board from the orderly room on the way to the kitchen for mess duty. I waited until all the

My Story

other workers were inside, then went in, got a cup of coffee and sat down at a table at the rear of the Mess Hall. Whenever a cook was near, I would write stuff on the paper. I had drawn a rough diagram of the Mess Hall room, and placed the counters and stuff on the drawing. I did not have to work at all, but it was a harder day than if I had just done the KP.

I did not take much leave time while I was in the Air Force. Dona was there with me, and we were kept busy with our jobs and with Linda. I did take two weeks leave in the fall of 1954. We had just bought a new car, and I thought I would get a job at the local canning factory to make extra cash for a couple of payments. I worked the night shift, which meant I went in at 4:00 PM, and would work until the produce was all gone, usually around 3:00 AM.

One night we finished around 1 or 1:30 AM, and when I went to get in my car, I had locked the keys inside! I walked a few blocks to the Puyallup City Police Station, and told the officers on duty about my problem. They said, "No sweat, we have a device that will open anything". They had this little device that you pumped up, stuck a pointed shaft into the selected key hole and pulled the trigger. The air pressure would shoot little gadgets out that were supposed to open the locks. They showed me how it worked on several cell doors and cabinets around the station, and sure enough, it worked. They drove me down to where my car was parked and

My Story

tried the driver's door. Nothing. Around to the other side to try the passenger door, again nothing. We tried the trunk, and that did not open either. Dona had a set of keys at home, but that did not do me any good here. I could have broken a window to get in, but the car was new, and I did not want to do that. I decided I would call my friend Jim Terrill, have him go to our house and get Dona's keys, and drive them to me. I decided to wait until around 6:00 AM to call Jim.

I spent the rest of the night at the Police Station, shooting the bull with the two on duty cops. They showed me they had a game to keep themselves from becoming too bored. They would take a heavy rubber band, cut it so that it was a straight piece, and use it to shoot flies. They had a score sheet that had been running for several months. They scored sure kills, probables, and clean misses. A kill had to be witnessed, and the shooter had to show a corpse. A 'probable' had to be agreed to by at least two people. Since 'clean misses' were also scored the shooters would normally wait for a sitting duck (fly). I suspect the Police Department in Puyallup, Washington, is busier now than it was back then. Eventually, Jim arrived with my keys. (Dona's keys)

While I was at Scott AFB, I had to buckle down to keep up with my studies, as I did not want to wash out. I did get into mischief a few times over parking my car, but I have already confessed to those hi-jinks. In addition to

My Story

my studies at Scott Field, my main objective was to be married to Dona. When I got to my duty station, McCord Air Force base, I faced an entirely new world. I had responsibilities on the flight line, lots of new duties to learn, and completely unsupervised life in the barracks. Of course, I missed Dona, but I stayed completely involved in Squadron duties and working on my Auburn Speedster. When Dona joined me in the spring of 1952, and we lived off base, it was like a civilian job. Dona had her job, I had my work at the base, and we had our limited social life with our friends. I liked the Air Force well enough to be very interested in re-enlisting. Since I had only seen one duty station so far, I wanted to enlist for a tour in Alaska. My superior officers wanted me to enlist to fill my own vacancy, in other words, stay where I was. They kept cutting sample checks of what my reenlistment bonus would be, and the $12,000.00 was looking pretty tempting, plus they guaranteed me a promotion to Tech Sergeant. I finally agreed to sign a paper that said I could get out for 90 days, and if I did not like civilian life, in other words, did not find a job, I could re-enlist with all the benefits they offered.

My Story

CHAPTER 17: I AM A CIVILIAN AGAIN

When I got out of the Air Force in mid December, 1955, I had a fair amount of pay coming because I had not taken all my leave. As I cleared the base, they paid me in 100 dollar bills and several 20 dollar bills. They were all brand new and crisp. Little did we know what trouble they were to bring us. We planned to take a fairly leisurely drive back home, and planned to arrive in Ohio in time for Christmas. We stopped in Oregon to visit Aunt Lila and Uncle Bert, and spent a day or two with them. When we left them, we headed south to visit Verna and Ray at Hamilton Air Force base in California. The third or fourth day out, we were in a small town in Northern California late in the day, so decided to stay over night. Before getting a motel room, I decided to fill the gas tank. I stopped at a station and filled the gas tank, and when I went to pay the man with a brand new 20 dollar bill, he said "no way". It turned out that the little town had been stung with a rash of counterfeit 20 dollar bills just a few weeks earlier. I offered him a 100 dollar bill, with the same results. There was a bank in the town, but it was way past closing time, so getting the new bills changed there was not an option. I told him we were staying overnight, and I would pay him in the morning. He was pretty cool about that idea. When I agreed to get a room at the motel directly across the street, and add the gas bill to the room bill, he began to thaw out a little. I don't remember exactly how we worked it out, but the next morning Dona got into the

My Story

bank to change the new bills for some old ones to pay what we owed for the gas, for supper, for our room, and for breakfast. It sure pointed out that you could have a pocket full of money and still be poor!

We had an uneventful trip the rest of the way to Verna and Ray's place. They showed us around San Francisco, and we had a very nice visit. They got to meet Linda, and we got to meet our new nephew Raymond, who was about the same age as Linda. When we left California we sort of kept it moving because we wanted to be in Ohio for Christmas. There was snow in some places on the way home, but nothing like we had four years before when we were heading from Ohio to Wisconsin. We spent Christmas 1955 in Ohio with Dona's folks, and then headed up to Wisconsin. I was still undecided about reenlisting, so I had to try the job market.

In Merrill, once we had finished visiting, I began looking for a job, and looking for a place to live. I got a job at a plant in Merrill that made little metal things like screen door hooks and stuff like that. My job was in the plating department, where they used some kind of electrical system to coat the metal things with a coating that kept them from rusting. It was a terrible job. Everything stunk from the chemicals they were using, and you got an electrical shock every time you touched any metal equipment. I lasted about a week and decided the Air Force was a whole lot better that this. I happened to see Erv Zastrow somewhere, and he was delighted to

My Story

see me. I had worked for Erv for a short time putting roofs and siding on barns while I was in high school. I hit him up for a job, but he had nothing going at the time. He suggested I go see his brother, who was the boss at a wood working factory that made all kinds of small wood products. I went to see him, and I really laid it on about how bad I needed a job. He said he really did not have an opening, but would put me on any way.

I started the next day. My job was to off bear small pieces of wood that a man was sawing with a radial arm saw, and place them in a certain order on a wheeled pallet. The pieces would eventually be made into window frames. The sawyer had all of the fingers gone from one hand and two missing from the other. He would look at me and talk while fishing around the saw blade to get the ends of the material out of the way. I asked if that was how he lost his fingers, and he said yes, several different times! And he was still doing it! That seemed to be the caliber of the people working there. I was told that everyone was expected to work at top speed in order to compete with the 'cheap' wood shops in the south.

At noon on that first day, I was told to go to the Merrill Vocational School to have my hearing tested as required by state law. After having my ears tested, and on my way out of the building to return to work, I met Mr. Burchart, the vocational school Director. He was a friend of my parents, and of course he knew I had been

My Story

in the Service. He invited me to his office for a chat. He asked what my plans were, and I told him I had a job, but that I wanted to go to school on the G.I. Bill starting the next year. I told him I had been involved in electronics in the Air Force, and would like to continue in that field. He said "You should start right now". He said if I waited until next year, I would find some excuse to put it off again until the next year. I suppose he was right. While I was still in his office, he called the Wausau Vocational School, talked for a while, and when he hung up a few minutes later, I was enrolled in their electronics course starting the next day! Now I had to go back to my job and quit the job I had begged for the day before.

The electronics course at the Wausau Vocational School was a course provided by the University of Wisconsin, with credits leading to an Associate Degree. I drove every day, and to help defray gas costs, I had several Merrill students riding with me. I found the course pretty easy. I don't know if it was because of my experience in the Air Force, or because I had grown up a little, but I thoroughly enjoyed the course work. Although I had started at the beginning of the 2nd semester, I had no trouble catching up with the class. In fact, I signed up for several additional classes, one of them being public speaking. The G. I. Bill was paying my tuition plus $105.00 a month, which was not enough to live on. Dona worked at the Red Owl Grocery Store several nights a week after I got home from school, and

My Story

also had a job typing at my Dad's office when they needed extra help. Erv Zastrow called and told me he could use me on weekends, and also during my summer break.

We were paying $50.00 a month for a lousy apartment, and my Dad said he thought we may be able to buy a house for less than that. I did not believe we could, but we started looking at houses. We found one that was pretty badly run down, but was fairly well built, and was pretty large. We found the purchase price was $3500.00, and could be bought with a 10% down payment. I did not have the $350.00. We went to the local bank to see what we could work out, and I think some one had greased the skids for us. The banker said since the State of Wisconsin had never paid a Veteran's bonus, they had made arrangements for low interest down payment loans. He further said they could make the down payment loan, and then since we had the down payment, they could loan us the money to buy the house. We left the bank owning our first house, and the monthly payments were $35.00!

We immediately began making improvements to the house. Dona cleaned and papered several of the downstairs rooms. There was really no kitchen, just a sink hanging on a wall. We wanted regular cupboards and cabinets, and decided we would have to build them ourselves. I knew that Otto Peterson at Irma had a lot of rough sawn lumber piled in his farm yard, so we went

My Story

up to see if we could buy some. I told him that we would be building cupboards with it. He agreed to sell us lumber for the ridiculous low price of $100.00 per thousand board feet. We went to the pile and were loading lumber when he came out to watch. I had been laying the really nice wide boards aside as I felt for the low price we were paying we should take the narrow stuff. Otto said "If you are going to build cupboards, you are going to need those wide boards, so put them on your load". When we got to Merrill, Dad called a man he knew who had a planeing mill to see if he could plane the lumber, and what it would cost. The man said he did not have time to do it, but if we wanted to do it on a weekend, we could do it ourselves for free. We did, and it was really first class lumber. We built a very nice kitchen with it, and had lumber left for the next project.

The house had a large 2nd floor that was sort of divided into two rooms. We further divided them into a kitchen, a living room, two bedrooms, and a bath room. When finished, we rented the upstairs to a couple for $50.00 a month! The upstairs bathroom was a major project. A local plumber had given us a price of $2500.00 to do the job, plus he was going to leave the drain pipes below the down stairs ceiling where they would show. We did not have that kind of money, and we certainly did not want the drains hanging below our living room ceiling. I was discussing our problem with Mr. Dan Brace, who was one of Dad's Supervising Teachers, one evening at Dad's office. Dan said, "I used to do plumbing, and I

My Story

will help you do it". He and I worked several evenings, but we put in a first class bathroom, and the drains were hidden within the floor joists the way they were supposed to be.

Some of the other upgrades were a new roof, and a new paint job. We put in a lawn, and rebuilt an old shed out in back that I could use as a garage. The location of our house was in a pretty well run down area, but our efforts seemed to be catching. Both of the adjacent houses went through a refurbishment, as well as several houses across the street. I remember the Merrill Postmaster and his wife came strolling by one evening when Dona and I were working on the lawn. He was sure full of praise for what we were accomplishing. He said our efforts were affecting the entire area. When I left to join IBM, we sold our house after being in it only 11 months for $11,500.00. We surely had learned a lesson about renting versus buying.

When my Dad and I looked at that old house the first time, we found that the owner had leased it to the county, and the county had people living in it because there was no room for them at the 'County Home'. The people were all elderly, and they had been told the house was up for sale. I think there were three or four ladies and a couple of men. They told us the house was in bad shape, and that none of the lights worked and none of the electrical outlets worked. They had temporary electrical cords running all over the house. It had a

My Story

basement, and when I went down with a flashlight, I soon found the trouble. Every one of the circuit breakers was tripped! I flipped them back on, and lights came on all over the house. Of course the house had to be rewired which I could do.

When we moved in, I had to learn how to fire a coal furnace. Where I grew up we always had wood fired furnaces, and I knew how to 'bank' them so that they would carry some fire through the night. The first night it got really cold, I got up early, went to the basement and shoveled coal into the furnace. I mean I shoveled coal! Then I ran back upstairs and jumped into bed to get warm. I had not been in bed long before there was a tremendous explosion that shook the house. It also filled the house with heavy smoke and BLACK soot. I had smothered the flame in the furnace, and the heat built up until the fire broke through and caused the explosion. It blew the door of the furnace open, but did no other harm. Also, there was no fire, just the smoke and the soot. Some readers may remember in old houses you would put a circular cover over the chimney openings that were not in use. Well, this old house had those in all of the rooms, and the explosion blew them out along with all of the soot from the chimney from many years. Linda's bedroom (and her crib) was completely covered with soot. Once I realized that there was no danger of fire, I escaped off to my classes at Wausau and left Dona to clean up the mess.

My Story

CHAPTER 18: IBM BECKONS

Near the end of my 2nd year at vocational school, I began to look for a job. Most of the students in my class were preparing for jobs as TV repairmen. I was not too excited about that as a career. I heard that National Cash Register Company was hiring, so I applied for, and was called for an interview. When I finished the interview, they asked me to take a test. It was primarily a mechanical type test, like "if this gear goes this direction, what will this lever way out here do?" It was pretty easy, and they offered me a job that day. The job would start after I was out of school, and would be located in Gary, Indiana. I sure was not anxious to go to Gary, Indiana but a job was a job. I don't remember what my starting pay was to be, but it was pretty low. About a week later I got a call from the Manager at the local National Cash Register office. He asked me if I could come in that afternoon to meet their Division Manager. I went to see him, and he told me they were making some changes that would affect me. They had decided to start a one man office in the northern part of Wisconsin, and were promoting one of the men in the Wausau office to that job. That left an opening in the Wausau office, and I was to have that job. Wow! I had a job, we would be able to stay in our house in Merrill, and we would not have to live in Gary, Ind.

Well all that changed about a week later. It turns out that IBM was recruiting for people to work in a new division. The new division was called Federal Systems

My Story

Division, and it would concentrate on doing electronic jobs for the government. I applied, took the test, and was accepted to start as a Systems Engineer Trainee at Kingston, New York. After training for nearly a year at Kingston, my duty assignment would be Madison, Wisconsin. My starting pay was double what National Cash had offered, plus they would pay $11.50 per day per diem while I was in training. Now again, I had to resign from a job I had accepted but not yet started. I was to report to start school at Kingston, New York on July 17, 1957.

I knew that I had done fairly well in school, but I was surprised when I was named Valedictorian, and was asked to give a graduation speech. My primary electronics instructor taped my speech (without my knowing it) and presented the tape to me after the ceremonies were over. I guess my speech went over OK, but I had a scare when the ceremonies first started. The graduates were to walk into the auditorium in single file. I was to be the first in line. When I got to the area where the graduates were to be seated, I was to continue on straight and climb up about 5 steps onto the stage where the dignitaries were already seated. I forgot that I had a long gown on, and as I started up the steps, I tripped on the gown. I didn't fall all the way down, but whatever composure I had was lost when people in the audience laughed!

My Story

We now had a job and it was not in Merrill, so we put our house up for sale. It sold almost immediately to a newly retired Air Force Colonel. We left Wisconsin in time to stop for a while in Ohio, and then proceeded on to Kingston, New York. Kingston was a fairly small town where IBM had built a new plant. They had been hiring for the new division and had brought in a large number of new hires from all over the country. The result was that there were precious few places to rent. We had arrived in town several days early so that we could find a place and get settled before I started school. We looked and looked and could find nothing. We even had some doors slammed in our faces when they found out we had a baby.

On the last day before starting school, a Sunday, and we were about exhausted from searching for a place. We pulled into a parking place to re-look at the newspaper we had, when I noticed something. We had inadvertently parked at a place that sold mobile homes, and they had some parked with for sale signs on them! We went to the office and told the man we were looking for a trailer. He showed us one we liked, and he said if we had the money, he could locate it in his trailer park the next morning. I told him we had the money, but it was in a bank in Wisconsin. He made out the papers to loan us the money until we could get our money from the bank in Wisconsin.. After all the signing was done, he said "Son, I hope you haven't signed something that is going to get you in trouble". I guess he was not sure

My Story

we really had the money. It all worked out OK. I started school the next day, while Dona got moved into a space in the trailer court and started making the trailer into a home. The trailer was a 40 foot by 8 foot Vindale, and was nicely laid out for our family. A man who owned a restaurant had bought it and used it just for sleeping. He slept on the couch, and he must have been very heavy because the couch was squashed flat. The dealer put in a new couch for us. I don't remember what the price was, but we sure thought it was cheap. Although it was small by today's standards, it worked out really well for us.

There were other families who were new IBM employees in the park who we neighbored with, and my drive to work was only a mile or two. Some of the IBM employees had come from Lexington, Kentucky, and were in training for the Typewriter Division. I remember seeing one young man walking around the trailer park picking up stones. I went out to talk to him one day, and found out that he grew up in Kentucky, and the stones he was picking up were ammo for his sling shot. He hunted squirrels with it. One family we met in the trailer park wound up working for me many years later when we were in Auburn, Washington.

The first day of 'school' at the IBM plant was orientation day. There were about 30 of us who were assigned to System Engineering class. Several older IBM employees came in to talk to us about what we could expect and what would be expected of us. One of

My Story

the things they told us was that the originator of IBM, Mr. Tom Watson, was a teetotaler, and he would have anyone who cashed his check at a bar fired. They also said no alcohol 'on your person or in your person on IBM premises. They also informed us the company insisted that IBM employees dress like their customers would be dressed. That meant white shirts and business suits! There were a number of us in the group who were wearing sports jackets, and a few had on sweaters. We were told to be in class the next day in proper attire. That was a problem for me. I had no business suits, and not much money to buy one with. That evening we found a men's shop in down town Kingston that had a special on men's suits. We bought one that cost a little over nineteen dollars. It was a stupid sort of grey color that I hated, but I could afford it. Guess what? Next day in class there were four of us with the same cheap suit on! I think mine lasted to the first payday, then was quickly replaced.

The classes at IBM were very difficult for me. I had breezed through the material in the school at Wausau, but these classes in the new computer technology were tough. At one of our early class briefings, our class manager told us that for every person in the class, there were about 30 who had applied, but had not been selected. A number of the class attendees had been out of school for several years, and had been employed by various technical companies. I recall hearing several discussions between some of them about how difficult it

My Story

was to live on the small salary we were getting. Small salary? Dona and I were in pig heaven. We had been living on the $105.00 per month G.I bill money, plus whatever else we could scrape up. Now our salary was $81.50 a week, plus per diem of $11.50 per day! We lived on the per diem, and we stashed the salary. I got several raises during the 9 months I was in school, and by the time I was finished, we were making around $125.00 a week. The first time I was called out of class and told I was getting a salary increase, I thought I was called out to be fired! We had frequent tests to check our progress, and I had failed a few of them miserably. They had invited a couple of our classmates to try some other kind of job as they were doing poorly, and I thought that was what I was in for. Can you imagine my surprise when instead of firing me, they gave me a raise?

I studied most of the time both evenings and weekends, but we did get to see a little bit of that part of New York State. Kingston is in what is called 'upstate', and is a kind of rural area. It was heavily wooded, and because it was near the Catskill Mountains, it was a vacation/recreation area. I hunted squirrels a few times, and what I learned was that although it was heavily wooded and looked rural, it was still crowded. I would find a place that looked fairly wild to hunt in, but invariably, if I climbed over a hill, I would be in a housing development.

My Story

I was interested in airplanes, so naturally, I found a small airport to hang around at. It was the Catskill Airport, a small grass strip with about 5 old dilapidated T Hangers. The owner had a number of old WW1 airplanes. On some occasions, he and his friends would fly them and simulate dog fights. One day when I was up there 'hangar flying' with him, he had a fire going in a stove in a little office. The smoke stack stuck out through the wall where there had been a window. While we were talking, the area around the smoke stack began to smoke from being over heated. I commented that he should work up a better arrangement for his chimney, because of danger of fire. He said it had been that way for a long time and had never been a problem. Unfortunately, his place burned down that winter, and he lost those beautiful old airplanes. I am not sure the fire started at that smoke stack, but it most likely did. I never got to fly with him.

My Story

CHAPTER 19: ON TO WISCONSIN

I believe we finished the class in March of 1958. My duty assignment was at Madison, Wisconsin, at Truax Air Force Base. We were installing the SAGE Air Defense site there. SAGE was an Air Force operated national defense system. It used radar data inputs to track all aircraft coming into the United States, and was used to guide Fighter Interceptor Aircraft to intercept any that could not be identified any other way. It was a huge installation about the size of a city block in area and 3 stories tall. It consisted of duplexed computers. They were the largest and most sophisticated computers in the world at that time.

Dona, Linda, and I drove out to Madison, and had hired a mobile home mover to haul our trailer out there for us. We expected to have it located in one of the mobile home courts in Madison. We found that there was no room for our trailer. The one we liked the best was the nicest park in town, but they had a big stack of applications ahead of us. There were several trailer courts, but they were all full. We found out that the county had a moratorium on building new trailer courts, or even expanding the ones that were there. We understood the reason was that during the war people had flocked in to work in a munitions plant at Baraboo. When the war ended, they all left and left the County with huge bills for schools and other infrastructure that was no longer needed. I guess they felt trailers were too mobile.

My Story

We finally found a place for the trailer about 15 miles from Madison on a private farm. Before we could get it located out there, we had a strange piece of good luck. One of the couples who were also moving out to Madison were apartment hunting, and wound up looking at an apartment next to the trailer park we liked. When they were looking at the apartment, they noticed a large trailer being placed in the park. They commented to the lady who had the apartment that they had friends who were having trouble getting their trailer located. She said "Well, we can fix that", and she took them over to meet the trailer park owner. It turned out that they had just returned from vacationing together in the West Indies. My friend explained our problem to the park owner. The owner took one of the application forms, one of which I had filled out the day before, and wrote on the back "Give this guy attention". He told my friend to have me take it back to the park we liked, and hand it to the park manager. I took it back to the trailer park we liked, and handed it to the manager. He said "Why didn't you tell me you were friends of the owner". He put our trailer in the location we liked best in the park we liked best! It turned out that the park owner's name was Chet Bible, he was a county official, and he had arranged it so that he was the only one who could keep expanding his trailer courts. I believe he had three or four of them. We started looking for a house soon after we arrived at Madison. We were able to sell the trailer for much more than we paid for it because it was already located in a

194

My Story

prime spot, and the new owner would not have to move it.

We soon found an old farm house that needed some fixing up, which we knew we could do. The farm land had all been developed into housing units, but the old farm house had a large yard. We did the normal upgrading to make it comfortable, and also rented the upstairs apartment out for what the house payments were. I bought a Cessna 140 airplane, and was soon back to flying. Although I worked at the Truax Airport, I had the airplane located at a small grass strip at Monroe. I practiced flying until I was satisfied I was qualified to fly my family up to Merrill. We did that several times.

One day when I was at the little airfield, I noticed that several of the airplanes were damaged. I was certain it was vandalism, and I made arrangements to base my airplane at the civilian side of Truax Airport. Then I found out that the airport owner had put his horses in the airport area, and they had chewed on the fabric wings of the airplanes. I decided to move my airplane out, and was glad I got mine it before it suffered any damage.

Since I had never flown into an airport with a control tower, and had no training on communications, I called the Truax Tower by phone and told them I would be flying in and asked what I should do. The guys told me they would turn on their low frequency receiver and talk me down on that since my transmitter only had one low frequency channel to use. On the appointed day, I flew

My Story

in toward Truax. From a few miles out, I called for
landing instructions. I got none. I called several times,
always with the same results. Nothing. I continued on
until I was in the vicinity of the airport, and decided to
do what I had done when flying into Renton Airfield in
Washington. I would circle the airport while watching
the tower. They would shoot a red light at me until I was
in line with the runway they wanted me to use, then
shoot a green light at me. I started circling Truax, and
sure enough, while I was on a cross wind for the runway
I expected to use, they shot me a green light. As I made
my approach, I finally heard from the tower. His
instructions were to continue on for a landing on the
runway in front of me, but to expedite my landing. Now
I got nervous. When he asked me to expedite, I knew he
had some one landing behind me, and since my normal
landing speed was about 50 MPH, and any thing big
would be coming up behind me at about 200 MPH, I
increased my speed to around 75 MPH. The result was
that when I touched down, I bounced and was flying
again. Unfortunately, I did that several times before I
finally was able to stay down. When I rolled to stop, the
controller in the tower came back on the radio and said
"OK Cowboy, you are cleared to taxi across all runways,
and you can put him in the barn"! When I got parked
and tied down and inside the pilots lounge, I called the
tower to see why I could not contact them when I was
inbound. They told me someone had turned the volume
down on their low frequency receiver. It turned out that

My Story

that was a recurring problem nearly every time I went out to fly. I would call them on the phone and tell them I was going out flying and to turn on their low Freq. radio. They would turn it on long enough to give me taxi and take off instructions, then while I was out flying around the country, they would turn it off. When I would come in and start circling, they would call "OK Cowboy, we turned it on, do you read me"? I guess the low frequency radio made a lot of static, and it was a nuisance for them. I eventually solved that problem by installing a very basic VHF radio. It actually had four VHF transmit/receive channels, plus an omni receiver. Now I was really in pig heaven. The omni system was the first navigation system that actually gave me a heading to fly to reach a destination. I had learned to navigate by 'dead reckoning' which is based on a time/speed/heading calculation, and was usually backed up by following a major high way or a set of railroad tracks.

I pretty well covered southern Wisconsin in my flights around the area. One day, I decided I would fly across Lake Michigan. I headed east at around 2000 feet altitude. I was surprised at the size of the body of water as I proceeded out from shore. It was not long before I was out of sight of land behind me, and I could not see land in front of me. The horizon looked completely different when all I could see was water. Then I noticed my engine began to sound funny. Sort of a miss. I checked for carburetor ice, and it was clear, but the miss

My Story

continued. Not wanting to proceed, I turned around and headed back to the west. I soon had the west shore of the lake in view, and since the miss was no longer evident, I turned back to the east to continue on across the lake. Would you believe, when I got out of sight of land I could detect the miss again. Since I did not know what caused it, I decided to head for home. When I got back and was describing the problem to Louie Willomier, the fixed base operator, he laughed, and said most engines went on 'automatic rough' when flying single engine over water or mountainous terrain, because you unconsciously listen closer. I have had that experience several times with several airplanes in several different settings, but all of them occurred when it would be bad news to have to land.

After flying the Cessna 140 for about a year, I got the 'bigger faster' bug. We had been flying up to Merrill for weekends, and with Dona and I in the seats with Linda on Dona's lap, and a fair sized dog in the baggage area behind the seat, the airplane was too small. I began to think about a 4 place airplane that would also go a little faster. The answer was a Piper Tri-Pacer. The one I bought was newly rebuilt and repainted Piper's red and white scheme. It was certainly a pretty airplane. It was a four place, so now Linda had a place to sleep when we flew somewhere. I think by that time we did not have a dog. This airplane had a tricycle landing gear, and I found it much easier to both land and take off. Being

My Story

somewhat heaver, it was also more stable and smoother. All in all, I liked it very much.

My airplane story got me a little ahead of my chronology. I liked what I did on my first duty assignment at Madison. We worked shifts of 8 hours, and covered the operation 24 hours a day. Initially, we were installing and testing these gigantic computers, so we were the only users. When we had the installation complete, and had the bugs worked out, The Air Force came in to operate the system. It was their installation, but we had a hard time letting them operate 'our' machine. Our bogy was to have one of the two computers online at all times. Our contract with the Air Force only allowed about 5 minutes of down time a year! We kept one machine online at all times, and the other machine was in scheduled maintenance or on 'stand by' monitoring the operations. On first shift, the IBM crew provided operations directly for the Air Force, while on the night shifts we did maintenance on which ever machine was off line. Life was good. I liked working second or third shift, so I could fly during the day. In addition, I liked the challenge of finding and fixing electronic problems on the maintenance shifts. Many of the people on my crew out ranked me with regard to work experience. Some of them were sort of loud mouthed, and were pretty good at bragging about their abilities. IBM's policies required periodic evaluations which would/could result in being fired, having a salary increase, or be promoted. One night my

My Story

Manager invited me in for my scheduled evaluation. These times were always sort of tense. As I remember, he complimented me on my performance, and he made a sort of weird comment. He said "The squeaky wheel does not always get the grease". About a week later, as I was going off third shift to go home, I was invited to go with my manager to the Site Manager's office. I was thinking hard about what I had screwed up. When we got there, the Site Manager told me I was being promoted into management because I had demonstrated that I could lead other crew members in diagnosing and fixing computer problems. I could not believe what I was hearing. I had been at the site for just over a year, and I felt there were several others better qualified to be managers than I was.

After flying the Cessna 140 for about a year, I got the 'bigger faster' bug. We had been flying up to Merrill for weekends, and with Dona and I in the seats with Linda on Dona's lap, and a fair sized dog in the baggage area behind the seat, the airplane was too small. I began to think about a 4 place airplane that would also go a little faster. The answer was a Piper Tri-Pacer. The one I bought was newly rebuilt and repainted Piper's red and white scheme. It was certainly a pretty airplane. It was a four place, so now Linda had a place to sleep when we flew somewhere. I think by that time we did not have a dog. This airplane had a tricycle landing gear, and I found it much easier to both land and take off. Being

My Story

somewhat heaver, it was also more stable and smoother. All in all, I liked it very much.

My Story

Chapter 20: ON TO NORTH DAKOTA

 I had not had the Tripacer long before I was promoted to Group Supervisor at the Grand Forks, North Dakota SAGE site. It was almost Christmas, 1959, and they wanted me to go up there immediately to relieve a management problem. We had been planning on spending Christmas in Merrill that year. I made arrangements to fly the airplane to Grand Forks and take Dona and Linda with me, work the three days they wanted me to work, then fly back to Merrill for Christmas,. Then I would fly back to Madison, put our house on the market, and then finish the move to North Dakota. It was a good plan, but did not work out that way.

We flew to Grand Forks with no problem, and worked the three days there. On Christmas Eve Day, we headed for Merrill, Wisconsin. There had been a severe snow storm through the area, moving west to east as was normal. At the airport prior to take off, I did my weather check and found that the storm had moved through Minnesota the night before. It was cold but there would be no weather problems through Minnesota. I planned a refueling stop at St. Cloud airport, about the center of Minnesota, and would check the Wisconsin weather from there. That all went well also. On checking the Wisconsin weather prior to take off from central Minnesota, I found that the storm had passed through Wisconsin, and there should be no problems. We took off and headed for Merrill.

My Story

On arriving about 20 miles west of Merrill, I called the Wausau airport, the only aviation communications available in that part of the state, and asked for information on the runway at Merrill. Specifically, I asked if it had been plowed. After a delay, the radio operator came back on and said he had checked with the Merrill airport operator, and was told the runway was plowed. Good News. We proceeded to Merrill. I flew low over my parents' house as usual to let them know we were in the area; then flew on to the airport a few miles out of town. On arriving on the downwind leg at the airport, I noticed snow on the runway. I decided to continue my approach to a low altitude to check the runway condition. At a fairly low altitude, I could see tracks on the runway, and since I had been told the runway had been plowed, I deduced that the tracks were from other aircraft either landing or taking off.

We proceeded to touch down. Then all hell broke loose. I had touched down in nearly 18 inches of loose snow. The drag on the main gear pulled the nose gear down and we decelerated so quickly that the plane nosed over. We wound up upside down off to the side of the runway. We had stopped from about 60 miles per hour to upside down in a distance of about 50 feet. Of course, we were belted in so none of us was hurt, but it sure scattered our baggage and wrecked my beautiful airplane. The prop was badly bent, both wings had severe damage, the vertical stabilizer had whopped down so hard that it too was badly damaged. We climbed out, and then had to

My Story

walk the entire length of the runway to the operator's office because they were not expecting us. I called my parents' house to tell them we were at the airport and needed a ride home. I did not tell them we had crashed. Of course we told them as soon as they got to the airport. We had the normal Christmas evening celebration with the entire family, but it was not much fun for Dona and me. The next day, Christmas Day, 1959, I went back out to the airport to try to rescue what I could of my airplane. We got it up on the main gear and found that the nose wheel gear had failed. I got a hold of the airport operator and demanded to know how come he had reported the runways plowed when obviously they were not.

Here is what I learned. The operator had called the City of Merrill and requested the plows according to their normal procedure. The city responded that they were dispatching the plows immediately to the airport. That is when I had radioed the Wausau Control Tower to get the runway condition information. Since the city had told the airport operator that the plows were on the way, he reported to Wausau that they were plowed. That would have put the plows on the runway when we arrived, and we would have seen them. At that point I could have circled and waited for them to finish, or go back south to Wausau to land. The problem was that when the plows started out for the Merrill airport, they were diverted to the County Manager's residence to plow out his drive way as he was expecting "company" for Christmas

My Story

dinner! To finish this story, we loaded my airplane on a trailer and hauled it back to Madison, to Louie Willomier's Four Lakes Aviation, where I had bought the plane several months before. They rebuilt the airplane, and I flew it up to Grand Forks late the following spring. When we moved from Grand Forks to Great Falls, Montana, in 1962, I sold the Tri-Pacer to an outfit that had a contract to teach ROTC students at the University of North Dakota to fly.

I flew the Tri-Pacer around North Dakota a fair amount. I found that that flat country could certainly be rough flying in the summer time. You had to fly above 5000 feet to get away from the thermals. I and my boss had made a flight out to the western part of the state to check on some deer hunting possibilities. On the way back east, to relieve the boredom of flying in flat country, I was using my shadow on the ground to fly some patterns. Eventually we came up on U.S. Highway 2. I decided to put my airplane shadow on the highway and see how long I could maintain it. All was going well until my shadow met a car coming the other way. All of a sudden, the car veered off the roadway down though a ditch. I was amazed at why he ran off the road. Soon another car met the shadow and did the same thing. Then it dawned on me that they were veering off the road to miss that "thing" that was coming at them. That was kind of sobering, and I quickly departed the area of the highway.

My Story

The job at Grand Forks was completely different than working on the computer. My first good lesson in management came shortly after I got to Grand Forks. My crew, working nights on maintenance, had been wrestling with a pretty bad electronic drum problem. In fact, the problem had been passed on to us from the preceding maintenance shift. When my crew took a break for lunch, I went out and did some tests and found the trouble and fixed it. When my crew all came back from lunch, I noticed they shortly left the area and went back to the lunchroom. I went out to the drum area and found a note that said "you turned in your tool kit". I took the note and went to the lunchroom to talk. What I found out was that they recognized that I could fix the problems, but they wanted to fix them. I told them they were right, and that in the future I would 'coach' instead of 'fix' unless a problem jeopardized our ability to maintain our on line status. I soon found out that by managing several people to do what was needed, I could accomplish much more than doing it myself.

Managing people to get vast amounts of work done was a new experience to me. First of all, in the Air Force I had been taught to follow orders. As I gained rank, I got used to giving orders, usually with the implied authority of a Commanding Officer. At IBM, I was trained to do whatever it took to get the job done. Now, I had to learn how to get others to 'do what ever it took to get the job done'. This would have been easy in a military organization where you held a threat of some sort, but

My Story

IBM would not allow that. You needed to make an entire group (shift) think that getting the job done was the most important thing to do. One way I found that worked was to create a little competition between the members of my crew, and create a lot of competition between my crew and the other two crews at the site. Apparently I was at least somewhat successful, as I was promoted to Group Manager in a fairly short time.

We spent about 4 years in North Dakota, and it was one place we did not relish going back to. We bought our house in January of 1960, and because of snow, did not see our back yard until the next June. I had a sort of standing agreement with Linda, who was about 6 years old, that when it warmed up to 20 degrees BELOW zero, I would take her ice skating. The ice rink was about a block from our house, and it had a small warming shack. I would get Linda's skates on her and send her out on the ice, and I would sit in the warming shack until she got cold and came in. Then it was off to our house.

On New Years Day, 1961, the local newspaper had an advertisement from a used car lot that they had some 1951 automobiles for sale for $61.00. Since we had been talking about getting a car for Dona, we went to look at them. They had a 1951 Chevrolet, much like the first Chevy we had, so we said we were interested in it. The salesman tried and tried, but could not start it because it was extremely cold. He also had a 1951 Ford, so we said

My Story

if it starts, we will buy it. Same deal. He could not start it. As we left, he said" I have a 1951 Studebaker", we said naw, and kept walking. He turned on the key, and the Studebaker started immediately. We stopped in our tracks, and went back and bought the Studebaker!

On the way home with it, I found that the shift lever was stuck in high gear. Try as I might, I could not get it out of high. I had to slip the clutch at several stop signs or stop lights to get going in high gear. When we got home, I had Dona open the garage door so I could get it inside to work on it. Since we had a one car garage, our real car, a 1954 Chevrolet had to stay outside in the cold. When I tried to open the hood, I was having trouble finding the hood latch. Dona was inside the car marveling at her new wheels. I asked her if she could see a lever that said "HOOD". She said yes. I said pull it. Then I said pull it harder. She said like this, and she was holding the damned lever up by the windshield! The cable had broken. Now what to do. I couldn't get the Studebaker out of the garage because it was stuck in forward, and if I left the Chevrolet outside overnight, I would not be able to start it to go to work the next day. I looked all over the front, and short of breaking the grill out with a sledge hammer, I could not see how I was going to get under the hood to find out why it was stuck in high. I was really exasperated when Dona suggested I call the salesman and ask how to get the hood up. To show her how dumb the suggestion was, I called him and told him my trouble. I guess he recognized my

My Story

frustration over the phone, because he said if I would simmer down and take a screwdriver and remove two screws at the top of the grill, the entire grill would come out and I could easily reach the hood latch. I did, and I could, so I did. With the hood now open, I found that the shift linkage was worn so that if it opened more than required for high gear, it would stick there. I cut a loop out of an old rubber inner tube and tied it so that it could shift into high, but would not over extend. The fix worked great.

Dona drove the old Stueddy all the while we were in North Dakota. When we left, we sold it for $61.00 to the boy next door who was just starting college. We found out years later on a stop in Grand Forks that when the first boy was graduating from college, his younger brother was just starting, and he used the car. It eventually wound up being the family hunting vehicle, and they told me all they ever did to keep it from jamming in high gear was replace the rubber band when it got rotten!

My Story

CHAPTER 21: MONTANA, HERE WE COME

In late 1962, the job in Grand Forks was pretty well finished, and my boss was looking for a new assignment for me. My boss's name was Fred Keck, and I very much liked his management style. I had learned a lot from him. Fred had been born and raised in New York City, and although he had worked many locations, including in Europe, he never lost his desire to get back to New York City. He found an exciting job for me designing a reservation system for a major airline company. It was to be the first automatic computer operated passenger reservation system, and would have been a real feather in my hat, but the office was on the 32nd floor of a sky scraper in the middle of Manhattan. I said no. We discussed it long and loud, and Fred could not understand my absolute refusal to take that job. I guess I finally convinced him that if I could not drive my car to work, and park it near my office, I would be completely lost.

The job I eventually took was doing about the same thing I had been doing, but now at the Great Falls SAGE site at the air base in Great Falls, Montana. The difference was that by that time, the Air Force had decided to take over the maintenance in addition to the operations, so my job was to train the IBM crew to be 'trainers', and then to oversee the training of the Air Force crews to do the maintenance. That job took a year. We liked Montana very much. We traveled around the

My Story

state a fair amount. I did quite a bit of trout fishing in several great streams.

Mom and Dad came to visit us, and I had told Dad that we would be doing some trout fishing from the bank or wading. He reminded me that he was a "boat" fisherman. When they got there, he and I went trout fishing on the Missouri River where it came out of the mountains just south of Great Falls. We drove along the river road, and at one of the pull offs, we tried fishing. I had previously had good luck using Mepps Spinners on spin cast rods. I went down stream a little ways and watched Dad as he began casting his Mepps. About the third or fourth cast he hooked into a trout. I watched him fight it against the current for a while, then walked back to where he was. He said "I had a good one on, but now I think I have got bottom". About that time his "bottom" took off again. Eventually he brought it close enough so I could net it. It was a beauty. It was a Rainbow Trout, and it weighed about 7 pounds. Dad was excited now. He said "let's go to town and buy some tackle, then go home and get the girls (Mom and Dona) then we can stay out all day". We did that, and then went back out to the river road.

The fishing was so good, that we would stop at the first place where we could get the car off the road, fish until one of us caught a fish, then proceed on to the next wide place. We both got our limits that way, and had a great ride into some beautiful Montana country. While my

My Story

folks were with us, we went to Glacier National Park, saw the scenery and did some fishing.

Dona, Linda, and I went camping on many weekends, sometimes by ourselves, and sometimes with our friends. One favorite place was west of Great Falls in the Bob Marshall Wilderness. We usually camped at the top of a pass in the mountains. The unique thing about that spot was that the CCC had built a small lake up there by damming a mountain stream. They had a dam at each end of the small mountain pass, and the thing that made it unique was that the water running out of the west end dam flowed into a stream that eventually emptied into the Pacific ocean, and the water that flowed over the east end dam eventually wound up in the Atlantic ocean. It was seldom fished, and the trout were always hungry!

I had sold my Piper Tri-Pacer airplane in North Dakota, so I began looking for a replacement when we got to Montana. I found a Cessna 140 on a ranch in the northern part of the state. It had only a few hundred hours on it, and was in very good shape. The rancher had purchased it in 1946 with his mustering out pay when he got out of the service. I based the airplane at Gore Field, on a mesa, west of town. Flying around Montana's mountains was definitely different then flying over North Dakota's flat lands. I was not terribly anxious to fly into and over the Rocky Mountains, but I did fly over and around in the mountains to the east and south. I liked to fly the rivers to see the scenery. I found

My Story

if I took off to the east, and made a continuous climb at about 300 feet per minute, I could just barely clear the highest point of the Little Belt Mountains. I could look down and watch the elk herds, and there were lots of them!

Several of the guys that were on my crew had gotten into a Sherriff's Posse before I became the manager. Shortly after I arrived, they invited Dona and I to some kind of function they had. It was out of town quite a distance, and was where they kept their horses. It was a picnic thing, and after we ate, they got all the horses out and saddled them up. Guess what, they had one for me. I said "I can't ride; if that horse runs I will fall off". They said "That horse is too old to run, he can just barely walk". About the time I got into the saddle, someone swatted the horse on the rump with a hat, and he showed them he could run! I hung on for dear life, and Dona started yelling "he can't ride". The horse was heading for a fence and I was starting to wonder if he was going to try to jump it, when one of the guys caught up with us and got the horse to stop. Needless to say, I did not join the Posse. I did ride a horse on a real ranch roundup and branding operation that I will talk about later.

On one of Mom and Dad's visits to us while in Montana, we took a side trip to Glacier National Park. It was in August, and would you believe we got caught in a blizzard on the 'Going to the Sun Hhighway'? It is an extremely high two- lane highway from the west side of

My Story

the Park to the east side, and crosses the northern Rocky Mountains. We were able to go on through, but to see that kind of weather in August is sort of different. Of course we showed them the old store at Polebridge, an old fashioned store outside of the western edge of the Park. The store still had old fashioned milk pails and strainers and the stuff the stores in Irma had when I was a boy. On the way north, and following the Flathead River, we found a huge bear in some brush just off the road. Dad wanted pictures so we got out of the car. He took several, and then decided he wanted to see the bear move around. I threw a rock at him, and the bear reared up on hind legs and looked at us as if to charge. We quickly got back into the car. When we got to Polebridge, we mentioned seeing the bear. They asked us what color he was, and we said he was a very blond color. They got pretty excited and begin making phone calls to local people. It turned out that the bear was wrecking cabins which people had for rent all along the river. They were trying to get some men together to shoot him. They told us they figured someone had fed him from one of the cabins when he was young, and he was robbing the cabins looking for food. The problem was that he would completely tear them up. Several days later, when our camping trip was over, we left the Park on the same road heading south.

When we got to approximately the same place, there was the bear, but on the opposite side of the road! As soon as I got home I bought a bear permit so I could go

My Story

back up to try to get him. I guess I spent the next several weekends looking for that bear. I would camp in one of the old buildings left over from a logging operation. The logging camp had about a dozen buildings still standing. Some in a dilapidated condition, but all lined up on the road going through the camp. At different times there would be several parties camped there. One time there was an official State Bear Trapper camped there. I spent a fair amount of time talking to him. His job was to trap the bears, inject a drug to put them to sleep, then check their general health, put a tag on each ear to identify them, and he had medicine he could use if they had some sort of infection. He was a small man, and well into his 60s, and he had been trapping bear most of his life. I asked what he did when he got Grizzlies in his trap, and he said he handled them the same way as any other bear. He said the Black Bear which were more common came in all colors from black to various shades of brown to light tan. That was what we called the blond bear. He showed me one of his 'trap sets'. He had most of the teeth cut off from the leg traps so they would not cripple the bear's legs. He would set some kind of bait in a cramped location, then use small tree trunks to build what almost looked like a funnel laying on its side, with the small end encompassing the bait. The trap would be located so that the bear would spring it when going for the bait. He would fix a chain from the trap to a small sapling that would 'give' instead of being rigid when the bear pulled on it. If it were rigid, the bear could pull

My Story

away free. As a safety measure (for him) he would also have a chain about 15 feet long attached to the trap on one end and to a large treble hook on the other. The treble hook was left lying loose. The way it worked was if the bear, usually grizzlies, were to pull loose from the springy sapling, they would chase him until the treble hook snagged on something. Then he could outrun them! I asked if it always worked, and he said "it always has".

One evening I drove on an old logging road that wound up the mountain behind the logging camp. About a mile up I came across a cow moose with a calf. She was reluctant to move off the road, so I almost bumped her. Finally she allowed me to pass and I went on up the mountain. Sometime later, and just before dusk I was on my way back to the logging camp and my cabin, and as I came around a sharp turn in the road, there was my moose cow. Again she was reluctant to leave the road. This time she did not have her calf with her. I drove up close to her, and tooted the horn. That started her running and I followed close behind. I thought she would leave the road, but no, she stayed on the road but ran faster. Her udders were full, and as they swayed back and forth as she ran, the milk was squirting out of her. She could run at exactly 25 miles per hour! She had several opportunities to leave the road, but she continued around each turn as we came to it. Finally I could see the logging camp about a quarter mile away and below us. I began blowing the horn to get the attention of the men at

My Story

the camp because I figured they would never believe I had chased a cow moose. She ran right down through the middle of that camp with men on both sides looking out of the doors of the cabins. When she got a little east of the camp, she veered off the road and down into a small creek bed and continued on down. Some of the men in the camp told me she was a nuisance in the camp. If you left an ax or a shovel out, she would chew on the handle, apparently for the salt. I hope she got back to where she left her calf.

On my first trip into that country to hunt bear, there was still a fair amount of snow in the high country. The rule was that you were supposed to stop at the Flathead Ranger Station and register. That was so they knew who was in the country, how long you intended to be there, and roughly where you intended to hunt. All of that was to exercise some control if someone violated game laws, but also for a start if someone got lost. When I stopped at the Ranger Station and we were talking, his wife came out. They had been snowed in for over two months, and had not yet had a chance to get into town. I was the first person she had talked to other than her husband in over two months. She said "Next time you come, bring your wife, I want to talk to a woman!" I did take Dona up there with me on one of my trips. When I was talking to the Ranger, he said the bears were just coming out of hibernation, and they would gather on the south slopes where there was a little grass. He said they ate the grass as a tonic. He said "There will be some grizzlies in there

My Story

with the black bears, and the grizzlies are mean. They will come right after you, you will have to shoot them, then I will have to come after you, so don't go after any black bears if the grizzlies are around". I never did see a grizzly bear up there.

On that first trip into that country I drove my station wagon with street tires. The road was made of what they called Montana Pea Gravel, which was fist size rocks crushed from boulders. They were pretty hard on ordinary tires. The first day I punched a hole in a tire, so I had my spare on. Late in the day I realized the spare was leaking, so I dashed for the Ranger Station hoping he would have the stuff there to repair the tire. He did not have any, but told me he was going into Flathead the next day and would take my tire in to get it fixed. When he found that my spare was leaking, he said I will take them both in. Problem, I needed tires. He had spare wheels with tires on them in his shop, and they fit my Chevrolet. He loaned them to me until he came back with my tires. I would bet that no one would do that now!

When I left for home from that hunt, I had a blown out spare, and before I got to Browning, Montana, another tire started to leak. I got about a block into town and the tire was clear flat. It was a Sunday, and most places were closed, but there was a service station about a half block from where I was, and it was open. I walked down there to see if they had tires. I made the mistake of

My Story

telling them I had two flats. They had tires. New ones were over $50.00 each, and skins (worn out ones) were 25 dollars each. They were trying to gouge me! I could see a Gambles Store across the street with a sign that said tire sale $25.00 each. The service station guy said "Too bad its Sunday, everyone else is closed". I walked about a block on down the street thinking I might find another station, and I found one that had a sign that they had a 'special' on retread tires. I went back and drove my car (on two flat tires) down to that station. If I remember correctly, the operator said the retreads were like $20.00 each, but he had new tires for just a little more. I bought two new Miller tires for just under $50.00. Later, when I got home and had time to shop for tires, I bought two more Millers but they cost just a little bit more. How is that for changing from meeting nice folks (the Ranger) to meeting crooks (the first station operator) to meeting nice folks again, (the second station operator)?

When we bought our house in Montana, the Real Estate Agent was an old time cowboy whose family owned a huge ranch in the northern part of the state. He invited me and two other men from the SAGE site to go with him to a family gathering and cattle round up. The outing was to last four days. When we arrived at the ranch, we went to the cook house as he had directed. The woman who ran the cook house (actually a pretty good sized restaurant) told us that Mr. David had been sick and he was staying upstairs at the cook house. She

My Story

said he had told her to tell us to 'go on up to the big house' and just throw our sleeping bags wherever we wanted.

The 'big house' was absolutely gigantic! It was 3 stories high, and had about 15 rooms. We all spread our sleeping bags in the library, which was probably 30 feet square, lined with shelves all around and filled with books and records going back to the Civil War. The kitchen was also gigantic and looked like a full size restaurant kitchen. It had 3 refrigerators. One had meats and vegetables, one was full of cases of beer, and the third one was full of Champaign. It turned out the beer was for the 20 or so man crew that would work the round up, and the Champaign was for the party that would be held when the roundup was over. The Step Father's name was John B. David, and his name was on every building (in big black letters) in the little town except the Post Office and the railroad station. The ranch actually owned the entire town. The old man was high up in his 90s, and that year was the first he had not ridden a horse in the roundup.

They had horses for all of us, and I was a little spooky about getting on one after my experience with the Posse pony. They assured me the horse I would ride would not act up. These horses were not ponies, they were large draft type horses, and were about like sitting on a barrel. I asked about the size, and they told me "When we saddle up in the morning we are going to ride these

My Story

horses hard all day, and those little ponies you see in the movies would never last". After riding for two days to find and drive cattle into a holding pasture, they announced they would be branding the next day.

Early the next morning they asked me to drive an old ranch truck loaded with Mesquite wood to the branding area. I asked how I would find the area, and they said drive to the end of the road. It was not a road, just a two track across the prairie. I drove until I was sure I was lost and had gone too far when a fancy pickup came along side and said hurry up, you are late. When I got to the branding area, it was ringed by all kinds of vehicles, from fancy pickups to jalopies. The branding area was about 15 miles from the ranch buildings, and I asked how come the branding area was on the back side of the ranch, and they told me it was about 70 miles across that ranch! They already had a fire going and I parked the truck so that some of the young boys could keep the fire fed. My job, along with several others, was to hold the critters down while they branded them. I obviously was pretty clumsy, so some cowboys jumped into the corral to show me how to hold them. These guys and their families were neighbor ranchers, and this was the biggest and best celebration in the country, so many entire families came to help and then to party.

The way the branding worked was like this. The momma cows and calves had been separated from the rest of the herd and driven into a large corral. That day

My Story

we would brand about 200 calves, and that was just from one of many herds on the ranch. A cowboy on a horse would ride slowly into the corral, and with his rope would catch an unsuspecting calf by the hind legs. He would drag him into the part of the corral where we were waiting.

The object was to get the calf flat on his side and held so that he could be worked over. Keep in mind these are weanling calves and weigh around 250 pounds. To get him down, one person would pull one way on the rope that is around his hind legs, and another person would pull the opposite way on his tail. When you got him down, one knelt on his neck while the other used his boots to spread the calf's hind legs as far apart as you could. They wanted the calf on the ground less than 2 minutes, and here is what all they did to him. They put a paste on his horn buds, or if he had horns, they cut them off. He got 3 different kinds of shots. He got a 4 digit number tattooed inside his upper lip. He got an ear tag clipped on one ear, and the other ear was notched in a certain pattern. If he was a bull calf, there was a 90 % chance he was going to be castrated. They only kept a few as breeding stock. And last of all, every animal got a four digit symbol (brand) burned on his left flank. They only let two men do the branding because if the iron was too hot it could burn clear through into the innards and would be fatal, and if the iron was too cool it would not show the brand. The men worked really fast and I and my friends were mostly in the way. They had a couple

My Story

of boys who were supposed to catch the "Rocky Mountain Oysters" and get them into a bucket of water. Believe me, those boys were busy.

When all the calves were branded, they turned them back in with the momma cows then rode their horses around in the corral slowly. They told us that way they would move the herd enough so that each momma cow would find her calf, and they depended on the cow to lick and keep the new brands clean to prevent infection. When this was done, it was back to the main part of the ranch to party, and they did know how to party! Most of the beer had been drunk by that time, and the Champagne did not last all that long either.

The last day we were there, we were supposed to ride along to move a herd from one pasture to another. My two companions had gotten up early and left while I was still rolling up my sleeping bag and generally getting my stuff ready to head home. I was about bushed and did not plan to ride that day. To my surprise, Mr. David came into the room while I was there, and did I get a treat that morning. He showed me some of his old records that were stored in the library. One of them was a deed for 40 acres in Georgia his forebear had gotten for his service in the war of 1812. He also had bills of sale for mules one of his forebears' got for service in the Civil War. On one of the walls were a series of enlarged pictures and I recognized the airplane I had purchased when I first got to Montana. I asked him about it, and he

My Story

told me a few years back some of the ranchers decided to have an 'old timers' reunion, and they had it on his ranch. He said the family who owned the airplane were friends and were one of several who flew in. He told me that several of the pictures had been turned into wall murals and were mounted in the rotunda at the State Capital. Dona and I had a chance to verify that a few months later.

He begin to tell me stories of some of the other old timers who had been honored that day. One of them he called 'old one eye', and told me he had an eye put out by ranchers when was a boy. He was a Basque, and was a sheep herder. His family had driven a herd of several thousand sheep up into Montana from Arizona to cross the Milk River. The cattle ranchers did not want sheep in the area, and they hung his father and two brothers, and put out one eye of the young boy. Then Mr. Davis told me how he come to have such a gigantic ranch. His family were also sheep herders from the deep southwest, and also raised sheep in Old Mexico. He said the best markets for the sheep were in the eastern part of the U.S., and the only way to get them there was to drive them to a railroad head. Since sheep cannot cross rivers, they had to drive them far enough north to get across the Milk River, then they could head east. He told me that his family would have about a half dozen flocks of from 60 to 70 thousand sheep on the trail at all times. His family did not own the sheep, they were owned by British businessmen.

My Story

They could not make the drive from deep in the southwest all the way to the eastern markets in one year, so the British Syndicate put together this huge ranch so that the herds of sheep could winter there. They required that much area to have enough grazing for the numbers of sheep they were moving. They would drive them to the Milk River Ranch, spend the worst winter months there, then continue on east. Cattle ranchers did not like the sheep coming through and they would shoot or hang any drovers they caught alone. He said that eventually the sheep market dried up, and the British Syndicate broke up the operation.

One of the Brits kept the Milk River Ranch and started raising cattle. As a young man Mr. David had switched from being a sheep man, to become a cowboy. He said the British owner was killed when a horse fell on him, and at some later time, he married the widow, some years older than he was, and when she died the ranch was his. He was a vain old man, and very proud of his history and the fact that he had kept the ranch intact while most others had been broken into smaller spreads.

At about midmorning that last day when he finished telling me his story, he said "Let's ride out and see how they are doing with those cows". I about panicked. I thought he wanted me to saddle some horses for us, but he said go into that shed out there and bring that car. I got out to what he called a 'shed' and it was a large garage, and in it was a brand new Oldsmobile hardtop.

My Story

The keys were in it so I drove it around to the door. He got in and started it up then said "go back in and get them some beer". I went back to the kitchen and got a case of beer. He said "get another one", so I went back and got another case. He said "open me one" so I opened one for him and one for me. He set his bottle on the center counsel, started the car, selected Hi gear, and stomped the gas pedal. Naturally, his beer flew into the back seat and was gurgling all over and he said "open me another" and kept on going. We drove that new car across country looking for the cattle drovers, and finally saw them way off in the distance. He started off again across country and got almost to where they were and drove the car into a pretty deep arroyo. He tried backing out and couldn't move it. About that time his riders came to see what all the dust was about. They used their lassos to hook onto the bumpers and tried to pull it out but could not. Another man came up in a pickup truck, and as Mr. Davis climbed into the truck, he said "to hell with it, it shouldn't have got stuck". I guess it might still be there.

During my assignment at the SAGE site in Montana, the Air Force contracted with IBM to install a very large retrofit on the computer system. The Air Force had agreed to shut down the entire operation for two weeks so our crews could work a three shift (24 hour) day. About a week into the task, the 'Cuban Missile Crisis' erupted. My crew was working day shift when it all started. A Colonel was in charge of the SAGE site, and

My Story

about noon I was called into his office. He explained what was going on and said there was a high probability the Russians would take that opportunity to fly something into the middle of the U.S., and he had been directed to get the site back operational pronto. He asked me how long it would take to get back 'operational'. I explained that we had been taking things apart for a week, and it would take that long to put it back together. He said "I want it operational tomorrow at this time". WOW, 24 hours. I called in both of the crews that were off at that time, and everyone pitched in to patch the system together. We had cables running down the halls, through the offices, and dangling from the ceilings, but we had one computer up and running in about 20 hours. That took the pressure off from us, so we went to a 12 hours on and 12 hours off shift, and had the second computer operational two days later. We operated the system that way for over a month until the Cuban Missile thing subsided.

My Story

CHAPTER 22: OFF TO WASHINGTON DC

My job in Montana lasted just a year, so in late 1963 we were on the road again. This time we had to go back east, as that is where they wanted me to work. My new job was to be in the Washington D.C. area. We put our house on the market, hired a moving company, packed in the car what we did not ship, and headed east. I had contracted with a commercial pilot to ferry the airplane out to where we would be. He was to fly to his relative's home in Ohio and wait there until we got to our new place, and I would call to tell him where to deliver it.

We made a leisurely trip across country by car, stopping at Merrill, Wisconsin to see my family, and then in Ohio to see Dona's family. We had never been in the Washington D.C. area before, so when we got to Frederick, Maryland, we decided to get off from the super slab (highway) and drive a secondary road down through the country side heading for the Bethesda area. As we drove through Gaithersburg, Maryland, I noticed a sign pointing to the local airport. Since I knew we were in the vicinity of where we would probably live, I decided we should check out the airport. As we drove east toward the airport, we went through a tiny village called Washington Grove, and there on the edge of the little town was a new house with a FOR SALE sign on it. We proceeded on another mile and came to the airport. It was a small operation and was pretty new. It had a hard surface runway, but grass taxi ways. It had a maintenance hangar and small pilot's lounge, but no

My Story

hangars for personal airplane storage. They had a number of outside tie downs, and I arranged to rent one for my airplane. I told them I would be having my airplane delivered an a few days, and requested they take care of it while we were busy looking for a house.

When we drove back toward Gaithersburg, we again went past the new house that was for sale. Although it was getting late, actually, early evening, we turned around and went back to look at it. I parked in the driveway, and we looked around the yard. We were pretty impressed. Dona tried a door, and found that it was not locked, so we went in. Dona was checking out the rooms, and I had gone down into the basement, when someone yelled "who is in here"? We were both surprised to find that the owner who was selling the house lived in the house next door. He was also the Real Estate Broker handling the sale, and had neglected to lock the house after showing it that afternoon. He showed us through the house (even though we had pretty well looked it over) and told us that it was located on two lots, and had been positioned so as to have a nice view of a wooded area, and not block his own view of the same area. We told him we were new in the area, and would be buying a house as soon as we could find a suitable one. We made arrangements for him to show us the houses for sale in the area starting the next morning.

The next day we spent the entire day looking over the area, and looking at houses. We decided the best one

My Story

was the first one, and we were sure we could afford it, so we made an appointment with the local bank for the following morning. The bank business went smoothly, and we made arrangements to move in even before the closing. Our reason for this was to get our household stuff delivered as soon as possible. By the time I reported for work at the IBM offices on Wisconsin Avenue in Bethesda, we were the owners of a new house.

When I went in to work they offered me time to house hunt, and I told them I had already bought one. When one of the office managers heard we had bought a house just outside Gaithersburg, he shouted "There is no truth to the rumor that IBM will build a new plant in Gaithersburg". I guess he let the cat out of the bag. It turned out that IBM was in fact already negotiating on a large tract of land about two miles from where our new house was located. This guy had been telling IBM people, who were new to the area that they should look for housing in northern Virginia instead of in Maryland. Since I had bought the house before I reported for work, I had not heard his location recommendation. I never knew what his game was, but he sure was miffed because we bought in what turned out to be an ideal location, less than a mile from IBM's new location. I explained to him that my reason for buying where we did was because of the location of the airport, the beautiful little town, and a new house that we really liked. He didn't buy my explanation, and I didn't care!

My Story

While we were in Montana, we bought a little convertible for Dona. It was a Renault Caravel, and it was a little cutie. It was white with a black top, and a red leather interior. It was not a very good car for long distance driving, but was sure fun to drive around town. Shortly after arriving in Maryland, on the way to work one morning, I was involved in an accident with my regular car, a 1961 Chevrolet Station Wagon. I was not hurt, but my car sure was. The entire front was practically knocked off. Instead of totaling it, the insurance company wanted to have it rebuilt. We had shipped Dona's little convertible by truck, from Montana to Maryland, and it arrived the day I smashed my station wagon. I had to drive it many miles a day from home to our offices on Wisconsin Avenue, or to the Pentagon in Washington D.C. traffic. It could not go as fast as the normal traffic, and everybody wanted to be in front of me but they seemed to want to go over me instead of going around! It took some time to get my car repaired, and I was sure glad to get it back. I guess it drove ok, but we soon started looking for a new car. Dona was glad when my car got fixed, because now she had her car back.

I did not particularly like my new job. I was called a System Analyst. It seemed that everybody working in the D.C. area was a 'System Analyst'. The IBM offices were on Wisconsin Avenue in Bethesda, on the northwest side of Washington D.C. We were contracted to develop a computer based system to help the

My Story

Pentagon planners devise contingency plans for military actions at anyplace on the globe. We were specifically assigned to support the Air Force representatives on the Joint Chief of Staff. In short, the system was to have huge data bases containing information about every conceivable piece of Air Force equipment and personnel. The project would allow a senior officer to sit at a computer, and by using his knowledge and a keyboard, put together a plan that would identify every piece of equipment and every person required to conduct an operation to resolve any situation in any area in the world. For example, if the top members of the United States government decided to intervene in a situation somewhere, they would ask the Pentagon to come up with a plan or plans to resolve the situation. If the military decided the situation would require a 90 day intervention, the planner could identify the best Aircraft to conduct the flight operations. The system could then be used to find out where in the world those assets were located.

One example was the bombing of Libya in the 1960s. The best airplanes for the task were located on the west coast of the United States. The system then generated flight-plans to get them to Europe, and identified where they would refuel. Since the distance was greater than their fuel endurance, the system would identify what type of aerial refueling tankers would be used, where they were based, the flight plan to get them in place for the aerial refueling, and simulate the actual refueling. If

My Story

you remember, France would not allow the bombers to cross their territory, so the system could develop the alternate route, and again determine what kind of aerial refueling was required. The system could also determine how many of each kind of personnel was required, including mess operations, and medical equipment and personnel. The problem was that all the knowledge we needed to develop that kind of system was at the Pentagon in the minds of the experts. That meant that instead if working at Bethesda, a few miles from home, I worked almost fulltime at the Pentagon.

Even in 1964, when I got there, the traffic was terrific. To reach the Pentagon, I would have to drive just about all the way across the entire city. In rush hour that was impossible. I found that by leaving our house in Maryland about 7:00 AM, and by skirting around the city on the west and south sides, I could be at work in the Pentagon by about 8:30 A.M. I would take the beltway south to the George Washington Parkway to the Shirley Highway, and eventually into one of the several hundred acre Pentagon parking lots. Then I would have about a mile walk to the River Entrance.

At the Pentagon, I worked in an office with about 40 Air Force officers. They ranged in rank from a one star General down to a major. The One- Star ran every thing, and the major, the lowest rank there, did everything, including fetch coffee for the One-Star. I worked primarily with two Colonels. Col. Ellis was an expert in

My Story

Tactical Fighter Operations, and Col. Long was an expert in Aircraft Transport Operations. Other IBM employees were involved in developing support operations such as maintenance or medical. Computers were still sort of archaic, and the computer system we were to work with was a brand X. It was mostly a huge rotating drum that you could store data on electronically. Because of its size, it was never really operational. We were never real proud of the system operation. I heard several years later that an IBM crew went back in the 1970s and updated the system with more sophisticated computers, and the system worked great.

Col. Ellis and I became good friends, and he confided to me that he was trying to get to Viet Nam to get into a "shooting" war. He had been a Squadron Commander, had taught aerial combat tactics, and had done it all, but he said "I have never had my ass shot at, and that is what I have trained for all my life". He left for Viet Nam while I was still at the Pentagon, and he "got his ass shot at". He was shot down shortly after arriving in the war zone, and was killed in the crash.

I had some unique experiences while working at the Pentagon. I discovered that there was a service station a few miles from the Pentagon that would park your car and drive you to your favorite Pentagon entrance in a limousine for one dollar. Besides the convenience, IBM would reimburse the dollar! Naturally, I used that service on a daily basis. One day I had worked at the

My Story

Bethesda office for a few hours, then drove to the Pentagon to finish the day. I parked my car and jumped into the Limo. As we drove up toward the River Entrance, I could see something was going on. A Military band was lined up in a large grassy area on the right side of the driveway. I could also see that there were many ranks of troops standing at ease. Beyond the troops were several cannons. The River Entrance has about 30 full sized doors all lined up to accommodate the crowds going in and coming out, plus there are about 20 steps leading up to those doors. As the Limo driver turned toward the entrance, I could see that the stairs were all roped off with a red velvet rope except for a four foot wide area up the middle of the steps. There was also a red carpet from the parking area up that four foot space all the way to the center door. There were crowds of people standing on the steps on both sides of the red carpeted area. Guess what. My driver stopped with my door directly over the curb end of the red carpet. He jumped out, raced around, and ceremoniously opened my door. I stepped out, with my little briefcase clutched in my hand to a thunder of applause. The steps were absolutely crowded with people, probably several hundred, all clapping and yelling. What could I do? I ran up the red carpet as fast as I could, and was ducking through the door, when one of the officers I worked with grabbed me. It turned out that President Kennedy was supposed to come to the Pentagon to confer a medal on a Belgium General who had just retired as Chief of

My Story

NATO. They were late arriving, and the audience had been waiting for a while, and they could plainly see what my Limo driver was up to. They enjoyed my discomfort and that is why they clapped and hooted.

When the General and his escorts finally arrived, they put on quite a show. The Army band was all lined up on the lawn, as well as a large Color Guard. They had all the cannons out, and as the General arrived and was met by the President, they fired the guns. They gave him a 21- gun salute which, I believe is usually reserved for Heads of State. The President and the General and their entourages all trooped up and down the lines of the Color Guard, then there were speeches, at which time I and the officers I had come to see all went to our offices below and went to work. Many months later I was in the Pentagon working when President Kennedy was shot. I can tell you that that institution went into a "war operation". Our area was completely overrun with Generals, and our own lowly One- Star wound up hauling coffee to the Multi Stars.

Speaking of Generals, I have a sort of funny story. We frequently were called on to brief some of the military Brass about the progress of our project in the Pentagon. On one occasion there was to be an extensive briefing for the Air Force's Chief of Staff and his Aides. There were several of us scheduled to present 15 minute briefings. I and another Systems Analyst named Howie would brief on our project, he would go first then I

My Story

would finish. The schedule called for four 15 minute briefings before ours, Howie first, then me, then a 15 minute break. When it came time for Howie's briefing, he was not there. My brief was tailored to follow his. The General was not one to tolerate tardiness, and he was some perturbed. After scowling a bunch and scolding my boss, he said "Let's take a break now and somebody better be ready to talk when we reconvene".

This is scary stuff! About 10 minutes into the 15 minute break, Howie arrived. Our Boss cornered him and said whatever delayed him better be good. When the meeting reconvened, Howie went to the podium to begin, and the General started in on him. He asked Howie why he thought he was so important he could keep 30 or so busy people waiting. Howie of course apologized, and said he could explain why he was late, but it would take a little time to explain it. The General, sort of sharply, said "well you have made us wait this long, I think we will take the time to listen". Howie then told this story. Howie's home was in New Jersey, and he had taken his family to New Jersey over the weekend to visit his parents. While there, they decided to take his kids to the Catskill Game Farm to see the animals. One of the attractions was an elephant that was trained to do tricks. One of the tricks was to sit on a small red stool, and then lift both rear legs. Howie said they decided to leave early so they could beat the traffic because they planned to drive straight through to Maryland by Sunday evening. As they walked down the street to get their car

My Story

they heard a commotion behind them, and they learned that the elephant had gotten away and was running down the street. Howie had just bought a new car. It was a bright red Volkswagen Bug. You guessed it; the elephant spotted the bright red Bug so he sat down on it. Of course it caved in the hood. The trainers took the elephant and told Howie that someone would be along to get his information for the insurance. That made them late getting started for home. They got up on the Garden State Parkway heading south and all was well until there was a chain reaction accident somewhere up in front of them. Cars were hitting each other, but Howie got stopped without hitting the car in front, and the car behind them also got stopped without hitting them, but the accident continued on behind them. After things settled down for a minute, Howie started to pull out into the inside lane to continue, when a motorcycle cop stopped him. The cop told him to stay in line and someone would be along to take the information regarding the accident. Howie said he was not involved in the accident. The cop looked at the front of Howie's car and said "How do you explain this", Howie said "An elephant sat on it". The cop glared at him and said "Stay here, I will deal with you after we finish these other cars". Howie said he was the last car released, and he had driven all the rest of that day and all night to get to the briefing in time. The General said "I don't think you could have made that up, continue with your briefing".

My Story

Shortly after arriving in Maryland, I joined a Civil Air Patrol Unit at our local airport. We were the largest CAP unit in the area, having some 20 personally owned airplanes, plus two or three owned by the CAP unit. A number of the airplanes owners were Congressmen or Senators. Many of them were able to join us on searches. Our CAP Squadron Commander's name was Klaus something (very German), and one day I asked him if he had been in the Air Force. He said "yes, the Luftwaffe"! We were called to conduct search operations fairly frequently. Usually looking for aircraft that were down, but sometimes looking for lost hikers in the mountains of western Maryland, and sometimes looking for drowning victims in the Potomac River. We also practiced conducting search operations with the 26th Army, who was responsible for search and rescue on the east coast. They flew helicopters in their search operations.

We were called out to search for a downed B 47 some where in the mountains of western Maryland or in Pennsylvania. There was a three man crew aboard, and there was hope some of them may have survived the crash. We found the wreckage on the second day of the search, and when ground crews got into the area, they confirmed two dead. That meant there was a possibility of a survivor, so the search continued. He was found several days later, dead, but there were indications he had survived for several days. We all knew that we had not worked well with the Army units, and they realized

My Story

it also. It appeared that if we had coordinated better, we may have found him alive. The result was that we scheduled a number of training exercises with the Army helicopter units.

The procedure we worked out with the Army was that the Civil Air Patrol would fly the various assigned search patterns because our airplanes were faster than the small helicopters they were using. The Army helicopters would be assigned to fly to various positions around the search patterns and land. If the fixed wing aircraft spotted something that needed a closer look, the closest helicopter would be called in to take a look from a lower altitude, or even land if required. It seemed to work better than when each unit was doing its own thing. Another thing we did to get better working relations was to change places with the helicopter pilots. We invited them to come to our airport and fly with us. They in turn invited us to fly with them. That gave all of us a better understanding of what the other unit could do.

During this time, I again got the "bigger, faster" bug, and started looking for a four place airplane. I found a Piper Cherokee that was only two years old. It had fairly low hours, and was in good condition. They were willing to take my old Cessna 140 in trade. The Cherokee was located at Page Airways, which was the only fixed base operator at Dulles Airport at that time. Dulles had just been completed, and no airlines were

My Story

using it yet. Passengers liked the convenience of landing at the old Washington National airport which was practically in town. In addition, the new Dulles Airport was a Federal Aviation Administration (FAA) owned facility, and the Highway Administration had not yet built connecting roads from Washington D.C. to the airport. It was to be several years yet before any airliners began to use Dulles.

When I bought the Cherokee, I told them I wanted a checkout in it before I soloed it back to my airport. We took off from one of the parallel runways at Dulles, and while I was still on the turn leading to the runway, the tower operator told me to expedite my take off. I poured on the power, and we had lift off before I even got to the runway! I don't know why he told me to expedite, there was no one else using the airport! I made 3 touch and goes, and I never got to see either end of the runway. When we radioed that we wanted to land to a full stop, the tower directed me to the longest runway, and I landed to the west. The facilities are all located on the east end of the airport. The instructor said we had a 10 mile taxi back to the Page Airways hanger where he wanted to go. We parked on the ramp and went into a lounge for a cup of coffee. When we finished and came back to the airplane, I took a picture of it, and I have a picture of my little Cherokee sitting on that huge ramp all by itself. There was no other aircraft anywhere in sight! The various airport system operators needed to have a certain amount of traffic to stay current, so it was

My Story

not uncommon to be flying in the area and hear a request for airplanes to come to Dulles and shoot instrument landings. I did it a couple of times and if you told them you needed a 'no gyro' approach, they talked you right down to touchdown.

I based the Cherokee at the airport close to where we lived, and did a fair amount of flying around that area. I found Pennsylvania, the western part of Maryland, and the northern part of Virginia to be very pretty. The eastern mountains are not as intimidating as the western mountains. The last time I flew in to Dulles for a business meeting in D.C., it was on a commercial airliner, and they were extremely busy. The ramp which had been empty when I checked out in my Cherokee was jammed with all huge airliners, and the terminals were full of passengers. I caught a taxi into Bethesda, and the cabbie was driving on an eight lane highway where none existed a few years before.

While we were in Maryland, we made some neat vacation trips. One such trip was to the Outer Banks of North Carolina where the Wright Brothers took their first flight. We also spent some time on Virginia's eastern shore. Linda was already interested in horses, and she wanted to see the wild ponies on Chincoteague and Asoteague Islands. Our neighbors in Washington Grove had a beach house on Maryland's eastern shore, so we also spent some weekends and vacation there. The sea shore is OK I guess, but I would much rather be in

My Story

the north woods, or in any of the western mountain states. On the several assignments I had on the east coast, I was always conniving to get assigned out west.

When IBM opened the new facility in Gaithersburg, all of the IBM projects from all over the Washington D.C. area were assigned there. That is all but the 473L project which I was a part of! The people who lived in northern Virginia, or over on the northeast side of DC, now had to drive through a bunch of traffic to work and then back home. If that stupid 'office wonder' who initially was telling newcomers there was no truth to the rumor that IBM was going to build out there, at least some of them would have bought houses out there. As for me, my office stayed on Wisconsin Avenue and at the Pentagon, so I still had the commute. What I finally decided to do was to leave for work early before the traffic built up. I never had to worry about traffic going home as it was almost always late when I left for home.

One thing that I distinctly remember about the traffic on the south side of DC, was that there were from four to six lanes of traffic on the George Washington Parkway, and about that same amount of lanes on the Shirley Highway. Overpasses had not yet been invented, so where the two highways crossed they merged for about 3 miles, then separated and went on their separate ways. They called the area the 'mixing bowl', and traffic could flow through the area at a speed of about 60 miles per hour. This was commuter traffic where everyone knew

My Story

exactly where he/she was going. You could get through that area pretty fast. Come Spring, and the first Cherry Blossom, and it would take hours to get through. The problem was tourists. They had no idea what lane to be in to go where they wanted, so they slowed way down and sometimes stopped on the highway waiting to change lanes. One vehicle at a stop in the middle of the mixing bowl snarled traffic in all four directions for miles!

The little town of Washington Grove was pretty unique. It had started in the early 1800s as a Methodist Church camp. Apparently, the church had bought the property so that the church families could get out of the city of Washington DC during the hot summer months. They had built a small Fellowship Hall, with narrow lanes radiating out from it in all directions. The families would pitch tents along these narrow lanes. Over the years, they began to convert the tents into small houses, often in the same shape as the tents had been. They had enacted several rules to govern the encampment. One rule was that there was to be no commercial venture of any kind in the camp. Another was that there was to be no alcoholic beverages of any kind sold within a quarter of a mile of the town. They accomplished this by buying a one quarter mile wide swath of land all the way around the town.

By the time we arrived, they had changed the town to include several wide 'avenues' that were about 60 feet

My Story

wide, but were only pathways and not for automobile traffic. The few streets were still the narrow lanes that had room for single lanes of traffic. The town meeting was conducted once a year, and all business was conducted at that time. There was much vacant land in the town, and they had decided to allow two or three new homes to be built each year, with the proceeds from the sale of the lots to go to the maintenance crew, which consisted of two old men who mowed the vacant areas and raked up the leaves. Our house was one of the few that had been built, and it was positioned so that it had a great view of the wooded areas on both sides. In front of our house was a two lane road that skirted the town, and across that was the quarter mile wide wooded buffer zone. A few hundred feet into the woods was a spring fed lake that had been developed into a great swimming hole. Linda learned to swim there under the tutelage of a swimming instructor. Linda walked to school which was about a quarter of a mile away. She could walk there on the 'avenues' without having to cross any major streets.

During our first year there, we went to a PTA meeting to show interest in the school. During the meeting there was a rather heated discussion between a couple of women about where to plant some azaleas that had been donated. The discussion went on and on and it seemed like it was going to take up the entire meeting period, and the election of officers for the next year was still to be conducted. I broke into the argument, and suggested that the Chairman appoint the two arguing women to a

My Story

committee to decide where to plant the flowers on their own time. There was a round of applause when the appointments were made. On the next order of business, I was one of several people nominated to be Chairman. I accepted the nomination because I expected someone who had lived there awhile would also be nominated, and would win the vote. It was not to be. I guess my suggestion to appoint the arguing women was popular. I was probably not a very good Chairman, but I had two unique experiences because of that position.

First of all, the entire area around us was growing exceedingly fast, and it had been determined that our school would have to be expanded. It went from 11 class rooms to 23 rooms during the summer, and that fall when it opened, it was already too small! The other experience was an eye opener for me. The Principle was a very strong- willed lady who had been involved in trying to find a way to educate the kids from the DC slums. She asked me to go with her to visit some of the schools in downtown Washington DC. I resisted, but after getting a phone call from our IBM Division President who said "do it" I agreed to go with her and some other PTA officers. We found that the little kids (black) who were starting school had never seen a pencil. They had never seen a crayon or coloring book. They did not know what scissors was, nor had they ever heard of paste. We also noted that most of their talk was swear words! What our school principle was trying to do was get a program started that would teach these kids

My Story

the things that parents usually taught their kids before they started school. The idea was to get them on an even playing field. About that time, I found out that IBM was trying to do the same thing. (Thus the phone call) I guess that is why the school principle had pushed so hard for me to get involved. We called the effort by the schools 'The Leg Up Program'. IBMs efforts included the kindergarten age children, but also tried to reach the hardcore unemployed young men and women from black DC. IBM ran busses to the slum areas and brought those unemployed folks to various IBM projects to teach them how to work. Most of them did not even know that you had to be to work at a certain time, and that you had to be there every day. Many of them had police records for drug use, but also for theft and larceny. IBM did not allow anyone convicted of a felony to be part of the program.

I remember two individuals in particular who were a part of the program. A black girl about 20 years old was assigned to our group. Her job was to answer the phones when you were not there, and take messages. She had been taught to sort of type, so we also expected her to do some typing for us. I think her name was Alice. It was not long before we noted that she was not dependable enough to take messages for us. When she was asked if some one from our group was available to talk on the phone, her answer was usually "I don't know". If asked to take a message, you usually could not read it. When she began missing about every other day, IBM replaced

My Story

her with another candidate. We had a serious discussion with one of IBMs top Division people about our getting our work done versus the value of the experiment. His answer was that IBM had decided if they could train one person out of five candidates to work steady and be able to support themselves, the experiment would be a success. He also said IBM was in it for the long haul.

Another situation I became aware of was a young black man who was assigned to a group managed by a friend of mine. My friend told me that he had gone over the normal IBM benefits with the young man, and his take was "no company is ever gonna do all that for a black ass". Several weeks later the young man came to his boss and asked for some days off. My friend asked why he needed the time off, and the young man said "my Mama died". My friend offered his condolences, and said he could have enough time to go home (Mississippi) for the funeral. He also asked for the address so that IBM could arrange for flowers to be sent. He got the address, and went through the normal process. About three months later the same young man came in and asked for time off because his Mama had died. My friend said "Wait a minute, your Mother died several months ago". In talking with the young man, it became apparent that 'his mamma' had not died at all, he was just testing to see if big IBM would do as it said it would do. My friend asked if the flowers had arrived for the first 'funeral'. When the young man said they had arrived, my friend ask then why did he try it the

My Story

second time. The young man said he thought the first time was a fluke, and he wanted to see if the benefit was real. When my friend asked him if he had thought that he could be fired for lying, the young man said every black person he knew who had ever worked had been fired for less than that and it was no big deal! He expected to be fired every day. He also told my friend that he was a professional pick pocket. He said "I won't pick your pocket here at IBM, but if you come downtown, you be in my territory, and look out"! When the Government got involved they called it the 'Head Start' Program, and the 'Equal Opportunity' Program.

My Story

Chapter 23: NEW JERSEY?

There came a time when the 473L project started to man down, and I grabbed at the chance to get on a new project. The new project was located in New Jersey, which was not my favorite place to be, but the project intrigued me. IBM had won a competitive bid to develop an Air Traffic Control System which would be computer based, and stretch from coast to coast. The idea was to track all commercial air traffic from take off to landing, and provide ground based Air Traffic Controllers with accurate positional and altitude data on every aircraft in the U.S. sky. Further, all data on every airplane would be passed automatically from one control sector to another within an Air Traffic Control Center, and from one Air Traffic Control Center to the next Control Center all the way to the planned landing. Air Traffic Controllers were already trying to do their jobs with only raw radar data (radar blips), and very inaccurate altitude data. Our project would convert that raw radar data to digital data which could provide printed information on each airplane to each controller as the plane entered and traversed a control sector. Big job!

The project was located at NAFEC (National Aviation Facility Experimental Center) near Atlantic City, New Jersey. It was located on a one time Naval Air Station. Our office buildings were WWII barracks, and the main building was a mock up of an actual Air Traffic Control Center. Initially my job was to help design the overall system. Once the programmers began to get software

My Story

tested and running, I was assigned to start testing the system. I had a crew of brand new IBM hires. Some were college graduates, some were ex- military, and I think some were dropouts. We worked at night where we had full use of the computers. It was the crappiest job on the project. First of all because I had to train everyone of the crew and some had to be replaced. Secondly, every time we found an area of software that did not meet specifications, the software managers would attempt to change the specifications instead of fixing the problem. Most of them had no flight experience, and it was hard to convince them why the specifications were written as they were. Eventually, IBM agreed to get some experienced controllers in from the various field locations, to work with us. They were truly professionals who wanted a system that worked instead of something rushed out the door.

When we got to the point where we were ready to do some real life testing, we installed a partial system at the Air Traffic Control Center in Jacksonville, Florida, and we installed airborne equipment on Eastern Airlines aircraft. For awhile we just tracked the system, but eventually we got ready to exercise some control over the aircraft. At first the Eastern pilots were wary of the system, but finally began to help us complete our testing. One of the reasons the pilots did not like the system was that we could track them very accurately, including their altitude. They were some times sloppy about flying the assigned altitude. If assigned to 32,000

My Story

feet for example, we would track them flying any where from 30 thousand to 34 or 35 thousand. When we would call them and tell them we had them at 30,156 feet instead of the assigned 32, 000 feet, they would say "what have you got down there?" We had installed altitude encoding transponders along with our tracking gear. It finally got to be a matter of pride for the pilots to fly the specific assigned altitude.

When the system was far enough along to begin installation in sites further west, I requested that I be the manager of the Seattle Air Route Traffic Control Center in Auburn, Washington. It took awhile but eventually we were on our way back out west to Washington State.

The house we bought in New Jersey was in a small town, and was inland from the beach a few miles. It was called Northfield, and was pretty quiet, as it was not on the main highway leading into or out of Atlantic City. We bought it from the original builder, and I guess he thought he would live in it forever, as it had several special touches. It was fairly large, and was on a large lot that was heavily wooded with oak trees. Linda was in junior high school, and was at the age where she was interested in going to the beach. Most of the beaches were a place where you did not want your youngsters to go. To solve that problem, we put in a swimming pool. It was not a large one, but it was deep enough to dive in, and was made to fit into an ell of the house. A large sliding glass door opened onto the pool deck, and we

My Story

sometimes had our breakfast out there. It was a great place to just lounge. In summer, Linda could have her friends over to play in the pool. They had fun, and we knew where she was. We were there when Ray and Verna and their family came back from four years in England. Ray was mustering out of the Air Force from Fort Dix, so they stayed with us while he was winding up his affairs. Their boys were - - - well they were boys, and they tried daily to splash all the water out of the pool! They all had fun, and we enjoyed having them there. While they were there, The Worlds Fair was on, and we decided to go to New York to take it in. That was a busy day, but the thing I remember most was that Raymond accomplished something that hundreds of thousands of people had not accomplished. He broke the escalator leading to one of the major attractions! How he did it, I don't know, but he sure enough broke it.

While we were in New Jersey we went through a couple of pretty severe Nor'easter' storms. We were far enough inland so we did not get any flooding, but the flooding on the outer islands where Atlantic City was located was pretty bad. There would be heavy rain along with the wind, but the flooding came from the tidal action. When the wind blew as hard as it did in a typical Nor'easter, the tides would be driven higher than normal onto the low lying lands, then when it was time for the tides to go out, with the wind still blowing onshore, they would not go out. Next high tide would just add water to what was already there, then, you guessed it, the wind would die

My Story

down and all the tides would whoosh out all at once. Most of the damage would be caused by the tides going out, not coming in.

I flew back to New Jersey from Jacksonville in one of these storms. I usually did not get concerned about rough air (turbulence) because I understood what caused it, but coming into the Philadelphia airport that night in total darkness, in a horrible rain storm, with the wind tossing that airliner all over the sky, I was pretty apprehensive. We did land safely, then I had to fight the wind out to where my car was parked. I drove the Expressway toward Atlantic City to my turnoff for Northfield, but they had the exit blocked at the exit toll booth! They said the whole town is flooded, and you can't go there. I said I live there, my family is there, and that is where I am going. Actually, the only impassable streets were where the roadway dipped under a railroad. I knew of a way around, and when I got home, Dona and Linda were trying to catch water pouring into the basement through the basement windows. We all worked at it until we were exhausted. We also had a sump pump in the basement, so with our efforts and the sump pump working, we did not suffer any major damage.

I flew my Cherokee up to New Jersey when we moved up there. The nearest airport was Bader Field right in downtown Atlantic City. It was surrounded on 3 sides with ocean, and was about 4 feet above sea level. The

My Story

runways were only about 2000 feet long, which you can usually get away with at that low altitude. Taking off was never a problem, but on landing you had to touch down on the extreme lip of the runway to have room to stop. On approach, you flew down between the high-rise hotels, which often generated some vicious cross winds. If you took time to look, you could see right into the 13th or 14th floor windows! I did not like that airport. One day I was out to change the oil in my plane, and found some damage on one of the wings. While I was working, I kept hearing something hitting some of the planes tied down near mine. I thought kids were throwing rocks. Finally I noticed that seagulls were picking clams up from the water, then flying up over the airport and dropping them on the tarmac to break them open. Some of them were hitting the airplanes. I knew I had to move my airplane, but to where?

The building I worked in at NAFEC was called Building 149, and was located adjacent to one of the huge runways on the aviation facility. The runways were used by many airlines for training their pilots, and for giving the pilots periodic checkouts. There was a tower on the field to control the tiny bit of traffic they had. I decided to try to get my airplane located at the facility. I went to the head IBM guy, and he said the FAA would never allow it, but he did not care if I tried. I went to see the Facility Manager, (FAA) and found that he was in a flying club that had an airplane similar to mine. We did some "hangar flying", and when I left his office, I had

My Story

permission to base my airplane at NAFEC, and better yet, I could tie it down within 100 feet of where I worked. I was the only civilian airplane out there, and the tower couldn't have treated me better. I could go fly for an hour at noon if I was working days, but usually I would fly a while before starting in late afternoon.

We had purchased a small camping trailer while we were in Maryland, and had made several weekend camping trips with it. We enjoyed camping, and had sort of decided to try to find a larger one, with better facilities for longer term camping. One weekend we drove over to Ohio to see Dona's family. While there we were talking to her brother and brother-in-law about campers, and one said he had seen one advertised in a local newspaper. We read the Ad. and found that it was for a 26- foot Barth. The Barth Company only built trailers by special order, and they were beautiful. They had everything built-in, back then when no one else was doing that. I said "It is going to be way too high priced so there is no point in calling about it". Dona's brother said why don't you go and at least see it.

We finally agreed and called to make an appointment to see the trailer. We were told it was stored in the 'bus barn' in a small town nearby. We drove over there and met a very nice elderly couple. They took us to the building where the trailer was stored and we were awed at its condition. It was gorgeous, and it was brand new. Just for kicks, I asked what they would sell it for. They

My Story

said $4,500. I was flabbergasted! I had expected it would be around $20,000. The man said, "If you buy it, I will have my shop install a hitch on your car as part of the price". We said we would buy it, and made arrangements to have the hitch installed the next day. The man had built up a company that made special machines to support the tire industry in Akron, and his welders fabricated a special hitch that worked great. When we had the trailer hitched up and were ready to leave, I asked the man why he was selling the trailer at such a low price. He told this story: He said he and his wife had worked for many years building and operating his company. A few years back, they decided to take a trip to Florida, and they wanted to be comfortable, so they had the trailer built with all the amenities available at that time. When the new trailer arrived, they started on their first vacation. When they got ready to camp that first evening, they had to back the trailer into a parking space. Neither he nor his wife had ever had experience parking a trailer. She was supposed to guide him into the space, but she would disappear behind the trailer where he could not see her. He said they argued for the first time in their lives, and were angry with each other all the next day. He said that evening the same thing occurred when they tried to park it and they both agreed they wanted nothing to do with that trailer again. They drove it back home, parked it in the bus barn, and after it sat there a few years they had decided to sell it. It was our good fortune to be there at the right time. We used

My Story

the trailer for several years, and eventually sold it in Washington State after we moved there, for way more than we paid for it.

I was sort of agitating to get going to the Seattle site. Finally, about the middle of January, 1970, the project began making serious plans to man up a crew for the Seattle site. Dona and I agreed we should have a new car, a four wheel drive, and something big that would pull our 26 foot trailer. We ordered a 1970 Chevrolet Suburban 4x4, iridescent green, with every option on it. The dealer said we would have to pay for it before he would order it because he could never sell it if we did not take it. We told him we would pay up front if he guaranteed that he could deliver it by the 1st of June. Our plans were that I would fly out to Auburn, Washington to get the site started, then come back and get Dona and Linda after she got out of school in June.

 I made several trips out to get the site set up. I had to arrange for office space, hire some office help, and do all the stuff necessary to support a small off site crew. Back at NAFEC, IBM allowed me to interview and select my own crew. That worked a lot better than someone picking losers for me to work with. The members of my crew were recently hired IBM-ers, but they were College Grads, and had majored in software design. I hired one old time IBM employee to be my hardware expert. Would you believe he turned out to have been our neighbor at the trailer court where we

My Story

lived in Kingston, N.Y. when we first joined IBM many years before. We did not know it until we had a crew get together, and his wife was talking about a birthday party her kids went to while in New York at the trailer park. It turned out to be Linda's 3rd birthday party! We had taken movies, and when we dug them out, sure enough, there were the Nordstrom kids.

Setting up a new IBM facility was a sort of unique experience for me. My crew back in New Jersey had asked me to get information about the housing market, schools, etc., so I went to the Chamber of Commerce office in Auburn to pick up some packets to take back to them. The people got all excited when I said I was moving to town with some IBM families. One lady said, "Don't go away, I will be right back". The next thing I knew I was surrounded with real estate people and bankers. What I had not realized was that Auburn was a Boeing town with a huge factory. It, along with several others, all around the area had been closed, and Boeing was in a slump. As a matter of fact, there were billboards up saying "Will the last person out please shut off the lights". Many people had been laid off, not only Boeing people, but all the other industries, and companies that supported Boeing, had laid off people and several had gone out of business. And here I was saying "I am bringing IBM people into town"! I had to quickly explain that we were only going to be about a dozen families. When my crew members arrived, they

My Story

had a problem selecting which house to buy because there were so many on the market.

Dona and I had agreed that I would look for a house for us, and we had bought so many by that time, that I knew pretty well what we would both like. Linda's instructions were to find a place where she could have a horse. On my weekends, I looked over the areas within easy driving distance from work (and also from the local airport) and I found a beautiful area in the country a few miles east of Auburn. It was on a high hill, and the lots were all well over an acre, with many as large as 10 acres, so it was not crowded. The house I picked was a new one, built just before the big Boeing lay off, so it had been on the market for a while, and the price was right. It was a large one story, with a 3 car garage. It was built on a slope, and had a full basement that opened to the lower back yard. The main part of the house had windows the full length of the east side, and glass sliding doors leading out of the dining room and out of the master bedroom, to a veranda that ran the length of the east side. We had an unobstructed view of Mt. Rainer from every room in the house. Linda's request was fulfilled, because we now had enough room for her to have a horse. Both Dona and Linda were well pleased with my purchase when they saw it a few months later. It turned out that our new neighbors also had horses, so we eventually pastured Linda's horse with theirs on both of our lots.

My Story

When my crew arrived in May and I got them started on
our task, I was free to go home to get my family. We
wanted to license our new car in Washington State,
rather than licensing it in New Jersey, then redoing it a
week or two later. I got all the information I thought I
would need about the car and went to the Department of
Motor Vehicles in Auburn. The man took all the info
and messed around behind the counter a while, then said
"How much does it weigh?" I didn't know, and I told
him so. I pointed out that the vehicle was still being
built, and that I would pick it up in a few weeks in New
Jersey. He said, "I have to have a certified weight slip
before I can issue a license". I was exasperated, and left
in a huff. I was driving down the street when I went past
the local Chevrolet dealer. I figured they would know its
weight, and I could get a document from them. I stopped
in and asked to see the truck salesman. I told him what I
was trying to do. He said that made too much sense, and
the DMV could not handle it. He said he didn't have any
documentation that would help me, because they would
insist on a formal weight slip. I was about ready to leave
when he said he had thought of a way we could work it.
He looked up the vehicle weight in his book, then took
one of his cards and wrote the weight on the back. He
said "Take this card to 'so and so' Movers, ask for Jack,
tell him what you are trying to do, give him this card
and five bucks, and he will fix you up. I found the
moving company, and did as the truck salesman told me
to do. "Jack" put a slip in the scales printer, messed with

My Story

the dials and pulled the lever. Out came a 'certified' weight slip. I drove right back to the DMV and handed all the stuff including the certified weight slip to the guy. He looked it all over and said "How did you get this?" I said I had the car shipped out to Washington, had it weighed, then sent it back to New Jersey. He reluctantly gave me a license plate. I flew back to New Jersey about the 1st of June to get the family and head back west.

I had about a week's worth of work to do at NAFEC before we would leave, and the first day I drove into work I went past the Chevrolet dealer where we had ordered the new car and there it was. It was all shined up and sitting on the front lawn in front of the building. I stopped, and said I would like to take delivery that afternoon, as I wanted to take it to a welding shop to have a special trailer hitch put on it. They said they would try to have it ready. That afternoon when I stopped, they did not have it ready. For the next three days they did not have it ready, but there it sat in front of their building. On the fourth day, I said I am taking the car because it is going into the welding shop today for the hitch. We planned to leave for the west coast that weekend. It turned out that they had the car all prepped and ready all the while. They just wanted it to sit on the lawn as long as possible to sell additional cars like it. When we had ordered it several months before, they told us there were no other vehicles like it anywhere in the area for us to look at. I should have charged them a

My Story

commission because they ended up selling several vehicles like ours. We got the hitch installed, and also a special air conditioner.

When I got home that afternoon, the moving van was in the yard loading. When we had started planning our move, we had requested the largest moving van they made, because we knew we would have a full load. The van that was in the yard loading was NOT the largest van they had, and I knew all our stuff would not fit. I sort of blew my stack and started bawling out the driver. I said I was going to call the moving company and cancel the move and hire one that had a larger van. The driver said the size of the van was his fault. He told me the company had a larger van scheduled but he convinced them to let him take the load. He was a recently fired Boeing employee who lived in Auburn. He had started driving the van to feed his family, and he had a six week old new baby at home that he had not yet seen because his loads were taking him the wrong direction. When he saw the posting for a load to go to his hometown, he begged the moving company to let him take it. I relented and let him keep on loading. I told him that I had bought a house and that we wanted him to unload into the new house instead of our stuff going into storage. Since we planned on stopping in Ohio and Wisconsin, we knew he would get there before us. I had made arrangements with the realtor to let the driver into the new house. He noted the room that each item came out of, and marked it on each crate. When we arrived at

My Story

our new house several weeks later, we marveled that nearly everything was located in the correct room, and there was absolutely no breakage. That had never happened to us before. I was glad that we had let him take the load. The stuff that did not fit eventually got delivered via another van, but with some breakage.

A year or so after we arrived in Auburn, I stopped to buy gas, and a guy approached me and thanked me for allowing him to haul the load from New Jersey to Washington. It was our van driver. He had quit the driving job after he delivered our stuff because he said he was never at home. He was pumping gas, and waiting for Boeing to start hiring again.

Our trip to Washington State from New Jersey was without incident after we got a tire problem squared away. I don't remember exactly what the problem was, but we had three flat tires on the new vehicle before we got to Ohio. It seems there was a problem with the valve stems. We drove up to Wisconsin to see family on the way, then took our time enjoying the country we passed through. We pulled into a campground just east of Yellowstone Park one afternoon intending to stay the night. The campground owner met us at the driveway, and said he would like to have us stay but that the Yellowstone River was about to flood its banks, and his campground was going to be flooded. He suggested we drive up the road further to where there was a wide place on the side of the mountain where there would be a safe

My Story

place to park for the night. The trailer was equipped for camping without the need for hookups. We found the place he had described and stayed there that night. While there we watched his campground flood with several feet of water.

I mentioned earlier that Linda had ordered a lot large enough for a horse. Well ours was, so she immediately began looking for a horse. She would grab the daily newspaper and look for 'horse for sale' ads. We went to look at a couple, and were dissatisfied with what we were seeing. Finally she found an ad that sort of described what she was looking for. We went to look, and found this big Paint mare. She was about six or seven years old and seemed to be pretty gentle. The owner said she was a mountain horse, so she was sure footed. He also said she would pack. His little daughter was out there climbing all over the horse. She would climb up her leg to get on, or grab her mane and swing up or down. I did not know a thing about horses, and neither did Linda, but I figured if that little girl could climb all over her, she must be pretty gentle. We bought her, and the man delivered her in a day or two.

Linda immediately tried to catch her to put a bridle on her, and the horse resisted. First of all, she would walk away from Linda; just enough so she could not catch her. If Linda got her in a corner, the horse would lay her ears back, bare her teeth, and start bouncing her rear like she was about to kick. She really looked mean. I

My Story

thought, what have I done, this horse is going to hurt Linda. I went to see a neighbor who raised horses, and told him what was going on. I told him about the little girl that had been climbing all over her and she did not seem to mind. He said, well you are new to her, and she is testing you to see what she can get away with. He said I should get a fist sized rock, and when Linda had her cornered, and she started acting up, to throw it at her as hard as I could. I did. I hit her in the ribs, and you could hear a 'chunk'. She settled down immediately. Linda and the horse, named Lady, got along great after that.

Lady turned out to be a blessing for all of us. She was a nice pet for Linda, and gave Linda something to do evenings and during summer time. They rode pretty much all over the area. Linda took her to college with her, and eventually down to Las Cruces, New Mexico. I think Lady was about 35 years old when she died. While in Auburn, Linda asked about raising a colt. I told her no way, that our place was a one horse farm. Lady had other ideas. She surprised us early one morning by presenting us with a new baby. That was a little bit of a challenge, because the weather was getting cold, and we did not have a place inside for them. Linda arranged to rent a neighbors garage to use as a barn. She also agreed that it was her responsibility to take care of both of them. She did a good job of that, getting up early enough to feed them before going to school.

My Story

I really enjoyed the challenge of operating an IBM off-site project. I had a fair amount of management experience by that time, but always with a more senior manager on site. Now I was the senior guy. The job was very complex. The Air Traffic Control System was the largest software program ever attempted at that time. To make it even more complex, it had to operate in conjunction with 24 other Air Traffic Control Centers scattered across the continent. Each Control Center had hundreds of inputs, or data sources, from all over the country, and the system was responsible for accurately tracking everything that was airborne in the U.S. The on-site FAA Controllers only had contact with the commercial airliners or with aircraft flying with IFR (Instrument Flight Plans). General aviation aircraft not on IFR flight plans, of which I was one, was a nuisance. The basic project software was not ready when we got to the site, so in addition to working to get our site unique data working, we were working on the project software. My crew became very adept at resolving problems experienced at other locations, which pleased me greatly, as that is what I gained a little fame for when I was a SAGE Systems Engineer, before I went into management. In addition to the capability my crew developed, we encouraged the customer FAA personnel we worked with, to get involved in resolving some of the software problems. That more than doubled the manpower we could use to test and repair software that was not working correctly. The result was that Seattle

My Story

Air Route Traffic Control Center went online with full scale Air Traffic Control in the shortest time of any of the other 23 sites. I was pretty proud of that.

My boss's' boss was not happy that I had involved the FAA customer in resolving the problems. His standard approach with the customer was that there were no problems of any kind, when they, as well as we, knew there were still lots of problems to be resolved. I never knew how he could take that approach when the entire project was way behind schedule, and we were working on customer locations. How could they keep from knowing we were having problems? Since his approach was to lie to the customer, I never allowed his security clearance to be filed at my site. That meant when he came to the Auburn site, I had to escort him when he went to call on the customer management. At our quarterly management meetings, he would complain that the Seattle site was the only one of twenty three Control Centers where we were not smart enough to get his clearance on file. He never knew that over half of the site managers asked me how I was able to keep him away from my customers. It was easy. When they sent his credentials (clearances) to the site ahead of his visit, I threw them into the waste basket! Eventually, his boss, an old friend of mine from our SAGE System days, removed him from the project.

I had a few interesting experiences while working, or observing, on the control floor. I was watching the

My Story

controllers doing their job when the first aircraft hijacking occurred. That was when D. B. Cooper hijacked the flight coming to Seattle from Salt Lake. He had the aircraft land at Portland and let the passengers and all but the flight crew and the head Stewardess leave the aircraft. Then they flew on to SeaTac (Seattle) where they landed and he demanded four hundred thousand dollars, and parachutes. When they took off, we tracked them heading back toward Salt Lake where the plane eventually landed. They claim the hijacker jumped out over eastern Oregon. Our Control System taped all aircraft activity that took place in every 24 hour period, then we would rewind the tapes and use them for tracking the next day's activity. One of my crew was smart enough to quickly dismount the tape and save it. The officials re-ran the tape many times to try to determine where the hijacker jumped from the aircraft. The theory was that when the pilot slowed enough to drop the rear hatch for him to get out, it would show on the tape.

My theory is that there was never a hijacker. The flight crew had flown as a unit for a long time, except for those they let off in Portland. It all went too slick for it to be accomplished by a guy acting alone. The officials did not find the money because they never inspect the map (brief) cases the flight officers carry, and there is ample room for the money in those brief cases. After all, four hundred thousand dollars is not that large a bundle.

My Story

For several years after that hijacking, when I would be flying into or out of SeaTac, I would hear them paging D.B. Cooper. (D.B. Cooper, please come to a white telephone) There were a spate of hijackings all over the country for a while, and it became a federal offense to even joke about it around an air terminal. My friend Jack Dewey was the manager of the Control Center in Oakland, California. Frequently when we were scheduled to attend our quarterly Site Managers meetings, Jack and I would arrange to meet at some terminal, usually at Denver, then fly the rest of the way together to discus common problems or fixes to common software problems. I remember meeting him in Denver on one of those occasions, and as I was walking toward him in the terminal, he began waving his arms and yelling "Don't say it, don't say it". When I asked what that was all about, he said "You usually greet me by saying Hi Jack, and I don't want either of us to go to jail!

We fully enjoyed our stay in Washington. One of the main attractions for us was the drive east to the Snoqualmie National Forest. It was only about a dozen miles away from where we lived, so we could drive out there in the evenings. The lower area was called the Green River area, and we could see elk and deer every time we drove out there. Our neighbors all would go out then complain that there were no animals. Dona and I would take them with us, and show them how to spot the animals. I was lucky enough to shoot a huge elk in that

My Story

area, on the only elk hunting trip I was able to put together. I use the antlers for a hat rack in my office today! I also fished for trout in the mountain streams, and often could fill my limit within a few hours.

The guy I had chosen to be my 'hardware' expert at the Auburn Air Route Traffic Control Center turned out to be the guy who lived in a trailer at the same trailer court when we first started with IBM at Kingston ,New York. Linda played with his kids there, and we did not realize that until we had our first crew get together, and the wives started comparing notes. His name was Roy Nordenstam, and he was the only one on the crew about my age. We also shared an interest in the mountains and hunting. He convinced me that we should try for a mountain goat. They had a season in the late fall in the North Cascade Mountains. We applied for permits and found that they were easily obtained because the terrain was so rugged, most people did not even try for them. The first time we hunted for goats we had four days. We would climb to about where they were, then pitch camp and hunt from our camp. We had to pack everything we would use, and I was used to camping with a camp trailer, so I packed lots of stuff. My pack weighed a little over 70 pounds! When we got to the jumping off place, we had to sign in at the Ranger Station. We checked the weather with the Ranger, and while talking to him, I asked how long it was going to take us to get to the area we wanted to hunt. He looked at me and said "you are not going to make it up there". The climb was from

My Story

about 1000 feet to 9000 feet in about 5 miles. If he had not said I couldn't make it, I would not have made it! I have never worked so hard in all my life.

Once we reached the area we were looking for, we pitched camp on a narrow shelf just wide enough for our tents. It was probably 10 feet wide and had a drop off of over 500 feet on one side and a sheer rock wall on the other side. There was a glacier about 300 feet above us with much water shooting out from under it. It was very cold, although there was no snow on the trails. After breakfast the following day we started out to hunt. We decided to stay together until we sort of had a feel for the area we were in. We climbed higher on a narrow ledge which eventually widened out. As we climbed, we noticed that fog was moving in. It did not worry us because we knew our camp was on the only trail back down the mountain.

At some point, the fog cleared a little, and we saw a small cabin perched on a rock peak several hundred feet above us. You could see a sort of a trail heading toward it, so we started climbing up. We walked through an area that had a lot of broken plastic and small metal pieces, and what seemed to be oil soaked soil. When we got near the cabin, we found that it was on a different peak than the one we were on, but there was a set of steps cut into the cliff side that led to the cabin. You had to actually duck down to avoid the overhanging rock as you climbed the last several feet. When we got to it, we

My Story

found that it was a fire lookout, about 10 feet square. There were windows on all four sides which gave a clear unbroken view of what seemed to be the entire world. There was a pedestal in the center of the room where the sighting device had been mounted, and counters with cupboards below the windows all the way around. In one of the cupboards was a supply of jars of peanut butter, with a notice to hikers to use what they needed, but save some for the next hiker. There was also a 'sign in' book where hikers had signed and added comments. About two pages back from where we signed were comments about a lost hiker, and the search attempts to find him. During the search, a helicopter crashed at the foot of the last climb, and that was the debris field we had walked through. One of the last comments told that the hiker had eventually been found dead at the foot of the cliff on one side of the peak we were on.

The cabin was about 10 feet square, and the rock peak extended out only a few feet beyond the sides of the cabin. You could walk all the way around the perimeter of the peak, but it was narrow. They had driven steel rods into the rock all the way around, and had a steel cable attached to the rods to make it safer to be outside the cabin. The steel cable also tied the cabin to the rock to keep the wind from blowing it off the peak. The log book indicated that the hiker's body had been found at the foot of the 1000 foot cliff adjacent to the entrance door.

My Story

We were sobered by reading the account of the hiker's death and the death of the two searchers in the helicopter.

As we stepped out of the cabin, Roy in front, his pants leg caught on the frayed end of the steel cable, and he tripped. He fell forward, and caught himself on the steel cable strung along the rods. As we looked down, we were looking at the place where they had found the hiker's body 1000 feet below only a few weeks earlier. We surmised that the same thing had happened to him. We hunted for the next two days, then started back down the mountain. I believe going down is harder on ones legs than going up. When we got to the Ranger Station we told the Ranger about Roy tripping on the steel cable end, and that we guessed that was what happened to the hiker. The Ranger had been involved in the search and recovery of the body.

After several weeks of recovery back at work, we decided to give it another try. This time we would only have 3 days, but we thought we could hike in one day, hunt one day, then walk back out on the third day. This time my pack weighed about 25 pounds. It is amazing what you can do without when you have to haul it on your back. The climb was also easier this time. We camped on the same narrow shelf, and started hunting the next day. We again climbed higher, because that is what everyone said we had to do to find mountain goats. When we got to where we expected to see the cabin fire

My Story

lookout, it was gone. We went up closer, and found a place where they had staged it as they took it down. We found out from the Ranger later that they agreed the anchor cable was probably what caused the hiker's death, so they tore it down and hauled it out by helicopter. We did not see any goats so we prepared to hike back down the next day.

On the way down on our last day, and about a mile and only a few thousand feet above our car, we saw some goats! We scoped them and there were 3 or 4 that would be good trophies. As we checked things out, we found that although they were only about 200 yards away, there was a canyon about that same depth between us and them. We looked for a way down and could find none, so it would have taken us several more days to work our way to them, then try to find a way back. We had already talked to a young guy who was on his third day of coming out with a goat on his back, so we decided we better try again later. Alas, the 'next' time never came. All in all, it was a wonderful experience. It taught me that I was not a mountain climber, although I did a little more of it years later when I lived in New Mexico.

I had hired a commercial pilot to fly my airplane from New Jersey to Washington, and I based it at a fairly new airport in Auburn. The airport had a nice runway, hard surface taxiways, and had covered tie downs. I enjoyed flying in the same part of the country that I had learned

My Story

to fly in 20 years before. The western mountains are a whole lot higher than the eastern mountains, and are a lot more intimidating. Unless you have to, it is fairly wise to not fly the mountains with a single engine, so I didn't.

As I stated earlier, I had hand picked a good crew. As they gained experience, they also gained professionalism. It soon became apparent that I did not have much to do and I was bored. My manager solved that problem quickly by assigning me the task of opening another off site location in Salt Lake City, Utah, to install the Air Traffic Control System. My main location remained at Auburn, and I traveled to Salt Lake frequently to oversee that operation. I used some of the people from my original crew to give them additional experience, and to help train both the new IBM people and the customer personnel. I had a chance to drive around the Salt Lake City area on my trips down there, and I much enjoyed seeing that country. I had driven through there in 1951 on my way home from the west coast, and I could see that it had changed considerably. On one of my trips to the Salt Lake Air Traffic Control Center, I decided to do some sightseeing in the mountains around the area.

One day I wound up in an old mining ghost town called Park City. It was certainly a neat little place. It was squeezed into a narrow canyon with a wider area at the mouth of the canyon. It appeared that it was starting to

My Story

be an artist colony. On my way out of the canyon I stopped to talk to a couple of young men who were working in an area that had a lot of building materials in storage. They asked me if I would be interested in investing $25,000 with them. They explained that they were developing a ski resort, and were starting to build small condos. They explained that the 25 thousand dollars would pay for the materials, and their investment would be the labor to build them. The condos would have a complete kitchen, two bathrooms, and three bedrooms. One of the bedrooms would have its own entrance so that it could be rented separately from the rest of the condo. The company they were starting would maintain the buildings, and would keep them rented. The owner could have use of the condo any time with appropriate notice so that it would not be rented at the same time. I talked with Dona about it when I got back to Auburn, and we decided it was too much of a long shot. We could not have been more wrong! Park City, Utah has developed into a first class ski resort. The last time I had any chance to check on the condo values they had increased to around a million dollars for the ones closest to the old mining town area. The area they were selling when I talked to them!

When we realized that our assignment in Washington State would soon end, and there was a fair chance we would wind up back on the east coast, we decided to sell the Barth trailer. We advertised in a small newspaper called the Barth Ranger, which was published by a

My Story

group of Barth owners. A sea captain from California read about the trailer and bought it sight unseen! He told us he had to buy the Barth because that was the only way his wife would accompany him on his annual fishing trip up the west coast from California to Washington.

That leads me into a story about some land in Arizona that we bought many years ago. When we bought the Barth trailer while we were in New Jersey, we were contacted by a club made up of Barth owners saying we were eligible to join an organization called the Barth Rangers. There was no fee to join, just express an interest, so we did. Each month we would get a copy of their newsletter giving details of what various owners were doing. In one issue, there was an article about the Barth Rangers having a winter convention in Aniston, Alabama. While there, the chairman of the organization informed the group that he was leaving for the desert of Arizona immediately after the convention ended. He invited anyone who was interested to join him. He and his wife would be camping on some desert land his family had homesteaded many years before. About this same time, we found out that most of the members were retired high ranking Naval Officers. A number of the members followed him to Arizona for the winter. In the next issue of the newspaper, there was an article saying they had decided to make the Arizona property a winter location for members. The owner, an Admiral, would donate 10 acres for a sort of convention center, and he

My Story

would make 40 acres available for members who would like to purchase 2 acres for $100 each to park their trailers on. The money raised was to be used to put in a well and build a community building. The original 40 acres were purchased immediately by the members who were there. It happened that a number of members who were NOT there complained that they did not have an equal chance at the 2 acre lots, so the Admiral decided to sell an additional 40 acres at the same deal. This was supposed to be a retirement village eventually.

Dona and I had no intention of retiring in Arizona, especially with a bunch of high ranking Naval Officers, but we thought if the land was all taken up and later newer high ranking Naval Officers wanted in, there might be a pretty good chance for a profit. I called the Maricopa County Assessor to find out if the development was legal. He said it was, but some of the lots were better than some of the others, and one should look before buying. We bought without looking.

At first our annual tax bill was 6 or 7 dollars a year, but eventually it began to increase rather steeply. We began to get letters offering to purchase our property, and many of them were from land speculators who told us they had 'foreign investors'. The taxes continued to escalate until we were paying about $150.00 for an unimproved lot. Then all at once the tax bill dropped to far less than the $150.00 we had been paying. Shortly after we had moved to New Mexico, we received a letter

My Story

from a real-estate company who asked if we would rather be annexed by Avondale or Buckeye. We decided we needed to go check on our land. We drove to Buckeye, Arizona, and tried to follow the directions we had received over 20 years before on how to find the location of our land. The directions said we should go to Rosa's Café on the main street, and ask Rosa how to get there. She could tell us, but she would also know the conditions of the roads. Well, of course there was no longer a Rosa's Café, so we tried to find it using a map.

We drove south from Buckeye on a highway that ran on the west side of the Estrella Mountains, to what looked like a county road into, or at least near to, our land. We found most of the roads were in pretty bad condition, with some of them completely washed out. Eventually we found a small collection of really ratty buildings, so I drove up and found a man working in a small shop. He was making an airplane out of aircraft wreckage he found in the desert. He was trying to make one airplane out of several light aircraft carcasses. I asked him about our lots, and if he were aware of any activity by an organization called the Barth Rangers. He said some outfit had tried to make a retirement community out there in the desert several years ago, but the project fizzled out. He said they had a well put in, and had built a Community Hall. He said, "If you climb up on that railroad embankment, you can see the remainder of the building". I asked if there were a way we could drive to it, and he told us the roads had been washed out a few

My Story

years back and not repaired. As we drove out, we drove through Avondale, and when we spotted a real estate sign, we decided to stop and see what we could find out about our lots. The Realtor was there, and he spent a fair amount of time with us. He told us that the reason the taxes began going up was because there had been a considerable amount of land speculation going on. A Mr. Keating (remember the Keating Five?) a California speculator bought a large chunk of land near our lots, and began building a planned community. The real-estate man suggested we drive out to the southwest on a 'Parkway,' and continue all the way to the end. We did, and we found what he had explained. Near the lower part of the development were a few hundred homes that were in the $100,000 to $200,000 range. There were schools and lots of open park- type spaces, and some lots that were reserved for churches. As we climbed higher, still on a beautiful Parkway, we found substantially larger homes, but not quite as many with more vacant lots. The homes here were in the $500,000 range. We continued up the Parkway, and eventually found a few homes that were gigantic, and were placed in prominent places on escarpments. There were only a few, and they were multimillion dollar homes. The Parkway continued about a half mile to the top of a divide. There the roadway was blocked by barriers and signs that said 'dead end'. As you looked over the top of the divide, you could see the line that marked the western edge of an Indian Reservation, and about a half

My Story

mile to the west, you could see a railroad track. Both of those lines narrowed like an hour-glass then widened into what looked like the country we had driven through to get up on top. Mr. Keating and his syndicate owned all of that land out in front except where it was squeezed between the railroad and the Reservation. Guess who owns that land? We own two acres of it!! The real-estate man suggested we hang onto it. He said "If they had not put Keating in Jail, you could be quite rich". He said some day that project will continue, and your land will go up in value again. Well, as I write this, it is near the end of 2012, and the taxes are back up to over $150.00, so I guess we will have to go look.

In early 1975 my job at Auburn was rapidly coming to an end. A new manager had been named for the Salt Lake City site, and my crew had done an excellent job of training the customer personnel. Bottom line was that we had worked ourselves out of a job. I was able to promote most of my crew, and we were lucky enough to get most of them to a location of their choice. Two of them wanted to go to England on a new project, and I was able to make that happen. One went back to his original location at St. Paul, Minnesota, and one went to a site near his parent's home in California. One I had to fire. She was fairly new to IBM, and to our crew, and she was dishonest. She cheated on her work records, and she cheated on her sick days, and she was GONE! As for my self, I wanted to stay in Washington. Linda was

My Story

just going into college at Washington State University, and I did not want to go clear across country at that time.

IBM had a small crew at the Boeing plant serving as on-site representatives for the AWAX project, an airborne radar system. They needed a new manager, and the job was within easy driving distance from our house. The project was managed from Owego, New York, and the Division Vice President said he did not want me on his payroll because I was too expensive. I guess he wanted an entry level, low paid manager.

Since I did not have any responsibilities at the Air Traffic Control Center, I started hanging around at the Renton, Washington, IBM Branch Office. The Branch Manager suggested that I go with the various sales people as they went their rounds. I did that for a couple of months, and that experience pointed some pretty sharp differences between the Federal Systems Division, which I was in, and the Commercial Division of which the branch office was a part. It is true that the Federal Systems Division (FSD) was the newest division in IBM, and we were considered mavericks. In the older divisions, everything was done as it had been for years and years. In our division, we did whatever had to be done to get a job done. I was being trained as a salesman in the old division, and I just did not fit. After I had convinced a couple of major customers that there was a better way to do their job than what the branch office was offering, I was invited to spend my time elsewhere.

My Story

Guess what? My next job was in Owego, NY, working for the VP who thought I was too high priced.

When our job at Auburn was nearing completion, IBM told us to start procedures to sell our houses. I supervised the process for my crew members, then started the process for myself. The process consisted of dealing with an IBM approved bank, and selecting a licensed Real Estate Appraiser. The approved bank would also select an appraiser. When both had completed their appraisals, the bank would average the appraised values, and then put the houses on the market at the "averaged" price. If the house sold for less, IBM would pay the difference. Also, if the two appraisals came in more than 10% apart, the employee could request another appraiser. The two highest appraisals would then be averaged for the guaranteed price. The whole procedure was to allow IBM employees to freely move to new jobs with out worrying about selling at a loss. IBM would also pay a reasonable monthly fee to a reliable company that would keep absent employee's homes in good condition while for sale. My task as manager was to see that all that worked smoothly for each employee.

I found in our several moves, that if you bought property that had universal appeal, and in reasonably respectable neighborhoods, you always made out OK. One of my crew members bought a poorly constructed house way out in the country at a lousy location. He also paid a

My Story

premium price. We had a bear of a time getting him a decent appraisal. One of the initial appraisers made a comment on her forms that she could not imagine anyone wanting to buy in such a remote location. She really gave it a low appraised value. Since she was the bank's selected appraiser, I was able to use her unsolicited comment about the location to delete her appraisal, and start over. The employee still lost money, but not as much.

In our own case, we made out like a bandit. Since I did not yet have a new assignment, and actually thought we may stay there for a while, I elected to not go under the IBM program. Instead, we invited a couple of Realtors to come out and make an informal appraisal. We picked the higher of the two, and said "Add ten thousand dollars, and go ahead and put it on the market". Would you believe it sold immediately to the first looker. He was a Government employee who had come from the east to take a job in the area. He had his family living in a motel, and they had horses, so our place was a natural for them. That quick sale created a problem for us. I did not yet have a job, so we rented a giant big house that was kind of decrepit, and moved into it temporarily. Since that was not an official move, we had to do it by ourselves. On top of that, our next door neighbor and very good friend, Verly Magnuson, died of cancer right at that time. We were in the temporary house only a short time and soon left to go to a new assignment at Owego, New York.

My Story

CHAPTER 24: WHAT? BACK TO NEW YORK

Ha Ha, the big gun at Owego who did not want me on his payroll got me anyway. It turned out when I got there they really did not have a job for me. My new manager tried to keep me busy writing specifications for projects that were not going anywhere! I did not like the place or the job. It was the first time in my career with IBM that I was working on IBM premises. All of my previous assignments were field assignments, and were either on off site locations or were on customer premises.

What I found at Owego, where the various group managers had worked together for a long period of time, was that they spent more time trying to outdo each other than they spent doing their job. Each manager seemed to feel that he was compelled to take advantage of other group managers. I was the new kid on the block, and I did not expect to have to compete with other IBM managers to get my assigned work done. I told the Plant Manager (Division Vice President) what I thought of his operation, that his managers were spending their efforts trying to make each other look bad rather than putting their efforts into doing a decent job for the customer. He agreed! I told him I wanted out, and eventually, that is sort of what happened.

We were in process of bidding a large project for the Air Force with Lockheed Corporation. I inveigled a place on the bidding team, and helped write the proposal. As

My Story

usual, there was a tight schedule, and we worked 16 and 18 hour days. I liked that better than not having any responsibilities. When the proposal was completed, and we got the job, I went to California to do some briefings with both Lockheed and with the Air Force. The Owego Plant Manager (the one I had told I wanted out) was head of the briefing team. When the briefings were finished, Lockheed and IBM decided to exchange engineers and have a representative in each other's plant. Guess who was named to represent IBM at Lockheed? I got out of Owego! The problem was that I still lived and worked in Owego, but commuted to California on a weekly basis. I would fly from New York to California on Monday, then fly back home on Friday. I did not like the project I was on. I thought early on that it was a loser, in that it was an experimental program and was never going anywhere. Even the Lockheed VP I was working with did not believe in it. It was called PELSS pronounced 'pells' and stood for Precision Emitter Location Strike System. It was supposed to be mounted on fighter aircraft, and would sense that the airplane was being 'painted' by a ground based missile system. Supposedly, before the missile could be launched, PELSS would launch its own missile and take out the ground unit. Eventually Lockheed dropped out. IBM redeveloped the system as WILD WEASLE. Now that was a system that worked, but by that time I was off on another assignment in the West.

My Story

When we initially arrived in New York on this assignment, we went directly to Owego where IBM's Federal System Division plant was located. Owego was a small town of around 9000 people, and nearly every other person worked at IBM. We rented a room at the local motel that had a restaurant. That same evening we met a real estate agent whose office was in the same building. We told him we would be buying a house, and asked if he was he interested in showing us what was available. He was interested, and suggested we meet him the next morning at 10:00 AM. I said," No, we will meet you at 8:00 AM". He said "I can't show you houses at that time, because people are not ready yet". I said, "They will be ready if they want to sell". We told him we would give him 2 days to find us a house, then we would go to someone else.

You must remember, we had bought a house at every one of our previous locations, and we knew exactly what we wanted. We told him in detail what we wanted, including no stairs in the house, a large lot, not in a development, and must have a garage. The first house he took us to was a split level. We did not realize that until we got inside, and there were three or four steps leading up and the same number leading down. The first thing Dona did was stumble going up the steps. We said that is enough, and we both left the house. The next one he took us to was a tiny little thing about the size of a chicken coop. It was cute, and well maintained. An elderly lady lived there, and it was evident to us from

My Story

the conversation between he and the seller that he had us there to prove to her that he was trying hard to sell her house. I told him I was aware he needed to show people that he was working for them, but that we wanted to buy a house in two days or less, and we did not have time to look at those he knew would not work. Then he took us into a development. The houses were very nice, but crowded on small lots. He said this is where you should live, all the IBM executives live here. We told him we would not even get out of the car. Since it was lunch time we went back to the motel restaurant. At lunch he told us he had never worked so hard before at showing houses. After lunch he drove us around and if we did not like the area, we did not even get out of the car. We had looked at several houses when he said "I have shown you all the houses that I know of except one that is way out near the Pennsylvania line, and I don't think you would like it". He said it was too large at 5 acres, that it had a built in swimming pool, and the décor was pretty wild. We said lets go see it. It was what he said, pretty wild; we bought it! We were in the local bank the next morning getting papers signed. We were able to get in quickly as the owners had moved to Florida and the house was vacant.

It was a Ranch style house, with all the living quarters on one floor. It was built on a slope, and had a full walkout basement. It had a large swimming pool built next to the house on the basement level. The pool was all enclosed as though it was part of the house. There

My Story

was a fairly large all glass greenhouse built on the same level as the pool. There were sliding glass doors all over the place. There were at least two on the main floor level opening onto a full length veranda which over looked the pool. From the veranda, you could ride a slide down to the next level and into the pool! I think there were at least a dozen ways to get into or out of the house. The basement had been finished, and the previous owner (the builder) made her family live down there so they would not mess up the upstairs. There was a two car garage on the main level. It was located on 5 acres of wooded land on the top of a hill. All of the lots around were at least 5 acres, and some up to 20 acres. It was pretty rural, but only a few miles from the village of Vestal, and about ten miles to work at the Owego IBM facility.

The inside décor was pretty different. The carpet in the living room was about 2 inches deep soft white wool with gigantic red roses on it. When you walked on it, you literally sunk in to your ankles. Some of the walls were painted dark red, and the main bathroom was all bright pink. Dona did some redecorating to tone it down a little. We liked the house, and especially the large lot. We had a two acre sized pond built in the woods at the side of the house. A doe and two fawns moved in to the pond area, and just stayed there. The pond was the one thing we missed when we moved out a year later. We were fairly close to the Pennsylvania line, and we used to drive down there on back roads to look for deer.

My Story

Actually, we had lots of deer on our place but enjoyed driving down there.

My routine was to spend the weekend at home, then go in to my office in the wee hours on Monday, get the material I was going to need in California that week, then go to the airport and fly out. I would spend three days in Lockheed's plant at Sunnyvale, California; then come home on Friday. Sometimes I would stay through the weekend in California, then come home earlier the next week.

After a while, I got tired of the long commute (coast to coast) so one Monday morning, very early, when I was ready to leave for the airport I taped a note on the VP's office door. The note said HELL'S BELLS, PELSS SMELLS. I thought the VP would find it when he came in later. I did not know it, but he was already at work. He was a loud, swearing, cigar chomping Italian, (we called him the 'Top Wop') and he loved to bellow. He found the note, and came stomping, bellowing down the hall before I left. He wanted to know what the @#$%^&* problem was. He reminded me that I had told him I wanted out, and he got me out. I told him that I had about all the air miles I wanted. I also told him that his customer, Lockheed, was not serious about the project and was going to leave IBM high and dry. We talked it over a while, and he suggested I stop at El Paso, Texas on my way to California, and drive up to the White Sands Missile Range, and look at a job that was

My Story

opening up there in a short time. He said if I liked it I would have that job when I finished what I was doing in California. When I landed in El Paso, I got a car and drove up to the White Sands Missile Test Range. I talked to the people there about the job and decided I wanted it. I called Dona and suggested she start thinking "brown". It was August, and it was hot and brown, and we had been living in 'green' states for over 10 years. I finished the job in California early that fall and started getting ready to move again. **This time back out to the west.**

My Story

CHAPTER 25: OUR FINAL MOVE (almost)

We arrived in New Mexico on October 4, 1976. It was our first experience in a desert area. Desert? We drove down from Albuquerque at night following a semitrailer because we could not see the road because of fog. We arrived in Las Cruces with the streets flooded. A day later at work, we held a meeting at which we agreed to work seven days a week because we were already behind schedule. The first Saturday, we could not get to work because of SNOW on the San Agustin Pass! Desert? The snow was not very deep, only about 4 inches, but it was slick, and very few New Mexicans know how to drive on snow. The problem was that cars were scattered every which way and had the road blocked. We got turned around and found a road several miles further south that crossed the mountains then turned back north onto the base.

We quickly found a house we liked, so it did not take Dona long to get a neat place for us to live in. It was a new house, in a new development, but Dona wanted some changes made in the interior. For some reason, they had the interior broken up into several small rooms. She devised a plan that would remove several walls to open up the inside a bunch. It took a while for the carpenters to get the work done, and Dona was getting impatient. One day she was scolding the crew foreman (a Hispanic man) for not coming to work the day before. She said "You told me manana, but you did not come the next day". He said "lady manana means not today".

My Story

Eventually they finished the work and we liked the new arrangement. So did the builder. He started building all his houses with an open floor plan for the main part of the house.

Since we had lived in a number of places, but never in the Southwest, and since we thought we would only be here for 18 to 24 months, we bought a small motorhome so we could travel around and see the country. We started in the extreme south west corner, and each day I had off, we would work our way a little further north. Our plan was to work our way up the west side of the state, then start on the east side. We had Honda trail bikes that we carried on the vehicle, so we would find a place to park the motor home, then ride the trail bikes to see the country. We rode the old railroad line on the Mexican border from the Texas line west to Rodeo in the New Mexico boot heel. The old rails had been removed but the road was still rideable with the bikes. The path was right on the U.S. Mexican border. You could not do that now because of drug traffickers. We also spent some days exploring the west mesa, a dessert area west of Las Cruces with a number of extinct volcanoes. We could climb right down into the craters, plus you could ride for miles on the lava beds. You had to be careful not to get lost, because you left no trail. We also spent some time exploring the Mimbres area. That is an area at the south end of the Gila National Forest.

My Story

Our project at WSMR was to build and install a system that could fly up to six obsolete jet fighter aircraft for targets for testing missiles. The current system, built by Bendix, could only control two aircraft, and being based on radar, it was so inaccurate they had to keep the drones several thousand feet apart. The Army, the customer for this project, wanted the capability to fly them 18 inches wing tip to wing tip. After watching a flight test with the Bendix system on my initial trip to WSMR (White Sands Missile Range) with the aircraft a thousand feet apart, I said "If you get two going the same way the same day, you call it a formation".

IBM had won the job on a competitive bid some time before and had spent considerable time developing a system that used pulsed transmissions to uplink commands to an aircraft, and down- linked resulting telemetry. The system was based on a large ground based computer located in the Range Control building, and smaller but high performance computers in each airborne vehicle, acting as auto pilots. Additional high performance computers were located on mountain tops on both sides of the Missile Range. The system was so fast that we could uplink hundreds of commands per second, and downlink an equal amount of telemetry for each of up to six controlled aircraft. We did not use radar at all because of its inherent inaccuracies at long distances.

My Story

The airplanes we started out with were the F-102 Delta wing, and a jet powered drone, the S-34, built by Ryan. IBM replaced the analog autopilots with the computers (digital auto pilots). North American Aircraft had the contract to make the necessary modifications to the airplanes. The planes were modified to replace the original auto pilots with the newly designed digital auto pilots, but still left room for a human pilot. All of our initial test flights were conducted with a human pilot aboard. He was there to save the aircraft and the electronics package if the particular thing we were testing did not work.

The pilots were all retired Air Force jet pilots, and all of them are a little crazy, but they also had to be a little bit brave to sit in an airplane through computer controlled take offs and landings without "clicking off". To click off meant that the onboard human pilot took control for some reason, and that action obviated the test. Once our system was completed and tested, the only time we flew with an onboard pilot was when we had made major modifications to the system, or were testing a newly droned aircraft.

We started out with the capability to fly only two aircraft, and once we had demonstrated that capability, the customer wanted to go operational. My job was to get the system installed and then train the Army personnel to operate it. In addition to the software in the ground based computer, and the software in the airborne

My Story

computers, we had to install ground based computers (tracking stations) on many of the mountain tops around the Missile Range. Most of the locations we selected for the tracking stations did not have roads, so the installation and maintenance of those stations had to be done by helicopter. Since there was no commercial power on those mountain tops, we pioneered using solar power.

When we had the system working fairly well, the customer, (the U.S. Army), scheduled a flight test to check to see if we had made the accuracy requirements that the specifications called for. The method of testing was to control an aircraft with the system throughout a typical 'missile test' flight. The method we used to fly the airplanes was to create a point in space (a rabbit) with the ground based computer, and move it through the required profile. The system would then control the aircraft to get on the 'rabbit' and stay there. Both the rabbit and the actual airplane location would be recorded, and were displayed on the Control Console. They could be played back later, or could be printed out.

The day of the first test, the flight went well, and I was certain we had met all requirements. It turned out that there was a man on the Army civilian staff who did not want IBM to have the contract. He showed up at the mission debriefing with a printout that he gleefully showed we were in error during the entire flight by from 100 to over 300 feet. I was quite surprised, and there

My Story

was considerable discussion. I finally asked what print out he had, as we had not yet had time to do our own print out. He showed it, and lo and behold, it was labeled BENDIX. I said "You actually tried to do an accuracy test with the system we are replacing because of its known inaccuracy? "He retorted that it was not a fair test for us to record our own position data. I agreed, and asked him what the most accurate tracking system on the base was. The Army personnel said that the missiles were tracked with a 'theodolite' line of sight system that was certified accurate, and the data could be recorded. I agreed to another flight, and this time we would have to fly the aircraft in a different pattern that had line of sight to the theodolite. We did that flight a day or two later. This time at the mission debriefing the same IBM 'friend' arranged to get the theodolite printout before any one else. Again, he said "Ha, you missed your accuracy specification again". You could see he was happy! We asked him what the error was, and he said "It varies around 18 feet". We studied the print out and it showed a consistent error of 18 feet, plus or minus up to 3 inches. My chief Engineer, Marv Hake, asked what the theodolite tracked on. The Army representative said it tracked the leading edge of whatever it was tracking. Marv then asked what it would track on an F-102. The guy said it will track the nose of the airplane. Marv then asked me to call our team member at Holloman AFB where the airplane was, and ask him to measure the distance from the nose of the

My Story

airplane to the antenna that our system tracked. Our man, Eldon Volgamore called back a few minutes later and said "The antenna is exactly 18 feet from the tip of the nose". Viola! We had flown the entire flight with an error of 3 inches or less! That sort of set the stage for two things. First, it established our accuracy, and second, it alerted us to the fact that there was a man on the customer staff who did not like us. I had to deal with him on several occasions during my 10 years at White Sands Missile Range.

We went operational with a four drone capability, and were regularly flying to test various missile manufacturers' products. Our original assignment duration was expected to be 18 to 24 months. Once we had the system operating well enough to test missiles, we began to try to train Army personnel to maintain and operate the system. It was not working. The military has this thing that says they have to keep their officers on the move, or so it seemed. We would find a good candidate for a specific job, have him half trained, and the Army would see fit to send him somewhere else. One day my counterpart, a Civilian Army employee came to me and said "You guys can't leave because we cannot operate this system". And they couldn't because they kept moving their people.

I wanted to stay as I was tired of moving, and I had enough engineers who wanted to stay to be able to maintain and operate the system. My superiors at IBM

My Story

said we would not be able to stay because up to now, we had been considered R & D, 'Research and Development', and that paid much more than O & M 'Operations and Maintenance', which is what we would be under a new contract. Our salaries were too high for an O&M operation. When I told my Army counterpart that we would not bid the new contract which was coming up, he said I have some news for you. The new contract was going to require that we do the required engineering to fly several additional types of jets, plus be able to remotely control up to 15 Sherman tanks for a special missile test that was coming up.

The aircraft types were the F-86 E, the F-100, F-104, and the F-106. Each of those airplanes, plus the Sherman tank would require a new digital auto pilot, and the associated software. It appeared we could be in an R&D program for several years. We bid the contract and won, and I was able to retire from IBM 10 years later, in 1986. The system we built was called the Drone Formation Control System (DFCS), and we gathered a certain amount of acclaim for some of the tasks we were able to accomplish.

First of all, we perfected a way of taking the aircraft off from Holloman AFB, over 45 miles away, with about a 15 second lapse between the start of each aircraft take-off roll. This was required when we flew all 6 aircraft. If we took them off at the Air Force recommended rate of one every 5 minutes, we did not have enough fuel on

My Story

board to make some of the sophisticated presentations the missile makers required. The normal fuel load would last approximately two and one half hours. For safety reasons the Air Force required we return to the air base with a half hours worth of fuel remaining on board. We were required to land the airplanes into a 'catch cable', and it took up to 5 minutes for the ground crews to unhook the cables and set them up for the next airplane. When you added up all the minutes it took to meet the Air Force requirements, there was precious little time left to make whatever number of passes the missile test required.

As a matter of fact on two occasions when we were flying multiple aircraft for special tests, we were "commanded" to make another pass, even after I had advised the officer in charge of the test that we would not have enough fuel on board to return to Holloman. In both cases the "command" was given by a high ranking General who had a personal interest in seeing the missile test completed. The gun system we were testing was the Sgt. York, which was an automatic, track-mounted cannon that fired high explosive marble sized 'buck shot' as thick as tooth paste. The system was a lousy system, and could not hit the ground, let alone a low flying, maneuvering aircraft. In the first case, after presenting the target aircraft one extra time, the General contacted Holloman and told them we were coming in on low fuel. They cleared the area of other aircraft, and we landed two drones on an emergency basis. In the second case about a week later, and still testing the Sgt. York gun system, the same General ordered another 'go around' after we reached our normal go home time. We flew the extra go around, and the Sgt. York again failed to hit the airplanes. The General said "go around again", and I said we will not reach Holloman. He said "they are my airplanes". We went around again, and the gun system again failed to hit anybody. The General said "Shit, take em home". We did not make Holloman with either aircraft. The number one aircraft, the first one off the runway, crashed in the mountains at the north end of the Missile Range, and the second one to take off crashed about 20 miles north of Holloman, in the White Sands Monument. There was a no-no directive regarding flying over the Monument with low fuel, but that is what the General ordered.

When we wrote up our portion of the test report, we recommended that the entire Sgt. York system be scrapped. We had lost two airplanes worth about a million dollars each including all the electronics aboard, and the gun system had not scored a hit in multiple passes on two separate test days. My engineers proved that the radar system the gun used to find the target and aim the cannons was not capable of meeting the requirements. The Army was proposing to buy 21 systems at a cost of about 4 million dollars each. Partly based on our report, the contract was cancelled and needless to say, the manufacturer was angry with us.

My Story

There was some talk about the General having to pay for two airplanes, but I think that went away.

I should explain that this particular test required that we survey a route through a canyon in the Oscura Mountains that the F-100s would fly through. The gun system under test was located on a mesa above the canyon, so the radar system would be tracking the targets with mountain terrain in the background. It was because the radars could not track the targets and aim the guns successfully at low altitude, that we reported the system was a failure. The successful flight of two high speed jet aircraft up through a narrow twisting canyon for multiple passes under control of a computer over 100 miles away was a first, and was highly acclaimed at that time by the industry. It seems that precise drone control is now an everyday occurrence.

We had a number of highly technical missions. We pioneered delivering ordnance by drone aircraft, which I understand they are now doing routinely. The test we did was to drop 500 pound practice bombs from several different droned aircraft onto a ground target up range. We found that once we discovered how to measure the wind very precisely, we could literally drive a stake with successive bomb runs. This test was put together to demonstrate the feasibility of using multiple bomb hits in the same place to penetrate heavily fortified bunkers, or to crater the runways of potential enemies.

My Story

Another test was to fly two modified F-86s through a simulated atomic blast. The Atomic Energy Commission had a need to know what would happen to a pair of B-52 Bombers that would deliver atomic or nuclear bombs on a target from an extremely low altitude. B-52s were too expensive to drone, and also too expensive to lose, if the tests showed they would be destroyed in the explosion. An engineering search showed that of the available aircraft, the F-86 most closely resembled the B-52 in construction and in shape.

At a briefing, we were told the AEC would construct a silo about 30 feet in diameter, and about 50 feet high consisting of ANFO (nitrate fertilizer), other explosives, and natural gas jets. It would be constructed so that the explosion would exhibit the same characteristics as a nuclear bomb blast except without the radioactive fallout. Our job was to fly two aircraft through the explosion at very low altitudes. They wanted one aircraft directly above the explosion so the shock wave would hit it from underneath, and the other aircraft was to be in a position so that it would receive the shock wave from directly behind. Both aircraft were to be at an altitude of 100 feet above terrain. They told us they would accept accuracies on station of between 100 and 200 feet. I told them that if we could find a way to control the aircraft in the area they had chosen for the test, we would deliver accuracies of less than 3 feet. They laughed Ha Ha. The area they had chosen was very near the area of the

My Story

original atomic bomb test in 1945, an area chosen because of its extreme remoteness.

We had demonstrated our ability to control the F-86s in several earlier missile test missions, so we knew we could fly the airplanes. The problem was that the F-86, being an old airplane, had no decent altimeter system that we could use to control its height above ground level. On previous low level missions, we depended on the number of ground stations used in calculating X, Y, and Z. The area of the test, being at the extreme north end of the Missile Range did not have any good locations to put temporary ground control sites. Compounding the problem was a range of mountains between our takeoff at Holloman and the test site. We would have to climb the aircraft up to around ten thousand feet, cross the mountains, then trim them down to the required 100 feet.

We built special auto pilots for the two F-86s, and installed state of the art, radar based, altitude encoding altimeters. The modern altimeters available at that time had a trim range of only 1000 feet. We flew a number of engineering flights, and found that we could fly the aircraft up through Mocking Bird Pass (through the mountains) then descend them down to 1500 feet. We would then trim them down the maximum of 1000 feet while flying a racetrack pattern that would take them over the blast area. On the first racetrack pattern, we accomplished the maximum trim down to approximately

My Story

500 feet, and on the second race rack pattern, as we started into it we flew over a previously located temporary ground station. It had the capability of accurately measuring the distance from it (on the ground) to the aircraft in the air. That accurate height data was used to calculate how much additional descent had to be made to get into the presentation box. Remember, we had to do this to two aircraft while accurately maintaining their respective positions.

There was another problem that had to be resolved, and that was mission timing. The AEC engineers had calculated exactly how many seconds it took from the time they lit the fuses (gas jets) until the explosives reached maximum shock. Our data was used to calculate where the aircraft had to be when the fuses were lit. The problem was we were flying in a real world, not in a laboratory, and the climatic conditions such as wind, temperature, and etc. all had some effect on the speed of the aircraft. We resolved that by doing precise timing on the first trip around the race track while we were trimming down. Based on that timing, we interpolated the time we would be on station.

The AEC was so certain we would lose the drones, that they prepaid the Army for them. There were over 200 items of data that were to be recorded on each aircraft, and the AEC wanted all data to be downlinked so that it would not be lost in the crash. That equipment caused the drones to be loaded to maximum. The reasons they

My Story

feared we would lose the drones were as follows: they would be damaged by the blast, they would be thrown around so violently that we could not recover before they struck the ground, and finally, they said the pressure change would be so violent that the flight sensors would be overloaded. We had thought of all those possibilities, and felt that the most likely was the last, that the flight sensors would be overloaded. We solved that by programming the auto pilot to 'freeze' all inputs from one second prior to the anticipated blast until 2 seconds after the blast shock wave passed. Come the day of the mission, it was a piece of cake. We flew the drones up there, did the presentation, survived the blast, and brought the drones home to Holloman. That was another day of great jubilation . The AEC treated us to steaks and beer at the Hitchin' Post, our favorite winding down place.

When we were doing some of the early engineering, I had arranged to have two Air Force B-52 pilots come to our offices to discuss the characteristics of the B-52. During the afternoon, it dawned on them how expensive the mission was going to be. One of the young pilots said "I can save you gobs of money. Just tell me where you want me to be at what time, and I will fly my B-52 through your explosion for a paltry one million bucks!"

Many of our missions were as complex as this one, usually because we would be flying more airplanes. A typical mission would start by being at work by about

My Story

2:00 AM. We had a rigid countdown, just like NASAs countdown for a space launch. Every entity that was involved in a missile test had its functions to perform at precise times, and there were around twenty organizations involved in most tests. Any organization who reported countdown steps successful, then failed to perform, could be made to pay part of the cost of a failed mission.

I remember a specific test we were involved in where things were not going well. There had been a number of 'holds' and delays for various reasons, mostly coming from the missile launch area. We were about 15 minutes from starting aircraft take- off operations, when one of my engineers called on the radio (everybody was on the same frequency) and asked me to go into my office so he could talk to me on the phone. It was a busy time at my Mission Control Console, so I said "Spit it out". He said "You better take the phone call". I reluctantly unhooked from my console and went to the office. As I walked in the phone was ringing. It was my engineer, and he said "They don't even have a missile on the launcher!" The missile maker had played the game as though he was ready to test because he was going to have to pay for much of the scheduled time. His hope was that during the countdown, someone else would develop a problem, and he would be home scott free. I learned that they called that kind of ploy 'Range Poker'. I called all of my guys together and old them we were the new kids on the block, and since we could never win

My Story

at Range Poker, we would never go into a missile test unprepared. In ten years, we never were unable to support a mission because of system troubles. There were a few times when aircraft were not ready, but they were maintained by others, and therefore not our responsibility.

My Story

CHAPTER 26: I GET TO DRIVE TANKS, AGAIN

Our tank driving operations were a welcome change from flying aircraft. Our most complex operation was to drive 15 tanks in single file in a race track pattern, with exactly 150 feet between them, and have them come out of the oval track into a target area with the center tank adjacent to a stake in exactly the center of a one mile diameter test area, at a precise time. The test was of a missile that was to be launched from Vandenberg in California, would fly to White Sands, arch over, and dive at the tank formation. At a certain distance above ground, the missile canister would open and a batch of mini rockets with armor piercing explosives, were to search out and destroy the tanks. The test was successful, but I am not sure the missile system was ever funded.

The problems of driving the tanks by remote control were many. First of all, we had to build auto pilots for them. Then we had to design a mechanism to shift into gear, press and depress the throttle, put the brakes on and take them off, plus engage the steering clutches for left or right turns. The tanks moved slowly enough so that we could use electric screw actuators to operate the controls. My engineers had to know what the control characteristics were so they could design soft -ware, so my old tank driving capability from the Wisconsin National Guard came in handy.

My Story

We mounted our tracking devices on a tank and I drove it. We had the tank on what was called the 'small missile range' because it was flat and had an area I could drive in without being affected by other base traffic. Once the system was tracking the tank, I would respond to actions requested by the software engineers. All the data was recorded so that it could be played back repeatedly. I would make a series of slow starts, then moderate starts, then maximum effort starts. Next it would be a series of left turns then right turns, etc. We devised the control software, and then had the tank transported up range to where the Space Shuttle had landed a few years before.

We would now be driving it by remote control from the main base, a distance of about 40 miles, so it had to be where it could not create damage if it got away. We kept a manned truck in the area, usually behind the tank so we had "eyes" on it. Of course, we also had a small tank depicted on our display consoles. When we had satisfactorily controlled one tank through its paces, we told the Army we were ready for more tanks. We had mounted our equipment in all 15 tanks. As they delivered them to us up range, we would put them through their paces. Guess what we learned? No two tanks are alike! I panicked. Did that mean we were going to have to develop a unique control system for each tank? Wow, there was not enough time, plus I had modified our contract to do the tank work based on our experience with the first tank. I was about to cost IBM our profit for a couple of years, and that was not going

My Story

to be popular at headquarters. My main engineer, Marv Hake, comes to the rescue!

Since the main problem was that the tanks cruised at different speeds for a given throttle setting, he devised a "crash avoidance" system that would make an overtaking tank pull over to the right to pass. Since the oval track we were driving on was a rough road about 30 feet wide bladed out of the dessert, with rough terrain on both sides, when the passing tank would pull over to the right, it would then be in rough terrain and would slow down, then pull back in line! The oval track that we drove on was measured to be two miles around, and at the south end was a circle, one mile in diameter, which was the target zone. It was perfectly level, and cleared of all brush.

After each test drive, the Army would drag the entire area to wipe out any tracks. The reason was that to score the tank presentation, they would measure the tank tracks; plus, if the ground had no previous marks, they could score where the bomblets hit. Incidentally, the bomblets had paint in them instead of explosives. That was a fun project! The 'tank simulator' we put together to design and test the tank autopilots was so successful that the Army gave us a contract to develop a simulator for a tank not yet built. They felt if they provided us the desired operating characteristics for the proposed tank, and we provided the simulator, they could determine if the tank would perform up to its requirements. Almost

My Story

the same thing had happened earlier when NASA contracted with us to provide software to allow a 'deadstick' landing. We developed the algorithms needed when we were doing the engineering flights on droned jet fighters. Our drones came in for landing with the engines rev'ed and available for a go around if necessary, but the Space Shuttle could not. They had to land on the runway at the end of their approach. We were able to provide enough engineering for them to perfect their deadstick landings.

When we had the tank driving system working and were preparing for our first operation, we had some heavy rain on the Missile Range for several days. Our tank driving area became a sea of mud, so the tests were delayed for a few days. Early on the morning of the scheduled test, my engineers who were up range radioed down that a significant washout had occurred in a portion of the oval track. They reported that a tank would not be able to cross the washout and still maintain its position in the formation, and worse, the following tanks would automatically be diverted to the right to avoid the tank in front of it. It appeared that we would have a whole row of 50 ton Sherman tanks stuck. When we were discussing how to proceed, someone on the radio said "what would General Patton do". I volunteered that he would have driven the number one tank into the hole and used it as a bridge to get the other tanks on with the mission. The Army elected to cancel the test and bring in road construction equipment.

My Story

CHAPTER 27: FORUM

Each year, IBM Corp. would sponsor a forum to 'Thank' those managers who had turned in outstanding performance during the previous year. The Forum was held in a different location each year, and always in a special place such as Reno or Las Vegas or Cancun, Mexico. I was invited to attend one year when it was held in Phoenix. It was held at the Biltmore Waldorf Astoria Hotel, which was originally built to be the winter home of one of the wealthy families of the 1800s. It was very lavish, and in addition to swanky rooms, there were golf courses, tennis courts, a livery stable, and more. The Forum lasted 4 days, and of course, was all free to the IBM attendees. Our first day's schedule consisted of the introduction of each attendee, and a story about what he or she did to earn the invitation. It turned out I knew several of the other attendees from previous projects. Then several IBM executives gave us a briefing on what some of IBM's future plans might look like, and then spent time visiting with us. After that, the mornings were unscheduled and you could do whatever you wanted to do. Of course if you were going to play golf or tennis, you had to have the correct attire. In the afternoon of each day we were entertained by business tycoons from several large companies, some inspirational speakers, and then in the evenings we had some outstanding performers entertain us. For example, one evening Dolly Parton sang for us. Another evening Crystal Gayle entertained us. The first or second

My Story

afternoon, General Alexander Haig was scheduled to talk to us. I believe he had retired from the Army to accept a position as Secretary of State for President Reagan, and had served as Chief of Staff under both President Nixon and President Ford. In any event, the day he was to talk to us I had left the auditorium to go to the restroom, and when I was returning, there was General Haig in the lobby. I went up to him, introduced myself, and pointed out that we had something in common. He said "What would that be", I responded that we were both working on International problems. I told him I was restoring an old International pickup truck, so we were both trying to resolve International problems. He said "How are we doing?" I told him we had been running neck and neck, both making progress, and then I ran into a tough problem so he got way ahead of me. He asked "What was your problem"? I responded that I could not make the windshield wipers work. He laughed and said that had to be a tough one.

Would you believe when he gave his speech that afternoon he recounted, the conversation we had had, and he used my name when he wished me luck! The crowds cheered and made me stand up!

My Story

CHAPTER 28: WE FIND CHLORIDE

We first saw Chloride on Labor Day weekend in 1977, about a year after arriving in New Mexico. The people I worked with had convinced me that we should spend the Labor Day weekend at a campground at Wall Lake in the Gila National forest. We stopped in Winston and talked to the elderly couple who ran the Winston store. When we left there, I should have turned to the right on NM 52, but instead I turned left onto Forest Road 226. After about a mile I realized we were on the wrong road and I began to turn around. Dona said "I see some rooftops, let's go see what there is, so we continued on to the west. At first, when we drove into Chloride, we thought it was completely vacant. We drove west to the end of the (only) street, turned around and parked in the road. Our next thought was that it was probably a deserted movie set. There were several False Front buildings along the street (dirt road), and it appeared that there was no maintenance being done on the yards. Almost immediately, Dona said it would be great if we had a place here. We drifted slowly down the street marveling about what we were seeing. Near the east end of the town we found an elderly man sitting in his yard. Mr. Hobbs was not too sure he wanted to talk to us. We found out later that people would sometimes come to the town to steal things, so he needed a little time to decide we were not going to do that. It appeared that Mr. Hobbs was not anxious to have us there. As Dona talked to him, he warmed up and finally said "Come inside and

My Story

meet mama, you will scarcely believe what she has".
We went inside and met Mrs. Hobbs. What a sweet
lady! Several things struck us immediately. One thing
we suspected was that they were very poor money wise.
Another thing we noticed from their speech was that
they were not educated. We also noticed even though
their furnishings were homemade, they were beautiful;
and both of them had pride in what they had.

Mrs. Hobbs had made all of the furniture throughout
their house, and both she and he were very proud of
their things. We were impressed. We were even more
impressed when I asked to see her workshop and we
realized that she had made her furniture with only a few
crude hand tools, a hatchet, a hand saw, a horseshoe
rasp, and a couple of paring knives that she had ground
down to carve with. We learned later that she also made
all of their clothes, including her own shoes! She had
also taught herself to paint using watercolors and oils.

When Dona said we would like to have a place here,
Mrs. Hobbs insisted that we use her phone to call the
absentee owner. Mrs. Hobbs warned us that the lady
who owned the property was not to be trusted as she
would lie and cheat if she could, and she would probably
swear at me. When we called the owner she was very
uncouth. She swore at me when I made a counteroffer to
her first asking price, but eventually we agreed to a price
for the property. Since we had been warned that she may
be less than honest, we hired a title company in Socorro

My Story

to research the deed for us. The deed history was jumbled and took a fair amount of time to unravel. During that time the owner called me repeatedly and using foul language, accused us of cheating her out of her interest money. I finally convinced her that we would pay her interest at the same rate as her bank paid, from the time we agreed to the price. If I remember correctly, that was the last phone call we got from her. When we finally received a clean deed, we called Mrs. Hobbs and told her we would be up to Chloride the following weekend. Since there was no traffic on the dirt street, we parked the motorhome in front of our new place for the night.

The following day we began to clear a significant amount of brush out of the way to get the motorhome up into the yard. As we worked, all seven of the elderly (we called them our Old Timers) came to see us, and they filled us in on the history of our new place. Because of the deplorable condition of the house, we had planned on pulling down what was left and burning it. As the history of the house unfolded, we decided that we could not burn it, but would attempt to restore it.

They told us the town Marshall had lived there, and he had a jail out in back of the house. We went out to look, and there was a tiny log building there, that was decrepit. I said "This would never hold anyone for long". One of the old men went inside and scraped the dirt on the floor until he found a handle. He pulled the

My Story

trap door open revealing a pit. He said "He kept his baddies down there until he could get them to Magdalena, where there was a real jail". We also learned that at the time the Gila Forest was formed, the first District Ranger lived there, so the house also served as the Ranger Station. We embarked on a rebuilding project almost immediately.

It took about 3 years of weekend labor to rebuild and restore it into a sort of weekend camp. We put in a well and had electricity put in, so we could be pretty comfortable when we were here. We were so sure we would be reassigned to some distant location that I made heavy- duty shutters for all the windows. We figured if we left we would close it up tight until we could get back. Eventually, we added more rooms to the house. When we moved here full time in 1986 when I retired, we needed the extra space, and Dona wanted a different kitchen location.

The little stone building was actually the first building we restored. I figured it would take less work, and it would be a secure place to store our tools and supplies when we were not here. We replaced the top layers of stone, using the native red rocks from the creek bed, just like the original town builders did. Then we replaced the roof using poles for rafters. While we were working on this little building, we found it had a basement. We also found out from the Old Timers that it had been originally built to be a chicken coop. It had also been a

My Story

whisky distillery, a gambling den, a school house, a first home for a newly married couple (a son of the town Marshall) and then a home for a family of seven whose name was Nichols. When we told the old timers we were fixing it up to store tools and materials, they said we would not have to do that. They said they would watch our stuff for us. One of them said "We will shoot first and ask questions later if someone messes with your place", all the while patting his 44 Cal. pistol! I now use the stone building for tire storage.

Our neighbors were delightful. They would come to visit during the daytime, and Dona and I would visit them in their homes during the evenings. Our neighbors across the street, and the first ones we had met, were Cassie and Earl Hobbs. Suffice it to say they were very special to us. We found that Cassie was multi-talented, and all Earl had ever done was cowboy. Cassie's brother and sister- in- law, Gene and Bessie Ramsey, lived next to them. At the east end of town on the north side of Wall Street lived Ted and Faye McBride. They had come to Chloride about 30 years before. Next door to us on the west side lived Tom and Blanch Walton. They had come to Chloride when Tom retired as Ramrod of the huge Ladder Ranch several miles to the south of Chloride. At the west end of Chloride lived Nellie Inman, and her companion Jake Parker. Nellie was a daughter of the infamous Inman lumbering family. Across the creek on the south side of Chloride lived Raymond Schmidt.

My Story

Although all of the old timers except the McBrides, were descendants of the original town builders, only Raymond cared about the history of the town and the town builders. He was our "historian". He had saved every relic that pertained to Chloride's early days, that he could get his hands on, and he knew all of the stories. Shortly after we found Chloride, we met Shirley and Dick Watson. Shirley was the only daughter of Harry James, who had arrived in Chloride in 1882 as a 6 year old lad. The William James family came from Pennsylvania in 1882 with 6 children, ranging in age from 10 to 2 years old. William James was killed in an accident at the Silver Monument mine in 1886. In spite of that tragedy, the family became very prominent in the area, and wound up owning a huge ranch surrounding the town, plus most of the town properties.

When it became apparent that IBM was going to be at WSMR for a while, and that there was a good chance I would finish my career here, we began to think about making our Chloride place our retirement paradise. We also began to develop a real interest in the history of both the town and some of the buildings. Two things struck us about the same time: One was that Winston, the neighboring village, was being taken over by the unwashed hippies living in little trailers with junk piled around; and, two, if this was going to be our retirement paradise, we had better try to protect our own little town. We began to watch for indications that places were coming up for sale.

My Story

We bought three parcels across the street from us from the same lady who owned our first house. A funny thing was that we bought these several pieces of property from her, and we never met her. We would go to her house in Magdalena to deal with her, but she always stayed behind a door. Her husband would fetch papers back and fourth, but we never met her. Weird! The last piece we bought from her was a few days after she had died. We had made an offer on it that she turned down. Her husband called one day, and said "If you want that land, come up and sign the papers, she died last night". We verified that neither her son nor her daughter wanted the land, then bought it. We bought some adjacent land by paying the back taxes, and paying the county a penalty fee. The hillside behind our house was being grazed heavily by a family who were using it without permission. I asked them to ease up on the grazing, because when it rained the hill was washing down into our yard. They refused to slack off on the heavy grazing, so we found the absentee owners near St. Louis, MO. and bought the entire hillside. That solved only one grazing problem, but there were others to resolve later. When Cassie and Earl Hobbs died, their sons were ready to discard all of the things Cassie had made. We bought the house, and Cassie's workshop, the Doodle Dum, primarily to save her things. Later we were able to buy the little stone house that was originally part of the property. Eventually we were able to buy the Pioneer Store, the Monte Cristo Saloon and Dance Hall, Pye's

My Story

cabin, the U.S. Treasury Mining Co. Headquarters building, the old bank building, several vacant lots, and acreage on both sides of Wall Street at the east end of town. Linda now owns the old Barracks and Armory building, and the first mining claim plus an additional claim of 20 acres each.

When we first arrived in Chloride, we enjoyed visiting the 'Old Timers' in the evenings, and listening to their stories. Our next door neighbor, Tom Watson had been the Ramrod (Boss) on the Ladder Ranch for a number of years, and he had lots of stories about cattle round-ups in the mountains, and cattle drives from Chloride to Engle to the train. The drive to Engle was about 75 miles, and took a couple of weeks, so it was quite an occasion. He told me they would sometimes include the neighboring ranches herds, resulting in several thousand head included in the drive. They would usually cross the Rio Grande downstream from present day Truth or Consequences at a place where the cattle could wade. On one drive they got to the river when it was in flood stage. They scouted both up and down stream to find a place to cross, but all would surely cost them several head of cattle, and may even drown some cowboys. The herd was on private land and could not stay there, so they arranged to cross on the newly constructed Elephant Butte Dam. The roadway was narrow, and the cattle were not used to being crowded that closely. The way he described the situation, it was bedlam, but they

323

My Story

finally got the herd across with minor scratches on both animals and cowboys!

Earl and Cassie Hobbs were our neighbors across the street. What stories they had! Cassie and her family, Mom, Pop and twelve children, lived in covered wagons pulled by oxen, as they wandered back and forth across Texas. She was fourteen years old when her family homesteaded on a section of land in the Dusty, New Mexico area. She said they built a small cabin that was large enough for her mother and dad to sleep in, as well as the girls, but the boys still had to sleep outside. She married Earl Hobbs when she was 16 years old. Since the family had wandered around Texas, she had not gone to school until they homesteaded in Dusty, and then it was a 15 mile horse back ride to school at Fairview (now Winston) so she only went sporadically. Earl's family came from Texas and originally settled in the Deming area. Earl never talked much about his father except to say that he never could hang onto any property. Earl told us that he did not get on with his dad, so he left home to go 'cowboyin' at the age of thirteen. I believe he was only 18 when he and Cassie married. He spent his young days as a broncobuster, and the other Old Timers around said he was a good one. We spent most of our 'visitin' time with Cassie and Earl. He and Cassie had the most wonderful stories about where they went and what they did.

My Story

Gene Ramsey (Cassie's brother) and his wife, Bessie, lived next door (on the east) to Cassie and Earl. We did not visit with them very often, but he told us stories about his family's wanderings in the two oxen drawn wagons. Actually, their father was a 'Sooner" from Oklahoma. About the time Mr. Ramsey started his family they drifted out of Oklahoma into east Texas, then across Texas several times for several reasons (Family fights etc.)

The McBrides lived at the east end of town. They had come to Chloride from Colorado many years before we arrived. We enjoyed visiting with them because they were nice people, but they did not have a history from Chloride.

Nellie Inman lived at the far west end of Chloride. She was from an old family who lived in the mountains west of Chloride. They were mostly woodsmen, and apparently were fierce. They were involved in shootouts and some say in plain murder. We visited a little with Nellie, but not about her family history. That came from some of the other folks around.

Then there was Mr. Raymond Schmidt. Raymond was born in 1897, and died in 1996. Nearly all of his life was spent in Chloride, or the surrounding mountains. His Mother died when he was an infant, and his father, Mr. Henry Schmidt, was an assayer and photographer, so his work frequently took him away from Chloride. Raymond was raised by his Grandfather, Judge Holmes,

My Story

We were able to buy the entire block across the street from our house. Part of it had been the Livery Yard, and had a couple of small wooden buildings on it that could not be saved. At the west end of the property was a large adobe building that was in poor condition, but I felt we could restore it to usable condition. The walls were tilting outward, so I put one inch pipes through the walls at both ends near the ceiling. By putting large nuts on the pipe ends, I was able to pull the walls back together. I used old woven wire fencing around the building corners to further bind them together. The wooden floor had been crushed by a local rancher storing too much cattle feed, so it had to be replaced.

The building looked horrible with the fencing tying it together. My friend Nick Ortega brought some Mexican workers up from his place, who wanted to make some money to continue their travels to Colorado. They said they could do stucco work. They also said they could make a cement floor. I hauled in many truck loads of creek gravel from Mineral Creek, and I had a semi load of cement bags delivered. The Mexicans were true to their word. They mixed the cement in a hole in the ground and made the floor; then did the stucco on the walls. I had a supply of tan stucco material, so that is the color of the building. It is now my wood working shop, and I am very proud that we were able to save it. Its history is fascinating. It was built in 1880 by Mr. Edwin

My Story

Holmes to be his law office. Mr. Holmes was a prospector/miner, but he had been elected to be the local Justice of the Peace, so he needed an office. He also ran a real-estate business in the building. The Post Office, which was started in the Pioneer Store in 1881, eventually was moved into the building. We know it was used as a dance hall, a gambling establishment, a Catholic Church, a Harley Davidson Dealership in 1914, again a dance hall, and then cattle feed storage.

Mr. Holmes was Raymond Schmidt's maternal Grandfather, so we learned the history from Raymond. One day I noticed a series of pencil lines on the door frame, with attendant dates and names. The dates start in 1904, and the names are Raymond, Amy, and Edwin. When I asked Raymond to 'splain' he said his Grandfather kept track of how much they grew. The others were Raymond's sister and brother. I promised him that I would not paint over that little bit of history!

The next building to get our attention was the Pioneer Store. It was built by Mr. James Dalglish in 1880, and was operated as the Pioneer Store all through the silver mining boom years until 1896. Mr. Dalglish moved to Hillsboro and started a meat market. We believe it is the building where Ben Lewis has his general store and restaurant. When the silver mining boom ended in 1897, Dalglish leased the Pioneer Store building to others for several years. One of the leasers was Phillip Winston, who was a brother to Mr. Henry Winston, for whom the

My Story

Village of Fairview was renamed in 1929. In 1908, Mr. Dalglish sold the Pioneer Store to the U.S. Treasury Mining Company. It was operated as a commissary for the James Brother's timber and ranch workers until 1923, when it was closed and sealed up with boards and tin over the windows and doors. All of the furnishings and the items of merchandise were left in the building. For nearly 73 years the rodents and bats had the run of the building. It was intended that the store would reopen when Chloride had a resurgence.

We bought it in 1988 from Mr. Edward James, Jr., who was the son of the family who had closed the building in 1923. Starting in 1995 all of the furnishings (except the 6000 pound safe) were removed from the building to be cleaned and refurbished so they could be replaced in their original location. The roof was replaced, the chinking between the logs had to be redone, and the interior had to be cleaned of rodent debris and sanitized. The large front windows had to be replaced, and the interior was painted to simulate whitewash which was the original wall coating. In addition to the furnishings and items of merchandise, many town, business, and personal records had been stored in the building. The stack of boxes had tipped over, and the contents were strewn about on the floor. These had to be picked up, cleaned, and re-boxed. At this writing, there are approximately 50 boxes waiting to be sorted and classified. Once the furnishings and items of merchandise were cleaned, and the interior of the

My Story

building was ready, the items were replaced as nearly to their original location as possible. The building was opened to the public as the Pioneer Store Museum in April, 1997.

The small wooden building near the west end of Chloride was built in 1884, to be the headquarters for the U.S. Treasury Mining Company. We restored it into a small house, and Daughter Linda lived in it when she first moved to Chloride. We anticipate using it as a vacation rental when Linda's house is finished.

The small log building in back of the Monte Cristo Saloon building was built by Harry Pye, the original finder of the silver. It was the first building in Chloride, and appears to have been built during 1879. Pye was killed by Apache Indians shortly after constructing the cabin. It was used as a home, first for miners' families, and when the mining was over, ranch workers lived in it. It stood vacant for many years, and was in danger of collapsing. We have rebuilt it into a rustic, but modern, two bedroom vacation rental cabin. The small adobe building adjacent to the Pye Cabin has also been restored and is also a vacation rental. The exterior of both buildings has been retained as near as possible to its original appearance.

The Monte Cristo Saloon and Dance Hall is a large adobe building. It was built in 1880 by Mr. Austin Crawford. In 1884, the building was leased by the city of Chloride to be used as a school. Eventually, it was

My Story

used as living quarters for the school teacher, a Mrs. Darr, and then was home for the senior members of the Edward James family. Lastly, it was used as a storage building for mining equipment. We have refurbished the building and it is now the Monte Cristo Gift Shop and Gallery. An art co-op of approximately 30 local artists and crafts persons display and sell their items there.

With the Pioneer Store Museum's popularity growing, it became apparent that we needed a modern toilet facility. To meet that need, we partnered with the Geronimo Trail Scenic Byway organization to construct a rest area that includes sheltered picnic tables and toilet facilities.

The large adobe building at the far west end of Chloride was built in 1884 to be the Barracks and Armory for the newly organized local militia. It was also the home of the militia Commander, Major James Blain. When we came to Chloride, Nellie Inman lived there with her friend Jake Parker. Jake was a Baton Death March survivor. After their deaths, the building was sold several times, eventually to our daughter. Linda is in the process of restoring and enlarging it for a house for herself.

We have completely resurrected the old bank building. It had been built in 1884 to be the bank, but failed before it could open because of a scarcity of cash in the area. It appears most people used the barter method for supplies. The bank building opened as the ninth saloon in Chloride, and operated successfully for many years.

My Story

Eventually, as folks left for greener pastures, the saloon closed and became a residence for several years. In the late 1940s the roof was removed to salvage the roof timbers. The timbers were used to replace some bridges that had washed away in a flood. With the roof off, the stone walls began to deteriorate until almost all of the side walls and the entire rear wall had disappeared.

Visitors enjoyed posing for pictures in the doorway of the front wall, but I feared that a stone may fall and hurt someone, so I hired some stone masons from deep in Old Mexico to 'point up' the walls with cement to make them safe. I asked the men to leave the remnants of the wall as they were. A day or two after they started work, one of them said they could finish the building to its original size using adobes. I replied I did not have any adobes, and he said "we make". Those four men made 6000 adobes in the yard adjacent to the building, and then built them into the remnants of the stone walls to finish the building. At this date, the building has been made into the Chloride Bank Café. It has a modern stainless steel kitchen, and an attractive 'period' dining room. It opened in late August, 2013, and was operated very successfully until the tourist count dropped too low to continue operation. It is now closed, but is ready to re-open when visitor traffic picks up.

There is an additional log building in Chloride which was not originally built here. We call it the Grafton

My Story

Cabin. It is located in the Chloride Rest Area, and is operated as a part of the Pioneer Store Museum.

Here is its story. It was built in the mid-1870s in a small mining town called Grafton. The town was located just a few miles from the Warm Springs Apache Agency, home of Victorio and his Apaches. The town was established there to support two active mines, the Ivanhoe and the Emporium, but it was also located in the Apaches' favorite hunting area. As a result, the town was attacked several times, and was overrun sometime in the early 1890s. Since the mining activity had diminished, the town was deserted, leaving the 35 or 40 buildings to the elements. Some of the buildings were taken down for the materials, and some washed away in floods. By the 1970s, only a few remained. One of them was relocated to Winston where it currently is used as a residence. In 1976 the last building was taken down log by log, and was reconstructed on the downtown Mall in Las Cruces, New Mexico. That activity was to commemorate the Nation's Bi-Centennial. They dubbed it the "Bi-Centennial Cabin",

The Las Cruces Museum system operated the cabin as part of their system until 2006. The city was planning street enhancements, and the cabin was in the way, and was slated for destruction. No one in Las Cruces would pay for its removal. The Pioneer Store Museum asked for the cabin to save it from being torn down, and the City of Las Cruces was agreeable except that the State

My Story

Statutes forbade the transfer because of the 'Anti-Donation Act'. The Sierra County Commissioners agreed to accept the cabin, if someone would pay the cost of moving it. The Pioneer Store Museum raised the $15,000.00 to relocate the cabin. It was selected to be an official New Mexico State Centennial project. After extensive overhaul, the cabin was dedicated on October 20, 2012, and is now operated as a part of the Pioneer Store Museum.

My Story

Chapter 29: OUR INVOLVEMENT IN THE COMMUNITY

In 1984, Sierra County was celebrating its Centennial by having many of its communities hosting Fiestas. Winston was no exception. Dona and I had not yet moved to Chloride, but we had been 'week- enders' for about eight years, and had been accepted as regular community members. We were involved in planning the Fiesta activities, which consisted of raffles, games for the kids, horse races, a pit barbecue, and a street dance in the evening. We charged a minimal fee for entrance to all the games or contests and for the barbecue meal. The affair was a spectacular success, and when the expenses were subtracted from the income, we had a profit of over $3000.00.

A week or two later we had a community meeting on the vacant lot where we had held the Fiesta activities, to try to decide how to spend the money. The meeting became fairly raucous because of the different opinions about the money. Dona and I had not realized it before, but a few thousand dollars up here was a huge amount! There were four suggestions for spending the money. They were: 1) start a community organization and work toward building a community center building; 2) start a rural fire department; 3) spend it to update a TV translator that a private individual had located on top of a local mountain; 4) throw a big party and spend it all. It was finally narrowed down to either start a community

My Story

organization or start a fire department. The community members argued so violently that the community became completely polarized. Members who backed the community association would not talk to the group who wanted to start a fire department. I tried to persuade them to stay together as a community and back one organization until it was started, then concentrate on the other goal. I tried to convince them that by working together they could have both, but to no avail. It was really sad to see neighbors who seemed to get along fine, all of a sudden would not even talk to each other. Some of our Old Timers told us there always had been factions. It got so bad that they decided if you were in the fire department, you could not be in the community association. Because of the way the Fiesta had been advertised, the folks who wanted the fire department insisted that they have all the money. They were more vocal, so they got it.

Dona and I worked with the group who wanted to build a community center building. We thought that was needed more, and we also knew the State would fund the fire department if they met certain requirements. We had a few meetings out in the open and only got rained out once. Because we wanted to attract members to the organization from all over the area, we decided to call it the WCC&D for the communities of Winston, Chloride, Chiz, and Dusty.

My Story

We eventually arranged to use an abandoned building in Winston for a temporary community center. Our rent was to be that we restore it. I worked on that with some of the local folks. I would bring the supplies up from Las Cruces on Friday evening and we would work on the building that weekend. I guess Dona and I supplied about half of the material because the group had no money. Once we had the building finished enough so it could be used, we began hosting enchilada dinners with a country dance following. Most of the locals, except the fire department members, would come, and lots of folks would drive up from T or C because of the novelty. (They could drink and there were no cops around) We charged a small fee and actually started to accrue a small building fund.

The lady who was elected to be the first Chairman had never conducted a meeting before, so she asked me to help her. I wrote an outline that roughly followed Roberts Rules of Order, and that worked pretty well. It was soon evident most of the local folks had never worked as a group to accomplish a goal. The meetings were positively ugly. If there were a difference of opinion, they would immediately engage in a shouting match. There was some cussing and lots of threats.

On occasion, there would be a slapping match. At one meeting an elderly Hispanic woman whacked a man over the head with her handbag for what she took as a slur about her ethnicity. It nearly knocked the man down

My Story

and he retired to a corner and sat down. Later I asked the woman's daughter what her mother had in her purse that was so heavy. The daughter said "her 45" revolver! I tried to encourage the attendees at the meetings to direct their comments to the chairman instead of at each other. That didn't work too well, as the Chair would also engage in the shouting!

It took about two years before we could have a serious meeting without the threat of a fight. We were still week-enders, and the Association Chairman (a woman) would watch for us to drive through Winston, follow us to Chloride, and lay the latest problem on us. One time she said "you have to make that woman stop". When I asked the problem, she pointed out she was the first in Winston to get one of those giant satellite antennas, and they really liked getting TV. The word got out that the antenna worked well, so another family bought one. The first lady swore as soon as the new antenna went up, her reception was weakened, and that the second woman was stealing some of her signal! It took us quite a while to persuade her that the TV signal came down like rain, and all antennas would receive the same amount.

In 1986, after we moved to Chloride full time, I was elected to be chairman. I was determined to prove that one could be a member of the community association AND the fire department. I immediately went to the Fire Chief and asked if I could join his department. He welcomed me. The next week, I called a community

My Story

association Directors meeting, and announced that I had joined the fire department and that I wanted both groups to work together. One of the most prominent ranchers in the area happened to be a Director. He swore at me, jumped up, took his chair, and threw it across the room. He stomped out and never came to another association meeting! We got along fine without him. It turned out he was not too well liked. He would get the poorer folks obligated to him somehow, by loaning them money, or using his equipment to help them with something, then hold it over them. When I was told I should not have crossed him, I said it was a new day, and I owed him nothing.

We had been quite successful at our enchilada dinners and country dances. Now a story about that. When we first decided to host a dance, we had no money to pay for a band. Someone suggested that we ask our local musicians. Several of our neighbors could play the guitar and some could play the fiddle. It turned out that they were willing, but some of them were feuding and would not look at nor talk to each other. When they played, they sat with their chairs facing out, with their backs toward each other! When they went to start a new song, they might start 3 different tunes, but eventually they would all wind up playing the same song. A favorite song was 'There were Seven Spanish Angels in the Valley of the Gun'. Our guests would say 'no, not again', and I would say, 'it is that or nothing'. Anyway,

My Story

the meals and the dances brought customers out from T or C and they would spend a fair amount of money.

In our meeting discussions we had talked about buying some property and building a nice building to be our community center. My friend, Nick Ortega, and I began looking for a piece of property that would work for us. We finally settled on a full block in the middle of Winston. It was vacant, and we had already used it for our Fiestas. It took several visits to the owner before he and his wife agreed to sell us the land. They both told us that based on the history of the town there was no way we could keep them from fighting among themselves and breaking up. He was also afraid he would lose control of the land, it would become overgrown with weeds, and become a dumping ground. Their house was directly across the street. I guaranteed the owners that I would personally mow the property and keep the weeds down.

We did not have enough money to buy the land and build a building, so the deal we made with the owners was we would enter into a 'Lease to Purchase' agreement for the land. The lease payment was $1000.00 per year, and the payment went toward the price of the land. The land was a full city block consisting of 16 lots, and we agreed to pay $1000.00 per lot for a total of $16,000.00. We also agreed that if we failed, the owners got the land back including whatever

My Story

improvements we had made. In addition, I guaranteed we would have them paid off within 5 years.

When I went to the Courthouse to register the deed for the land, I was told we could not hold title to land unless we were incorporated. (State Law) I contacted an attorney, and his price would have prevented us from achieving our goal of getting a building. I read in a local paper that there was a state community support organization in Santa Fe that was organized to help small communities build/restore their churches. I called them, and explained our situation, and they thought what we were trying to do was a good thing, and they agreed to have their volunteer lawyers help get us incorporated. Actually, they told me how to do it, and they checked my paperwork, then they even recorded us with the appropriate state department. They also showed me how to get our organization an IRS code 501 (c) (3). That made us tax exempt and also allowed us to accept donations that were tax deductible for the donors.

With 3 other couples working with us, Dona and I built the community center building. The total cost was less than $20,000.00 including the kitchen equipment which Dona and I bought at an auction. The bottom line is that we had enough money to build the building and pay off the land in just a little over 4 years. We found that saving money was a problem up here. Everyone would agree to save for something, but as soon as there were a

My Story

few thousand dollars, someone would try to work a way
to get it.

There were a few little problems to be worked out when
we first started the community center project. The land
we bought had a shallow ravine running pretty well
through the middle that would preclude using the lots as
a ball field, or even locating a building properly. It
needed to be filled. Dona and I found that just north of
Winston, the state highway crews had stored great
mounds of loose sand and gravel which had washed
across the highway during the rainy season. I stopped at
the State Maintenance Yard to see if the crews were
going to haul the fill dirt away. If they were, I asked if
they could dump it on our grounds. The boss told me
they would haul the dirt away and would have to find a
place for it, but that he could not dump it on private
land. He was sympathetic and suggested I call his boss,
the District Chief. I called the District Chief, and he
agreed that they should help us, but could not because of
their regulations. He suggested I contact the State
Secretary of Transportation, but said I should write him
a letter and explain exactly what we wanted. He gave me
the correct address. I did write the letter, and about a
week later I got a copy of the letter the State Secretary
of Transportation sent to the District Chief and the local
Yard Boss. The letter stated that if there was no need for
the state to use the fill in this sector, and if the haul to
our location was shorter than any other place on state
land where the dirt could be dumped, they should help

My Story

us. They used two trucks and hauled approximately 2000 yards, which I leveled with an old tractor I had. It completely leveled the grounds.

The next little problem arose when we started our building. I had scratched out a rough sketch of a building and our building committee approved it. Someone, I think Dona, made a fairly detailed drawing of our proposed building. Nick Ortega and I traveled from Las Cruces to Socorro talking with building suppliers to see if they would give us a price break. Many of them were very helpful. One outfit in Las Cruces told us they would supply roof rafters at two thirds the normal price, and would deliver them free. We had decided we would use cement block type construction, so we hit up the supplier in Las Cruces. Again we were lucky. They supplied the blocks for a dollar each and also delivered free. I contacted the cement supplier in Truth or Consequences and asked for a price break. He said NO. He pointed out that he 'donated in Truth or Consequences, and that was enough'.

There was a tiny cement supplier in T or C who was being put out of business by the big outfit, but I called him to see what he could do. He explained that the 'big outfit' had driven him pretty well out of business and all his drivers had found other jobs, but if we had someone who could drive the cement trucks, he would help us. I told him we did not have anyone who could drive the

My Story

trucks. Then he asked if we had a pretty good supply of water. I told him we had a pretty good water well, but he said "I don't think we can get water fast enough for what I am thinking". Then he told me what he was thinking, was to load his four cement trucks up with dry cement, ferry them one at a time, to our location and park them until we were ready the following day, then fill them with water and mix the cement on the grounds. He said the trouble was that the water had to go into the truck fairly fast, and a regular water well pump would not be fast enough. I told him we had a couple of old fire trucks that could supply about a thousand gallons fairly fast. He said "that will do it". Since we had discovered that the water in the fire trucks got pretty rusty sitting there, we drove them to the creek and dumped the water. Then we filled both trucks with fresh water. The next day, on a Saturday, neighbors came from all over to watch the fire trucks water up the cement mixers. Then they stayed to help pour the floor for the new building. Our cost was about half of what the 'big guy' offered. The Man's name was Don Holder, and he sure bent over backwards to help us.

Another small glitch was the building permit. The cost of the permit was based on the cost of the building. We had calculated that the building would be less than $20,000.00, so we sent the drawing and a check for whatever the amount was for a $20,000.00 building. I received a 'rejection letter' almost by return mail. The letter pointed out that the size building we were

My Story

contemplating was valued at $95,000.00, and our check was insufficient. The letter also pointed out that any construction in New Mexico that was valued at over $30,000.00 must be built by a licensed contractor. Further, any structure that was valued over $60,000.00 had to have a set of drawings supplied by a licensed architect. The rejection letter was sent by the Planning Department, but the Cabinet Secretary of Building Industries' name was listed at the top of the form along with the name of the State Governor. I called the Secretary and argued that no building in our area was worth ninety five thousand dollars, not even the State Highway Maintenance building a block away, and that if we were required to hire either an architect or a contractor our community would have to forget our plans for a community center building. We had a fairly long conversation, and he told me he had been Building Inspector in our area at one time, and he agreed with me that the valuation was too high. He said "I will connect you with the Planning Department and see if they can work something out". I said "No sir, they are the ones who rejected our permit request. If you can't help me I will call the other name on my form". He said I will call you tomorrow, then hung up. I was certain we had been brushed off, but early the next morning the phone rang, and it was the Cabinet Secretary. He said "How is your day going", and I replied it was a pretty day. He said "I am going to make it better" and he asked if I had the rejection form handy. I said I did, and he told me to

My Story

scratch out the $95,000.00 valuation, and write in $29,000.00, and resubmit the request with the appropriate size check. What he did was to decrease the value to just below the threshold that would have required a contractor. We received the building permit soon after. I guess our experience was that if you can articulate how regulations can hurt small communities, and if you can find people who try to understand the problems, usually there is a way to work them out.

After nine years as Chairman of the community association, Dona and I decided we had done all we could do so we both became more involved in the fire department.

We had joined the fire department in 1986 when we first moved to Chloride full time. The department was not much. We had an old Ford cab-over truck with a 1000 gallon water tank, but it did not have a pump. It was difficult to fill, and was just as difficult to get water out of it to fight fire. It had no brakes, and the only time we tried to use it, I drove it to the Garret Ranch on a fire call. The fire was in a tiny building that was burned down before we got there. The other fire truck was a hand me down from the City of Truth or Consequences and was pretty well shot. We did get it to a few fires. One time we responded to an automobile fire about a mile north of Winston. When the Chief got there, he set the parking brake and engaged the pump. He could not get any water flowing, and soon found that he had the

My Story

fire truck on fire. On that truck, the pump ran off from a power takeoff, but the parking brake was also on the transmission, so you could not use both. The way it was supposed to operate was to chock the rear wheels, then engage the pump. I have to give credit to the Chief. He was an old man who had never operated anything but junk, and that was all our fire department could afford. He held the department together until the late 1990s, then he retired.

We went through a succession of Chiefs who were not very interested in the department, and therefore not very successful. By the year 2000 we had a Chief who had decided to buy two fire trucks from departments on the east coast. I suggested he should spend department money to go back east to look at the trucks. I told him they used chemicals on the roads summer and winter, and any vehicles as old as the ones he was dealing on would be rusted out. He was a 'know it all' and bought them anyway. They arrived completely rusted out. They sat parked in an old adobe building we had modified so we could get the trucks inside. Both had dead batteries and/or flat tires. During this time, I and two others from Chloride decided we could build our own fire truck and base it in Chloride. We purchased a 1980 Dodge one-ton dually with a utility body on it. We welded a 400 gallon steel tank at the front of the bed, and installed a gasoline operated pump we had gotten from Bandelier National Monument. We got permission from a landowner in Chloride to build a tiny shed for the truck.

My Story

That truck was the one that responded to whatever fires we were called on. The Chief was pretty jealous of the operation in Chloride, and told us at one meeting that he was shutting down the Chloride station because the truck was an illegal homemade outfit, and was way overweight when full of water. All three of us from Chloride, the only members left in the department, said we would quit if he shut the Chloride Station down. To prove the truck was not overloaded we took the truck to the St. Cloud Mine, and asked if we could weigh the truck. The girl told us to drive up on the scales. With 400 gallons in the tank the truck was terribly overloaded, so we asked her not to record the weight. We drove the truck down into the creek and drained the tank. With the tank empty, we went back to the scales. This time it was just barely below the weight limit, so we asked her to print the ticket. We took the ticket back to the Chief and showed him it was not overloaded. All would have been OK, but the girl who ran the scales rode to church one day with the Chief and his wife, and she told him what we had done. It didn't matter anyway, as he was on his way out. Shortly after the catastrophe of 9- 11- 2001, President Bush, in a speech, pointed out that everyone could do something to make their community safer. That got my attention, so at the next fire department meeting I raised a stink about the abysmal condition of our fire trucks. I pointed out that the main trucks were unusable, and the only one operating was an illegal homemade. The bottom line is

My Story

that the Chief quit, and the members asked me to take over. I said I would do it for two years. My 2 years lasted 12 years!

My Story

CHAPTER30: MY TIME AS FIRE CHIEF

In December of 2001, I became the Chief of the Winston-Chloride Fire Department. The first thing I did was to have the best of the two rusted out trucks hauled to a fire truck repair shop in Belen, New Mexico, to have it put in useable condition. It was in such bad condition we had to pull it up onto a flatbed trailer. Then I called the State Fire Marshall and asked for help in building a decent fire department. He told me he could advise me, but that it would be up to me to do whatever was needed. He advised me to get rid of the homemade truck, and he would loan me a real fire truck. We went to a small department in the northern part of the tate and picked up our loaner. It was a beautiful 1955 Chevrolet fire truck, but it did not have as much capability as our homemade truck. Then he told me to work with the New Mexico Finance Authority to see about getting a loan to build new buildings. That worked very well. With the annual allotment we would receive from the state, we could build a main fire station at Winston, and a sub-station at Chloride. The main station would have 3 apparatus bays, an office, a store room, classroom, and a bathroom. The station at Chloride would be just a two apparatus bay building. I scratched out a basic design that the department members had discussed, and hired an architect to do a design for us. When I went to the county to get help, they said they were too busy but if we had the money and the OK from the State Fire Marshall to do it ourselves. So we did. We bought a

My Story

one- acre lot at the north end of Winston from a rancher, drilled a well, and started construction. At the same time we bought the two lots in Chloride that we had used for our little one space shed, and started construction. We tailored both buildings to look like they belonged in our little towns. The main station in Winston is stuccoed like the other buildings in Winston, and the sub-station in Chloride has a board and batten false front like many of the Chloride buildings. We needed new equipment of every kind. We had no PPE (Personal Protection Equipment) for either structure or wild-land fires, and no tools to fight either kind of fire. Except for the 1955 Chevrolet fire truck, we had no fire apparatus that could get to a fire and shoot water.

Earlier when I realized the fire department was not functional enough to provide fire protection for Chloride, I had purchased an antique 1948 International KB8 fire truck from a collector in Mount Vernon, Washington, because I like Internationals, and I felt we needed some fire protection in Chloride. I had no idea how long it would take to get the department up and functional. I drove a Jeep Cherokee up to Mount Vernon, picked up the fire truck, put the Jeep on a tow bar behind, and drove them back to New Mexico. The fire truck was in fairly good shape, and I had intended to use it for my own fire protection in Chloride. With the other fire trucks in such poor condition, I felt I could use it on any fires in the area. Then I decided that was not too good of an idea because of a liability factor.

My Story

I contacted the State Fire Marshal to get suggestions for finding good used apparatus to replace the rusted out trucks we had. He put the 'kibosh' on that idea. He said "We don't need any more junk handed down from some outfit back east, and you may not spend your funds on used trucks". When I protested that we would never be able to buy new trucks with our new building payments, he suggested I try for grant funds. I researched the possibilities, and found that FEMA had a grant program to aid fire departments to purchase the high dollar equipment we needed. I also found that the State of New Mexico was offering a grant program to help rural fire departments upgrade their equipment. These were both competitive grants, and the competition was stiff. The state grant program was going to distribute about a dozen tankers and about the same number of quick response type fire engines. I wrote applications for both grants. I did a fair amount of research on what was expected on the applications, and I emphasized the financial condition of our rural area. Would you believe my application was accepted on BOTH grant programs!

On the state grant, I had my choice of a 2000 gallon International tanker, or a Ford 550, 4 x 4, Quick Response Engine. I selected the International Tanker (tender) as the vehicle that would do our fire department the most good, because we have to carry all the water we need when we respond to a fire. The grant from

My Story

FEMA was a cash grant for about $90,000.00. I did not know how to write a specification for the type of fire engine we needed, so I contacted the State Purchasing Department to ask for the specifications they used to purchase the quick response vehicles. They sent the information, and I found out that the vehicle was very close to what our department wanted for a quick response vehicle. They invited me to 'piggy back' on their contract. The basic vehicle cost that the state was buying was $81,000.00, and I had a little over $90,000.00 of FEMA grant funds to spend. I worked with the vendor in Fort Gary, Canada, to upgrade our truck to be a quick response vehicle for either Structure fires or for wild-land fires. We upgraded the water tank from 400 gallon to 500 gallon, we had an oversized diesel powered pump installed, and we had it delivered with equipment ready to fight either structural or wild-land fires. The total cost came to a few hundred dollars more than the grant, but our department could make up the difference. The timing of the delivery of both vehicles could not have been better. They arrived within a few weeks of each other, and just as we were ready to move into our new Fire Stations. We based the tanker at the new Winston Main Station, and the new wild-land engine was based at the new Chloride Sub-Station. What a boost for the community!

Eventually I had grant applications accepted by both the BLM (Bureau of Land Management) and the U.S. National Forest. These grants were smaller in value, but

My Story

they allowed us to purchase all the firefighting tools we needed for both structure and for wild-land fires. Personal Protection Equipment (PPE) for structure fires is very expensive, costing about $25,000.00 per firefighter for 'Helmet to Boots' including SCBAs (Self Contained Breathing Apparatus). I wrote an application for complete sets for 10 firefighters, which came to a little over $250,000.00, and won. Another successful grant was for a high performance air compressor to re-fill the SCBA air tanks for $62,000.00. With our basic needs for vehicles, equipment, and tools satisfied, we decided we needed an additional 2000 gallon tender, and a high performance Urban/Wildland Interface pumper. I applied for grants for both vehicles, one in 2010 and the other in 2011, and would you believe both were accepted! These are $250,000.00 vehicles! Both trucks are now in our stations and have been used to respond to our neighbors' needs.

I found out early on that writing grant requests to FEMA was much like responding to government Requests for Bids for government contracts, much of which I did while with IBM. My records show that I have brought approximately $1,000,000.00 worth of equipment and buildings into Sierra County without spending a cent of local money. I decided to retire as Chief of the Fire Department as of the end of December, 2012. I will remain as a member of the department for a short time to help ensure a smooth transfer of responsibility, and I

My Story

have been asked to remain as a 'resource', which I am glad to do.

During my time here in Chloride, I have been asked to conduct two funerals. First, for Mr. Earl Hobbs, and then about two years later the Hobbs family asked me to conduct Cassy Hobb's funeral. Both of the Hobbs were very special friends of ours, and the request to conduct their funerals was very humbling.

One of the most emotional jobs I have had here in Chloride, yet the most satisfying, was building the coffin for one of our young men. The boy's name is Adam Petersen, son of a neighboring family. Adam came from North Dakota with his family when he was a year or two old. As he grew up he was very active, but well behaved, and was well liked by all. During summers when in high school, he worked with his father as a professional wildland fire fighter, and spent a fair amount of time using specialized equipment fighting wildland fires throughout the West. Shortly out of high school, Adam joined the Marines. After training he was deployed to Afghanistan, where he distinguished himself by fixing a mechanical problem on a fighting vehicle while under intense enemy fire, and by getting the vehicle and its crew back into a safe zone. He was awarded a Marine Corp. commendation and a medal. When his tour was over and he returned home, the community had a major "Coming Home Party" for him. He left to spend a few weeks at Twenty Nine Palms,

My Story

Calif. He was scheduled to come home for Christmas, and then join a Marine recruiting team. Alas, while on his way home just before Christmas, he rolled his pickup truck over a few miles from home. Adam was killed in the accident.

Adam's father asked me if I would build his coffin. I was both honored and terrified. Adam's family knew I regarded their son highly, but I did not know what they expected. Adam's Grandfather had some special lumber he had saved from a building project, and they asked me to use that. It was beautiful wood to work with, but was rough cut with a circle saw blade pattern. Since I did not know what the family wanted, I smooth- planed one side of each of the boards, and left the other side rough. I made it so that I could reverse the boards to use either side. When Adam's father and his uncle saw the completed coffin with the rough cut boards on the outside, they said that was exactly what they wanted. What a relief! Adam's mother also said it was exactly what she had envisioned. I made it slightly over-sized because Adam was rather tall. After the funeral, I had to remove the handles from each side to fit it into the vault.

Several weeks after the Funeral, the Funeral Director called me to say he did not have my bill. I told him that I had not intended to charge for my work. He explained that the Funeral was a standard military funeral, and he could not close out his books and get paid for his part without my bill. He said "The Marines insist that the

My Story

coffin bill be $2000.00". He suggested we submit a bill for the $2000.00 and donate it to the family or to the Wounded Warrior program. Adam's family liked the suggestion to donate it to the Wounded Warriors, so that is what we did.

My Story

MY ANCESTERS

I realize that my ancestors' go way back, and that their origins were in northern Europe; however this 'task' was not intended to be a complete family history but a sort of list of the high points of my life. With that in mind, I will provide some information that is readily available to me.

My Great- Grandfather on my father's side was Lars Peter Amundson. He was born on November 5, 1825, in a farming area of Sweden. He married Carrie Samuelson, who was born in 1836. They had eleven children, ten boys and one daughter. In 1869 they sold all of their belongings, and left Sweden to make a new life in America. Times were hard, and especially hard on children. Before they eventually arrived in Salina, Iowa, all but two of their children had died. The ocean trip took 20 days, and on arriving in New Jersey, Lars began looking for work. His forebears were 'Iron Mongers' so that is the type work he looked for. Among the tools he made were a pair of scissors and a sort of pliars, both of which are still in our family. The scissors were used by Carrie and her neighbors to cut the cloth when they were making clothing for their families. The pliars were given to me by my father, along with a metal box containing the pliars and several human teeth with gold fillings. The story is that the pliars were especially made for pulling teeth. When Lars pulled teeth, any that had gold fillings were given to him as his pay! Eventually, Lars moved on to Salina, Iowa, and started a new family. He

My Story

and Carrie had four more children, with the first one born in 1871, so it would appear that they did not stay in New Jersey very long. The four children were:

Samuel Otto, born in January 1871

Andrew Gustaf, born in February 1873 (My Grandfather)

William August, born in December 1875

Daniel Amos, born in September 1879

When Lars Peter Amundson became an American citizen he changed his name from Amundson to Edmund.

My Grandfather, Andrew Gustaf Edmund married Emma Bright in Parsonville, Iowa, on December 20, 1899. Andrew worked on the railroad for one dollar a day for a 10 hour day. When he was promoted to Foreman, he made $1.10 per day. He told us one day that his wedding suit cost him $10.00. Andrew and Emma had two sons, Carl Gustaf, born June 26, 1902, and Harold Rudolph, (my father) born on May 25, 1905, at Beckwith, Iowa.

Andrew moved his family to Irma, Wisconsin in 1911 to try to improve his health. I know for a fact that Grandpa selected the rockiest 80 acres he could find to homestead. He farmed that rocky place until just prior to his death at the wonderful old age of 99 years. The

My Story

reason I know he had the rockiest farm in the state is because as a boy I would help him 'pick rock'. He had a homemade 'stone boat' pulled by a two horse team that we would drive back and forth across his fields picking up the rocks. One day I remember protesting by saying "Grandpa, we cannot pick up all these rocks". He said "We are not going to pick up all of them, just one at a time". By the way, Grandpa's cousin John Samuelson homesteaded just a few miles away on a farm that had no rocks at all! Grandpa and Grandma's place at Irma was the family center for many years when I was growing up.

Grandma Edmund's forbearers also came from Sweden. Her father, Gustaf A. Bright, was born on February 16, 1844, the son of Peter and Anna (Peterson) Bright. Peter was a carpenter and worked that trade all his life in Sweden. He died in 1879. Anna died in 1901 at the age of 99.

Gustaf Bright worked in Sweden as hired farm help, and in 1872 he married Carlotta Johnson, daughter of John and Eliza Johnson, who were' landed' farmers. John died in 1857 and Eliza died in 1874. In 1876, Gustaf and Carlotta immigrated to America, specifically, to Jefferson County, Iowa, where he worked as a farm hand. He soon purchased his own farm, and became a noted agriculturist. Gustaf and Carlotta had six children, five girls and one boy. The third born, Emma E. (my Grandmother) married Andrew Gustaf Edmund in 1899

My Story

and moved with him and their two sons to Wisconsin in 1911.

My forbearers on my mother's side have had a long history in America. My sister Anne has done a great deal of family research and has records showing that we descend from members of the pilgrim ship The Mayflower, specifically, John Alden. Her research indicates we had ancestors in the Revolutionary War. My most recent forbearers arrived in Adams County, Wisconsin some time prior to 1850. Some of them were farmers and some of them worked in other trades. My Grandfather, George Albert Cummings married Verna Isadore Powers on March 30, 1904 at Kilbourn, Wisconsin (now Wisconsin Dells). They homesteaded in the town of Scanowon, Lincoln County, Wisconsin, where he farmed. They had four children, three girls and a boy. They were; Leila, Merton, Irma (my Mother), and Wilma. My Grandmother died when Mom was quite young, so I and my siblings never got to know her. My Grandfather Cummings was a typical 'Yankee farmer.' He was as strong as an ox, and was one of the last true rugged individualists. After his wife died, he raised the four children and farmed by himself. In his old age, his eyesight became quite bad, yet he continued operating his farm alone. When I was quite young he had an accident with a tractor. It tipped over, trapping him under it. He survived a night of cold rainy weather and was not found until late the following day when neighbors sensed that his cattle had not been tended.

My Story

Among other injuries, he had a broken back. I do not remember much about the days that followed, but I remember sitting on a bench at the hospital where my parents were visiting Grandpa, and overhearing the doctor tell my mother that Grandpa would probably never walk again. We were outside his door, and Grandpa was not supposed to hear the prognosis, but he did. He shouted "**The hell I won't walk again**" and he did! As a matter of fact he farmed for several more years after he recovered. He was as gentle as could be, but he was tough!

I do not know very much about Dona's forbearers. They lived in Ohio, and were involved in various industries there. Dona's Father, Norman Wise, served in the First World War, and while serving in France, he suffered from gas poisoning. He recovered, but it took a heavy toll on his health. He worked in the tire manufacturing industry, and liked to work night shift so he could tend a huge garden during the day time. Norman and Dona's mother, Hazel (Snyder) Wise, raised six children, three boys and three girls. Dona was the fourth born. Her father built the house she was raised in when he returned from World War I. It was located in a small village called Boston, Ohio, which was between the Cuyahoga River, and the old Erie Canal. Sometime after Dona and I left Ohio, the Government decided to make that entire area a National Historic Landmark. The Government purchased (or took) all of the properties in the little village including several that Dona's family had owned

My Story

for many years. We have since met people who are from Ohio who told us it is a rather special place where visitors can hike along the Cuyahoga River or along the tow path where the horses walked when towing the barges that plied the canal.

My Story

Lars Peter Amundson (Edmund) and wife Carrie Sammuelson

My Story

Andrew Gustaf Edmund & Emma (Bright) Edmund

66th Wedding Anniversary Dec. 20, 1965

My Story

**George Albert Cummings & wife Verna Isadore (Powers)
Cummings**

My Story

Andrew and Emma Edmund (seated)

Sons Harold and Carl (standing) *about 1920*

My Story

Harold and Irma Edmund *about 1970*

My Story

The Harold Edmund's 50ᵗʰ Anniversary in 1977

Harold and Irma seated

Left to right, Verna, Jerry, Don, Anne

My Story

Edmunds Celebrate 50 Years

Don and Dona Edmund of Chloride will celebrate their 50th wedding anniversary September 20. They were married in Dona's home church in Boston, Ohio, in 1952, while Don was serving in the Air Force.

They recently reminisced that they did not have much time to get it done. Don was stationed at Scott Air Force Base in Illinois, and had orders to report to McCord Air Force Base, at Tacoma, Washington. He could only get a few days off, so Dona had to make all the arrangements. She even had to arrange a special method of getting the marriage license and the required blood test. Don could not get home until Friday and the wedding was scheduled for Saturday.

The state required that both the license and the blood test results be delivered by mail. Since that was impossible, Dona arranged to pick them up, have a neighborhood postmaster put a stamp on them and then cancel the stamp as though they had been sent through the mail.

Now, 50 years later, they both think it was worth the trouble. Shortly after the wedding, Don left for McCord Air Force Base. Dona was able to join him the following year and they say they have never been apart for more than a few days since. Their daughter, Linda, was born at McCord Airbase Hospital in August 1954.

After four years in the Air Force and a few years going to school, Don was recruited by International Business Machine Corporation, to work in their new division that was dedicated to the 'new fangled' computers. Both of them say it was great to finally make enough money to live on, but then they found out that IBM meant "I'm being moved."

In their first 20 years with IBM, they lived in 13 states, often moving from coast to coast, doing various projects for the Government or the Military. In October of 1976, they arrived in New Mexico, assigned to work on a special project at White Sands Missile Range.

Immediately after buying a home in Las Cruces, they began to explore New Mexico because they expected to move again in a year or two. IN 1977, on Labor Day weekend, they accidentally found Chloride while looking for Wall Lake in the Gila National Forest. It was love at first sight for both of them (again) and they initiated the purchase of their current house that same day.

They spent the next several years as 'weekenders' in Chloride, restoring their house and out buildings. As luck would have it, they were able to remain in New Mexico. Don retired in 1986, and they then moved to Chloride full time.

Both Don and Dona keep busy with their involvement in community activities and their 'labor of love,' restoring the old buildings they own. They also enjoy showing visitors the Pioneer Store Museum in Chloride.

There will be an Open House at the Edmund residence in Chloride from 3 to 6:00 p.m., Saturday, September 21. Friends and family are invited to stop by and join Don and Dona in celebrating their Golden Anniversary. They request No Gifts, Please!

My Story

**Dona's father, Norman Wise (on the left) and a friend
during WW1**

My Story

Made in the USA
Columbia, SC
04 April 2019